RAF MARHAM

BOMBER STATION

RAF MARHAM
BOMBER
STATION

MARTIN W. BOWMAN

The
History
Press

First published 2008

The History Press
Cirencester Road, Chalford,
Stroud, Gloucestershire, GL6 8PE
www.thehistorypress.co.uk

British Library Cataloguing in Publication Data.
A catalogue record for this book is available from the British Library.

ISBN 978 0 7524 4694 3

Printed in Great Britain

CONTENTS

ACKNOWLEDGEMENTS

With thanks to the following: Dick Bell; Theo Boiten; Group Captain John Broadbent; Don Bruce; Chris Cannon, Countrywide Productions; Bob Collis; Ray Deacon; Grenville Eaton DFC; Alan Gardener; Benny Goodman; Nigel McTeer; Squadron Leader Rem Merrick, RAF Marham; Bernard Noble; Gary Parsons; Edwin Perry; Albert E. Robinson; Roger F. Sheldrake; Raymond W. Towler, Airfield Research Group.

1

BOMBER STATION

It was the first week in January 1939 when the bus from King's Lynn deposited Aircraftsman 1st Class, Fitter 2, E.C. 'Johnnie' Johnson, complete with all his kit, including a very heavy kit bag, outside the guardroom at RAF Marham. The station was comparatively new with traditional guardroom, barrack blocks and four hangars set on the edge of the grass airfield, 10 miles east of Downham Market and 9 miles south-east of King's Lynn in North Norfolk. Construction of the aerodrome had begun in 1935 when the RAF expansion programme began. It was envisaged that a home-based force of sixty-eight bomber and thirty-five fighter squadrons would be ready by March 1937. One third of the bomber force was to be equipped with aircraft capable of reaching targets in the Ruhr from British aerodromes. In February 1936 fresh plans called for a front-line force of 1,736 aircraft by 1939, and this was to include twenty heavy bomber squadrons. Modern aerodromes had to be constructed for the new bomber squadrons and Marham was one of these; by July 1936 two new public roads had been laid down round the aerodrome to replace country lanes that used to run across the site, including Old Dibbles Drove. When completed, the aerodrome was a completely self-contained township, with 13 acres of playing fields, a combined church and cinema, fire station, sick quarters, shops, stores and even prison cells with an exercise yard, beside the clutch of hangars. Materials used included 6½ million bricks, 3,000 tons of cement, 40,000 tons of ballast and sand, a million tiles and slates, 100,000sq.ft of glass, 2,000 tons of lead, 30 miles of electricity cable, 7 miles of salt-glazed drain pipes and 20 tons of nails. The aerodrome opened as planned on 1 April 1937, as a heavy bomber station in 3 Group, Bomber Command.

Marham was nineteen-year-old Johnnie Johnson's first adult RAF station. Born in North Walsham in 1920, Johnnie attended Paston Grammar School and joined the Royal Air Force in 1936 as an aircraft apprentice. He completed his three-year apprenticeship as a member of the 33rd entry of apprentices at No.1 School of Technical Training, RAF Halton, and was now qualified on both engines and airframes. In fact, this was the last entry to be trained in dual trades. Together with eleven others of his entry, on passing out Johnnie had, surprisingly, been

Handley Page Harrows in formation in May 1938. At Marham 115 Squadron flew Harrows from June 1937 to November 1938. (*Flight*)

posted to RAF Marham – surprisingly because he was a Norfolk lad, and the Air Ministry of the time was not renowned for posting airmen to the station of their choice. Marham in 1939 housed two squadrons: 38 Squadron equipped with twin-engined Fairey Hendons, the RAF's first all-metal, low-wing monoplane bomber, powered with two Rolls-Royce Kestrels; and 115 Squadron with Handley Page Harrows. 38 Squadron was the only squadron ever to be equipped with Hendons and it was the RAF's first monoplane bomber. Johnnie thought that it looked 'a large clumsy looking beast with a tall spatted undercarriage.'[1]

When 38 Squadron had first arrived at Marham on 5 May 1937 from Mildenhall they had been equipped with Handley Page Heyford biplane bombers. In June 1938 the squadron's 'B' Flight was used to form 115 Squadron, which used some of 38 Squadron's Hendons, to become operational until deliveries of Handley Page Harrow Is and IIs began. Even so, the Hendon and the Harrow were vast improvements on the types that had soldiered on in RAF service long after the First World War ended. In 1919 a grandiose plan had been formulated for an Inter-Allied Force to mount a combined bombing offensive against German industry, but the coming peace on 11 November 1918 had brought the great plan to an abrupt end. In Britain's haste to disarm, Marham and Narborough, along with many other aerodromes, were closed. Only a few months earlier they had been home to units of the Royal Flying Corps, flying on home defence patrols with an assortment of biplane fighters to intercept Zeppelin airships over eastern England.

The first airship raid had taken place on the night of 19–20 January 1915. Three Naval Zeppelins had left Germany on the morning of the 19th for England's East Coast. Two of them released a number of bombs, killing two people at Great Yarmouth and two more at King's Lynn. The inadequacy of the East Anglian defences against the 'Zeps' was evident, and in August 1915 seven night-landing grounds were created in Norfolk, one of which was Narborough, first used by the RNAS (Royal Naval Air Service). In the second half of

Fairey Hendons of 38 Squadron lined up at Marham in 1937. (RAF Marham)

A Fairey Hendon in front of the watch office (control tower) at Marham. (RAF Marham)

the year Royal Flying Corps aircraft also began using Narborough and an 80-acre field at Marham, a mile and a half to the south-west of Narborough. On 23 September 1916 flights equipped with B.E. 2b, F.E.2b, Avro 504K, Martynside G.100 and Sopwith Camel aircraft of No.51 Home Defence Squadron, which based aircraft at Thetford, Mattishall and Harling Road, arrived at Marham. They were joined in October 1917 by a night training squadron. The RFC airmen saw very little action, although some famous names served at Narborough and Marham. Early in 1917 Captain Albert Ball DSO★★ MC spent a brief period as an instructor at Narborough before he returned to the Western Front on 7 April. His forty-fourth and final victory was on 6 May. He was killed the next day and the posthumous award of the Victoria Cross followed. Lieutenant (later Captain) W.E. Johns, who wrote the famous *Biggles* books, was also an instructor at Narborough in 1918. Major (later Air Marshal, Sir) Arthur T. Harris, who became Chief of Bomber Command in the Second World War, commanded No.191 (Night) Training Squadron, which was at Marham from December 1917 to July 1918. In the summer of 1919 the Air Ministry announced that fourteen RAF stations were to be relinquished and disposed of, Marham being one of them. In the early 1930s the First World War sites at Marham and Narborough were surveyed, the former being chosen as the more suitable site for a new airfield. Work started in 1935, and when three officers and thirty airmen arrived on 1 April 1937 another chapter in Marham's long and distinguished history had begun.[2] 'Johnnie' Johnson continues:

When we arrived at Marham we found that all personnel had been confined to camp for the past two weeks or so. This of course was an extremely unusual situation as was the incident that had caused it. Apparently, or so we learned later, a few days before Christmas, 38 Squadron had been carrying out night flying with their Hendons. During the evening a Hendon had started up, taxied out and received a green Aldis lamp for take-off. It was then opened up to full power, rolled across the airfield and became airborne but almost immediately the engines were throttled back and the aircraft dropped heavily to earth, smashing its undercarriage and slithering to a stop at the edge of the airfield, extensively damaged. When the fire engine and ambulance arrived at the site, the aircraft and cockpit were found to be empty, with not a soul in sight. It was quickly established that no pilot had been involved in the flight, so the RAF Special Investigation Branch (SIB) were called in, but at the time of our arrival had failed to trace the culprits.[3]

This brings me back to Squadron life – one of the first jobs we inexperienced apprentices were given was to cut up the rear fuselage of the crashed Hendon with hacksaws! We were not welcomed with open arms, as an engineering officer was at pains to point out at our initial interview. We may have thought that we had been well trained but he had no intention of letting us loose on his aeroplanes until we had gained a bit of experience. This subsequently turned out to be cleaning oil drip trays and sundry other dirty and mundane jobs. Six of the new ex-apprentices, including myself, were posted to 38 Squadron and the other six to 115 Squadron. Here again we ex-'Trenchard Brats' were greeted with some reserve. This can be understood as the fitters and riggers on the Squadron were real old timers. Most of them had, over many years, managed to work their way from fitter's mate to mechanic, to airframe or engine finer and were entitled to regard this gang of young apprentices with some suspicion. It was well known that we were destined for quick and accelerated promotion when the expansion of the RAF took place, which even in those early days of 1939 was obviously to come.

Marham, after the last three years of rigid discipline of Halton, was to us heaven on earth, We were gradually absorbed into the Squadron and worked regular hours and had most evenings and weekends off. We could wear civilian clothes and a cheap bus service into nearby King's Lynn enabled us to go out and enjoy our airman's pay, which at around 26/- per week was wealth indeed after the 5/- paid to apprentices. Every other week we carried out night flying and this had the advantage that after Thursday's night flying had finished we were then free until start of work on Monday morning. A long weekend off every other week, with a lift home to North Walsham with a Sergeant airframe fitter, was a world away from Halton.

Night flying sometimes involved flare path duty. This necessitated the gooseneck flares having to be filled up with paraffin and then laid out in a line into the prevailing wind across the grass airfield with sometimes a hurried scamper to change the line if the wind changed. After dark the flares were lit and according to the Sergeant who was instructing us, as long as we stayed on the right-hand side of the flare path when aircraft were taking off or landing, we would be perfectly safe. I must admit it was a bit frightening to be in the middle of the airfield, with these huge aircraft hurtling towards you in the pitch dark. I wish that our Sergeant had instructed the one pilot who landed on the so-called 'safe side' of the flare path, causing me the fright of my life, as the wing of his aircraft rushed over my head.

So passed two or three months, and life was very pleasant. It was really like being a member of an exclusive and free and easy flying club. Changes were in the air but how fast and far-reaching and how long-lasting they were to turn out, we had at that time no idea. The first change was a rumour soon to become a fact that 38 Squadron was to be re-equipped with Wellingtons and we would say goodbye to the lumbering old Hendons.[4] With the rumblings of war, the news was greeted with great pleasure. Not least by the pilots and aircrew, who were only too aware that their chances of survival in a modern war would be very slim indeed, in their old underpowered machines, with World War One Lewis guns for their defence. The news was also welcomed by us ex-apprentices because we had been trained on hydraulics, retractable undercarriages, and radial engines, and were now on a par with our long-serving colleagues to whom all these modern innovations were very strange and new.[5]

Nos 38 and 115 Squadrons spent two years working up and taking part in the pre-war exercises. In December 1938 38 Squadron re-equipped with Wellington I bombers. 115 Squadron followed them in April 1939.[6] 'Johnnie' Johnson remembers the arrival of the Wellingtons:

Very soon the first Wellington Mk Is started to trickle in. Some of the landings left a great deal to be desired as the aircraft could bounce quite high if dropped too hard on the final flare-out. One of the early arrivals forgot he had a retractable undercarriage and landed without lowering it – although it's difficult to understand how he managed to ignore the loud klaxon horn that blew in his ear whenever the engines were throttled back with the wheels up. But he managed it! Sometime during the early summer we were completely re-equipped, the Hendons disappeared and 115 Squadron received their Wimpys – a name for the Wellingtons that was to become universal.[7] Indications of the coming war became stronger as summer went on. In August hundreds of reservists were called up and posted to Marham. The camp became crowded, tents appeared, the NAAFI canteen bulged at the seams – we'd always been served with tablecloths, cups, saucers and spoons and enjoyed personal service by the staff but with the sudden influx this obviously couldn't continue. Gradually the cloths and saucers disappeared, and even broken beer glasses couldn't be replaced quickly enough. At times we were reduced to drinking out of jam jars. The exclusive flying club atmosphere was fast disappearing!

During the evening of Wednesday 23 August 1939 RAF units in Great Britain and abroad were secretly placed on a war footing and mobilization of the Auxiliary Air Force and 3,000 members of the Volunteer Reserve began. The British public, probably aware they were enjoying the last days of an August at peace for some time to come, went about their business knowing they too would soon be called into the services. The fragile peace was quickly shattered during the early hours of 1 September. Poland was invaded by German armoured divisions, supported by the Luftwaffe employing Blitzkrieg ('lightning war') tactics developed from experience gained during the Spanish Civil War, 1936–39. In Britain full mobilization followed while units of Coastal Command began flying patrols over the North Sea. At bomber stations camouflage

A Handley Page Harrow of 115 Squadron at Marham in 1937. (RAF Marham)

was liberally applied to buildings and aircraft alike, and brown tape was stuck over every pane of glass in criss-cross patterns. On the afternoon of 2 September ten squadrons of Fairey Battles flew to France to take up their position as part of the Advanced Air Striking Force. It was a sombre Neville Chamberlain, the British Prime Minister, who announced his country's declaration of war over the air on the BBC at 11 a.m. the following morning, 3 September.

At the outbreak of war the overall strength of Bomber Command stood at fifty-five squadrons. On paper this sounds like a respectable figure but by the end of September it had been pared down to twenty-three home-based, first-line squadrons. These consisted of six squadrons of Bristol Blenheim IV light bombers of 2 Group and six squadrons of Wellington Is and IAs of 3 Group (with two in reserve) stationed in East Anglia. The rest of the force comprised five squadrons of Whitleys of 4 Group, based in Yorkshire, and six squadrons of Handley Page Hampdens of 5 Group in Lincolnshire. Wellingtons were first-line equipment for 9 Squadron at Honington, Suffolk; 37 Squadron at Feltwell, Norfolk; 99 and 149 Squadrons at Mildenhall and Newmarket respectively in Suffolk, and 38 and 115 Squadrons at Marham, while 214 and 215 (at Methwold) were similarly equipped in Reserve.

The President of the United States, Franklin D. Roosevelt, appealed to the belligerent nations to refrain from unrestricted aerial bombardment of civilians. The British heeded this request but the RAF was prevented from using a direct passage to the German industrial heartland because of the strict neutrality of both Holland and Belgium. France also requested that Bomber Command did not attack land targets in Germany for fear of reprisal raids on French cities, which her bombers could not deter nor her fighters protect. The only way to carry the war to Germany, then, was to make attacks on German capital ships. The task of bombing the German Fleet fell, therefore, to the Bristol Blenheim light bombers of 2 Group and Wellingtons of 3 Group in East Anglia, which were ideally placed to attack installations in the Heligoland Bight. However, British War Cabinet policy decreed that no civilian casualties were to be caused as a direct result of the bombing. RAF Bomber Command could strike at ships at sea or underway but vessels moored in harbours were not to be bombed for fear of injuring 'innocent' civilians. 'Johnnie' Johnson recalls:

I suppose the first effect of the war was that the aircraft were no longer put in the hangars at the end of flying each day. Daily inspections and rectifications were no longer undertaken in reasonable comfort, but carried out on the tarmac. Another shock was the appearance of a few WAAF mechanics who at that time, it seemed to us, were extremely toffee-nosed and never spoke to anyone below the rank of Squadron Leader. It was also around this time that our aircraft were returned to the manufacturers to have hydraulically powered gun turrets fitted in the nose and tail – then to be known as Mk ICs. Authority then decided that the aircraft lined up on the tarmac were very vulnerable to bombing and initiated a dispersal policy. Whoever thought of the idea of dispersing the aircraft every day to Little Rissington in Gloucestershire was obviously taking no chances! A one-and-a-half hour flight every evening for every serviceable aircraft was indeed dispersal! The disadvantages of this system soon became evident. Some pilots got lost and landed all over the place and then one of our aircraft landed at Rissington with a defective engine. On the day that this happened I'd been in bed less than an hour when I was shaken awake by the Sergeant engine fitter with the words, 'Get up and get dressed. I want you' and he named another couple of engine fitters, 'to go to Rissington to do an engine change'. We spent a large part of the rest of that night loading up a replacement engine with all the tools and equipment required, onto a lorry and in the early hours of the morning headed west to Gloucestershire. After what seemed to be endless hours of travelling, we refuelled at a nameless army base somewhere in Buckinghamshire, and arrived in the Cotswolds at Rissington. With stops only for food we carried on with the removal of the defective engine, which took most of that day. Later on in the war we could do the same job in about quarter of the time. We then prepared the new engine, transferring the necessary components from the old engine, hoisted it up, bolted it into position, reconnected all the pipes and controls and locked all the connections, re-checked them and declared all ready for a test run. It was now full daylight on the second or was it the third day? We were too tired to be sure. We pushed the aircraft out and carried out a successful test run, refitted the cowlings, summoned the pilot and saw him off back to Marham. We then re-crated the bad engine, loaded up all the equipment, cleared up all the spilt oil, climbed aboard the lorry and headed back to Marham ourselves.

It was obvious that dispersal required a rethink. Almost immediately, bulldozers appeared and opened up gaps in the hedges in the fields adjoining the aerodrome in the vicinity of what was then the bomb dump and thus began Marham's expansion. Aircraft were dispersed in these fields during daylight hours for servicing and refuelling. As winter advanced, my most vivid memory of this era is the cold and the mud. The mud was the worst, the aircraft bogged down, the petrol bowsers bogged down, lorries bogged down and they all had to be dug out. We were permanently covered with mud – eventually we had to have tractors fitted with tracks to move anything.

The winter of 1939 and the early months of 1940 were subsequently known as the 'Phoney War'. Day after day our aircraft were loaded with bombs, stood by and were then unloaded. However, we loaded millions upon millions of leaflets into the aircraft to be dispersed from the flare chute, together with the odd house brick, that we put in for the sleeping 'fatherland'. In retrospect, neither the leaflets nor the house bricks seemed to do much good. On the camp itself another aspect of the war had made itself felt. Overnight all the airmen flying on operations were made up to Sergeant – airman one day, Sergeant the next. Imagine the effect of this on the

Sergeants' Mess! It is doubtful if at that time any of its regular members had less than eighteen years' service, and then overnight they were swamped with large numbers of youngsters, to whom Mess tradition mattered a lot less than tomorrow's bombing target. The exclusive flying club had gone forever. Meanwhile Marham was still expanding. 115 Squadron had opened up its own fields for dispersal and metal tracking had been laid down to combat the mud – servicing outside had become the norm. Reservists and National Service men had come to swell the ranks of both ground and aircrew, and regular working hours and regular meals were definitely things of the past. It fell to the fitters and riggers to guard the aerodrome, on top of their other duties. I often patrolled alone around the bomb dump on the blacked-out station in the early hours of the morning, hoping that 'Jerry' wouldn't choose this moment to drop a bomb on it. We had had no experience of enemy bombs so we didn't know quite what to expect.[8]

The first RAF raids of the war took place on 4 September 1939, but the Wellingtons of 9 Squadron and 149 Squadron were thwarted by bad weather and two of the Wellingtons and five Blenheims failed to return. The following day 3 Group prepared for another shipping attack. Plans were quickly scrapped, however, when it was feared that the Luftwaffe was about to launch an all-out attack on bomber stations in East Anglia. On 16 September 115 Squadron received their first two Wellington IA aircraft, armed with the new Frazer-Nash gun turret. A combination of bad weather and the lack of suitable targets, as dictated by War Cabinet policy, delayed bomber squadrons from operating, and on several occasions during the next few weeks aircraft took part in sweeps over the North Sea. Otherwise, they were mainly occupied in bombing and firing practice and formation exercises.[9] On 8 October six crews of 115 Squadron took off from Marham to join a 99 Squadron formation in an attack on the German fleet off Norway, but no ships were found. On 17 November six Wellingtons of 38 Squadron searched for enemy ships near Borkum but, except for the fishing fleet off the East Coast of England and one motor vessel spotted on the return journey, no ships or aircraft were seen.

Meanwhile, under the RAF Bomber Command 'Scatter' plan, the majority of bomber squadrons were dispersed to satellite bases. For instance, Wellingtons of 38 and 115 Squadrons were sent to the 340-acre satellite site at Barton Bendish.[10] 'Johnnie' Johnson recalls:

Memories of flying club days were by now a very distant dream. For night-time dispersal the aircraft were flown into a large field about three miles away at Barton Bendish. More cold and more mud. Starting the engines at Barton Bendish after they had stood out all night in the middle of winter was quite an experience and required a special and a very, very unofficial technique. The Pegasus engine was primed for starting by pumping raw petrol into the top three cylinders, by means of a key gas pump fitted to the aircraft. The engine oil was of course by now thick and viscous, so that the trolley batteries could hardly turn the engine. The trick was to get the engine to backfire into the carburettor, where it would ignite surplus petrol in the air intake, let it burn for the requisite number of seconds to warm up the carburettor, and then extinguish it by placing your forage cap over the intake. All engine fitter forage caps had singe marks on them! If you misjudged it, you stood a good chance of burning up the whole aircraft but usually it worked pretty well.

All stories, even non-fiction so I'm told, should contain an element of tragedy and romance, to hold the attention of the reader. The tragedy occurred on the afternoon of 5 November 1939. A close friend of mine, John Bailey, who was one of the ex-apprentices who came with us to Marham, was one of six riggers detailed aboard a Wimpy being dispersed at Barton Bendish. It was not his aircraft but for some reason its own ground crew couldn't go to cover it up and tie it down as was the normal procedure. Ten minutes after take-off we saw in the distance, in the general direction of the dispersal, a towering column of thick black smoke. It was obvious that the aircraft had crashed. Later it appeared that the pilot, indulging in a bit of low flying, had hit a tree with his tail and the aircraft crashed in flames burning and killing everyone on board.[11] Imagine my feelings when a few days later, together with another mutual friend, we escorted John's coffin to his home in Beccles. Here we found his grieving family and the undertaker waiting in the sitting room with another coffin, to which the body was to be transferred, in front of them all. How I conveyed to the undertaker that injuries sustained in a crash in flames made it inadvisable to carry this out, I don't know. I was just nineteen years old, but I think I grew quite old that day.[12]

Flying in those days was subject to virtually no restrictions whatsoever. Providing the flight was authorised by the Flight Commander or his Deputy, a pilot could take-off and go more or less anywhere he wished. The favourite pastime was hedgehopping. Many times I have stood just behind the pilot, flying below the level of the Norfolk hedges, waiting for him to lift the aircraft above the line of trees rushing towards us, and dropping it down the other side. It was a breathtaking thrill, but then we were all very young and foolish. In later years, when I could appreciate how little flying training some of those pilots had done, I shudder at the risks we took.[13]

The Air Ministry planners were still of the opinion that close-knit formations of Wellingtons, with their healthy defensive armament, could survive everything the enemy threw at them, and penetrate heavily defended targets. Recent heavy losses in British merchant shipping, and pressure from Winston Churchill, the First Lord of the Admiralty, in particular, prompted the War Cabinet to order Bomber Command to mount, as soon as possible, 'a major operation with the object of destroying an enemy battle-cruiser or pocket battleship'. However, the directive added, 'no bombs are to be aimed at warships in dock or berthed alongside the quays'. The War Cabinet wanted no German civilian casualties. During the late afternoon of 2 December 1939, 115 and 149 Squadrons at Marham and Mildenhall were alerted that a strike would be mounted against two German cruisers moored off Heligoland. Immediately, twenty-four Wellingtons were loaded with four 500lb SAP (Semi Armour Piercing) bombs and 620 gallons of fuel, ready for a strike early the following morning. Leading the attack would be thirty-four-year-old Wing Commander Richard Kellett AFC, a distinguished pre-war aviator, now Commanding Officer of 149 Squadron.[14]

On the morning of 3 December the weather had improved and at 09.00 hours Kellett led his twelve Wellingtons off in four flights of three. He rendezvoused with three Wellingtons of 38 Squadron and nine of 115 Squadron from Marham, and the force flew out over the North Sea towards Heligoland in four 'battle formations' of six Wimpys each. Two cruisers were spotted at anchor in the roads between the two tiny rock outcrops that are Heligoland in the German Bight. Kellett prepared to attack from up sun. As a result of the early losses, the bombing altitude had been raised to 7,000ft (considered 'high-level' bombing altitude at this time). Hits were claimed on one of the warships and another Wellington attacked a large merchantman anchored outside the harbour, but a cloud obscured the targets and results were unconfirmed. Although Freya radar had warned the German gunners of the impending raid, the thick cloud at their bombing altitude had fortunately hidden the Wellingtons from view. Four Messerschmitt Bf 109Ds of 1 Gruppe Zerstorergeschwader 26 at Jever, led by Hauptmann Dickore, climbed and intercepted the bombers after they had bombed but their aim was spoiled by cloudy conditions. Even so, the two pairs of Bf 109Ds damaged two of the Wellingtons in the attack. One pair attacked from above and the other pair from below. Leutnant Günther Specht, who damaged one of the Wellingtons, was shot down by return fire from Corporal Copley, 38 Squadron, rear gunner in Sergeant Odoire's Wellington. One of the rounds from Specht's machine guns actually hit and lodged in the belt buckle of Copley's harness without injuring him. Specht ditched in the sea and was later rescued. The German had been wounded in the face and later had to have his left eye removed.[15] Luckily for the Wellington crews, the three remaining Bf 109Ds were low on fuel and they broke off the engagement, while sixteen Bf 109D/Es and eight of I./ZG26's new Bf 110Cs arrived too late to intercept the bombers.

Again the bombs were to fail miserably, although an enemy minesweeper was claimed sunk when one bomb went clean through the bottom of the vessel without exploding. It was, however, a trawler, formerly the *Johann Schulte*, which did sink to the bottom. Back at the RAF bases hopes ran high now that the bombers had penetrated enemy air space, duelled with the Luftwaffe and escaped unscathed. These hopes were to be short-lived.

On 14 December an armed reconnaissance by twelve Wellingtons of 99 Squadron proved disastrous when five of the Wellingtons were shot down by Bf 109Es of II./JG77 that had taken off from Wangerooge together with four Bf 110s of 2/ZG26 from Jever. Air Vice-Marshal 'Jackie' Baldwin, AOC 3 Group, was compelled to compare it to the Charge of the Light Brigade. Despite the losses Bomber Command opined that the Wellingtons had survived repeated fighter attacks; faith in the old adage that 'the bomber will always get through' seemed as unshakable as ever. Indeed, the debriefing report was to state later: 'After careful analysis of individual reports by all members of crews, it seems almost possible to assume that none of our aircraft were brought down by fire from the Messerschmitts.' At Bomber Command the consensus was that, in future, concealment was more important than defensive firepower. Henceforth bomber formations would fly at 10,000ft and crews were urged to seek the safety of cloud cover whenever possible. However, on 18 December 9 and 149 Squadrons were decimated by the Luftwaffe. The operation, in search of warships, carrying bombs quite unsuitable for such targets, cost twelve Wellingtons, eleven complete crews and several wounded. In addition to the twelve Wellingtons lost and the two written-off in crashes, three others were damaged in crash-landings in England. The RAF post-mortem into the disastrous raid had concluded that its Wellingtons and Hampdens could no longer cross German territory in daylight and expect to survive against Luftwaffe opposition. Meanwhile, ground crews at the Wellington and Hampden bases installed armour plate and applied self-sealing covering to fuel tanks. The losses seem to have shaken the War Cabinet out of its chivalrous attitude towards the German civilian population, but it would not be until March 1940 that the so-called 'niceties' of war were dispensed with and Bomber Command was allowed to bomb land targets for the first time. The RAF night offensive had opened in February 1940 with 'Nickel' raids with propaganda leaflets, or 'Bumphlets', being dropped on Germany. They at least provided an opportunity for crews to gain some valuable experience of flying at night.

In March the first Wellington ICs were issued to the squadrons. The Mk.IC had re-designed hydraulics and a 24-volt electrical system, which permitted the use of the new directional radio compass. Crews, ever mindful of the beam attacks made by the Luftwaffe, soon installed hand-held machine guns in the long narrow-side windows. With enemy warships massing in German ports and then sailing north for a possible invasion of Norway in April, 115 Squadron sent a detachment to Kinloss in Scotland to co-operate with the 9 Squadron detachment at Lossiemouth. On 7 April crews were brought to a state of readiness when it was realised that German ships sighted heading for Norway and Denmark the day before were part of an invasion force. During the afternoon Blenheims attacked but their bombs missed and another attempt by two squadrons of Wellingtons was thwarted by bad visibility. Two of 115 Squadron's Wellingtons, piloted by Pilot Officer E.A. Wickenkamp MBE and Pilot Officer R.A. Gayford, were shot down with no survivors by Bf 110s, and three others were damaged. The next day the Wimpys attacked and claimed hits on a cruiser in Bergen harbour. On 11 April six Wellingtons of 115 Squadron operating from Kinloss attempted to bomb Sola airfield at Stavanger, but only three actually bombed the airfield. Pilot Officer F.E. Barber was shot down and Flight Sergeant G.A. Powell's Wellington was seriously damaged, and he had to belly-land back at Kinloss without hydraulics. He was later awarded the DFM for this operation. On 12 April six Wellingtons of 149 Squadron took off from Mildenhall and followed in trail behind six Wellingtons of 38 Squadron from Marham, as part of a force of eighty-three aircraft seeking German shipping at Stavanger. No warships had been sighted when the Wellingtons were intercepted by Bf 110s. The enemy pilots, again employing beam attacks to excellent advantage, shot down two bombers of 149 Squadron and Squadron Leader M. Nolan's Wellington in 38 Squadron. Twelve Wellingtons of 9 and 115 Squadrons, which were ordered to make a bombing attack on two cruisers, the *Köln* and the *Königsberg* in Bergen harbour, fared little better. None of their bombs did any lasting damage. Altogether six Hampdens and three Wellingtons failed to return. On 13–14 April, Pilot Officer G.L. Crosby, operating from Wick, ditched 22 miles off Whitby. Wellingtons of 38 Squadron also operated against Sola airfield and flew the first of three operations to Stavanger on the 16th.

On 2–3 May twenty-four aircraft, including twelve Wellingtons, bombed Stavanger, Rye and Fornebu. In all, the Marham Wellingtons flew 173 sorties during the month to Norway, Waalhaven and oil targets in Germany, with the loss of five aircraft and crews. On 9 May a Wellington of 38 Squadron at RAF Marham was brought to readiness for a security patrol to Borkum in the German Friesian Islands. The front gunner, LAC G. Dick, recalls:

> The object was to maintain a standing patrol of three hours over the seaplane base to prevent their flarepath lighting up and thus inhibit their mine-laying sea-planes from taking off. We carried a load of 250lb bombs in case a discernible target presented itself. We took off at 21.30 hours. Holland was still at peace and their lights, though restricted, were clearly visible, the Terschelling

lightship in particular, obliging by giving a fixed navigational fix. After three hours monotonous circling and seeing next to nothing, I heard Flying Officer Burnell, our Canadian pilot, call for course home. The words always sounded like music to a gunner in an isolated turret with no positive tasks to take up his mind, other than endless turret manipulation and endless peering into blackness. I heard the navigator remark that the lightship had gone out and the pilot's reply, 'Well give us a bloody course anyway'. One only had to go west to hit Britain somewhere, or return on the reciprocal of the outward course – drift notwithstanding. After an hour's flying with the magic IFF box switched on for the past thirty minutes, I gave the welcome call, 'Coast ahead!' Much discussion occurred as to where our landfall really was. I told them I thought north of the Humber, which was 150 miles north of our proper landfall at the Orfordness corridor. I was told to 'Belt up'. As a gunner, what did I know about it? (I had flown pre-war with 214 Squadron for two years up and down the East Coast night and day and was reasonably familiar with it.) Probably pride would not let them admit that they were 150 miles off course, in an hour's flying. Eventually, a 'chance light' showed up and we landed on a strange aerodrome, which turned out to be Leconfield. Overnight billets were arranged at 04.00 hours for the visiting crew. However, others were on an early start. They switched on the radio at 06.00 hours and gave us the 'gen' that at around midnight Germany had invaded Holland, Belgium and France – hence the extinguished lightship. The odd thing was, we had returned with our bombs, as it wasn't the done thing to drop them indiscriminately. We returned to base later on the tenth to be greeted with 'We thought you'd gone for a Burton'. Good news was slow in circulating in those days.

The German violation of Dutch and Belgian neutrality had opened up a path for British bombers to fly directly from England to the Ruhr, where 60 per cent of Germany's industrial strength was concentrated. However, political infighting between the French and British commands delayed matters. The French, with their hands full trying to repel an enemy force from its borders, were alarmed at the repercussions of such an action and Bomber Command, with its sixteen squadrons of Wellingtons, Whitleys and Hampdens, was prevented from carrying out the action. For the time being RAF Bomber Command had to content itself with inland targets in Germany. On the night of 10–11 May 115 and 38 Squadrons contributed twelve and six Wellingtons respectively to the raid by thirty-six Wellingtons on Waalhaven airfield in Holland. The Wimpys carried twelve 250lb bombs in their bomb bays and all the attacks were carried out in dives from 4–6,000ft down to 1,200–1,500ft. Flight Sergeant L. Boore was unable to bomb when he found observation partly obscured by smoke from fires in the town, and he returned with his bombs. On the night of 14–15 May Wellingtons bombed Aachen and the following day the War Cabinet authorised Bomber Command to attack east of the Rhine. On the night of 15–16 May Bomber Command began its strategic air offensive against Germany when ninety-nine bombers, thirty-nine of them Wellingtons, bombed sixteen different oil and steel plants and railway centres in the Ruhr. No aircraft were lost over Germany but a 115 Squadron Wellington failed to return. Flight Lieutenant A.E. Pringle DFC had originally taken off at 20.55 hours but the aircraft developed engine trouble and, after landing back at Marham, the crew took off in another Wellington minus Aircraftsman Butler, who had gone sick. On the return trip the Wellington was blown off course by an unexpected wind and it crashed

Wellington IC P9249 HD-T of 38 Squadron suffered an engine failure and crashed at Marham Fen, on approach to the airfield during a transit flight on 16 June 1940. The pilot, Pilot Officer E.W. Plumb, was killed, and two of the crew were seriously injured. It is pictured here on a pre-war service test flight. (Vickers)

at Bernay near Rouen, with the loss of all the crew. By the end of the month Marham had lost another four Wellingtons.[16]

Throughout May 1940 the Wellingtons attacked tactical targets with limited success. By early morning on 2 June the remaining troops of the British Expeditionary Force (BEF) had been evacuated from the shores around Dunkirk. Thousands of French troops had still to be evacuated, and during the daylight hours of 3 June Wellingtons stood, bombed up, ready to attack German positions near Dunkirk. Italy's decision, at midnight on 10 June, to declare war on Britain and France caused Bomber Command to re-direct its bombing strategy. Mussolini's intentions had already been anticipated and it was agreed that as soon as Italy joined the war Wellingtons and longer-range Whitleys would bomb her heavy industry in the north of the country. On 11–12 June Turin was bombed by Bomber Command, a distance of 1,350 miles there and back. Marham's Wellington squadrons operated on fifteen nights in June, bombing targets in France and Germany. Sergeant L.A. Morris and crew of 38 Squadron failed to return from the operation to Baden-Baden on the night of 14–15 June. Two crew members were killed and four survived to be taken prisoner. On 16 June another 38 Squadron Wellington was lost, when Pilot Officer E.W. Plumb's aircraft suffered an engine failure during a transit flight and went out of control at 200ft before crashing at Marham Fen. Plumb was killed and two fitters on board were seriously injured.

During July 1940 the Wellingtons of 3 Group carried out attacks on west and north-west Germany, with the occasional raid on targets in Denmark. Unrestricted warfare now threatened from both sides of the Channel. On 10 July a German aircraft dropped eighteen bombs near Marham airfield, and a simultaneous attack was made on a decoy site at South Pickenham near the airfield.[17] On the night of 18–19 July Pilot Officer W.H.C. Hunkin and crew were shot down on the Bremen raid and taken prisoner. Marham's Wellington squadrons were operational on eleven nights in July, with a raid by twenty-four Wellingtons on the night of the 27–28 being the biggest so far when Cologne, Hamm, Soest and Hamburg were attacked, with nineteen Hampdens assisting.

On the night of 2–3 August, when sixty-three Hampdens, Wellingtons and Whitleys visited six targets in Germany, Pilot Officer R.T. Gerry's Wellington ditched in the North Sea off Wells returning from Germany. Two Wellingtons were sent out to look for the aircraft and the Wells lifeboat was also launched, but no trace was found of the crew. On the night of 14–15 August another Wellington was lost when Sergeant Gregory crashed at Brancaster while returning from the Lünen aluminium works, with the loss of all the crew. On 22–23 August Sergeant N.C. Cook of 115 Squadron crash-landed at Wood Dalling whilst returning from Mannheim; Sergeant H.V. Watts, the front gunner, was killed. On the night of 23–24 August the Luftwaffe rained bombs on London, the first to fall on the capital since 1918. Bomber Command was quick to retaliate, for on the night of 25–26 August it dispatched about fifty Wellingtons, Hampdens and Whitleys to Berlin as a reprisal. The flight involved a round trip of eight hours and 1,200 miles. Seven aircraft aborted and, of the remaining force, twenty-nine bombers claimed to have bombed Berlin and a further twenty-seven over flew the German capital but were unable to pinpoint their targets because of thick cloud. Five aircraft were lost to enemy action, including three which ditched in the North Sea. Bombing results had been unimpressive but the RAF had scored a great victory for morale. When Berlin was bombed again on the night of 28–29 August, crews from Marham were among the seventy-nine Blenheims, Hampdens, Wellingtons and Whitleys that took part in raids on the German capital and other targets. George Bury, Pilot Officer Barr's navigator in a 115 Squadron Wellington, recalls:

The target was Klingenberg Electric. Having been warned that the area was very heavily defended, we decided to fly at 15,000ft. That was 5,000ft higher than our normal height. At this height it was essential to use oxygen all the time, but after a few hours the masks became wet and uncomfortable to use. But, if taken off, frequent movement was very tiring. As it turned out the flight as far as we were concerned turned out to be fairly uneventful. Searchlights were very active. Although one did pick us up, he failed to keep us within his beam long enough for the others in the group to join in. When just ahead we saw a Wellington caught by two at the same time and quick as a flash many others concentrated on the same target and he was caught in a cone of at least ten searchlights. The whole area around the aircraft was as bright as day and no matter which way he turned and twisted, they easily held on to him. The last we saw of him he was in a steep dive with shells bursting all around. This was our eighth flight and the first time that we had seen another aircraft. We were beginning to think that we were fighting the whole war on our own.[18]

Berlin and Cologne and airfields were attacked again on the last night of the month. By the end of 1940 the 'Big City', as it was to become known to bomber crews, would have been bombed on ten occasions. In September Wellingtons of 3 Group made repeated night attacks on invasion barges massed in the Channel ports ready for Operation Sealion, the proposed German invasion of England. The Marham Wellington squadrons were operational on eleven nights during the month and 248 sorties were flown with the loss of just one aircraft. This occurred on the night of 11–12 September when Flying Officer Allen failed to return from a raid on Germany. The RAF bombing directive of 21 September gave support to priority attacks on oil refineries, aircraft factories, railways, canals and U-boat construction yards, while electric power stations and gas works in Berlin should also be bombed. On the night of 23–24 September Berlin was selected for a special retaliatory attack and was bombed by 119 Whitleys, Hampdens and Wellingtons. However, most of the objectives were missed and many bombs failed to explode. In September 1940 the Luftwaffe had been forced to abandon massed daylight bombing and the invasion fleet was dispersed. Bomber Command could again turn its attention to city targets.[19] Sergeant 'Johnnie' Johnson recalls:[20]

> So 1940 progressed with operations and losses increasing. Down south, Fighter Command, quite remote from us, had fought and won the Battle of Britain. War had become to ground crew a routine, albeit a routine with no time or work boundaries that could be defined. Feelings had to be hardened – there was no time or opportunity to grieve over that missing crew with whom a few hours before you'd been drinking and chatting. 'The Ship Inn' at Narborough had benefited from the influx of servicemen at Marham, becoming a favourite watering hole for the airmen. Robert Crisp had been landlord since the First World War, having served in the RFC as an aircraft mechanic. He and his wife had four children and Joan, the youngest daughter, later married Australian pilot Wing Commander Rodney Gibbes DFC.[21] Late in 1940 it was decided that all RAF aircrew were to be given NCO status. [22]

In October the Marham Wellington squadrons endured extensive cloud cover over German targets, and bombs were dropped instead on alternate targets. On the night of 30 September–1 October just over 100 aircraft bombed targets in Germany and the Channel ports. Three of Marham's Wellingtons were tasked with bombing the marshalling yards at Ehrang. Ten more were part of a formation of Wellingtons detailed to bomb the Reichsluftfahrt-Ministerium (German Air Ministry) in Berlin. Seventeen crews, including seven from Marham, claimed to have attacked this single building in the Leipzigstrasse. In fact, only six bombs fell on the German capital and the Air Ministry was not hit. Pilot Officer D. McLean's aircraft in 38 Squadron was shot down attacking Leipzig; he was killed but his five crew survived to be taken prisoner. Two other Wellingtons of 115 Squadron, flown by Pilot Officer A.J.J. Steel and Sergeant C. Wessels, failed to return from the raid on the Osnabrück marshalling yards. Steel and Sergeant R.P. Mogg bailed out and survived to be taken prisoner. All six men in Wessels' crew, who may have been shot down by a night fighter, were killed.

On the night of 7–8 October Squadron Leader R.O.O. Taylor and crew of 38 Squadron failed to return from the operation to Berlin, in which twelve individual targets were ordered to be bombed by over forty Wellingtons and Whitleys. On 16–17 October sixty-five Hampdens and Wellingtons attacked Bremen, Kiel and Bordeaux, while eight Marham

Wellington IC of 115 Squadron at Marham in 1941 (Rodney Gibbes is seated third from left). (K. Crisp)

Wellingtons were ordered to attack Merseburg. Some aircraft dropped incendiary devices into the Harz forests.[23] Only two of Marham's Wellingtons located the target at Merseburg. On 24–25 October Flight Lieutenant E.G.F. Chivers and crew were lost on the operation to the Blohm & Voss shipyards in Hamburg. Returning from the attack on oil refineries at Gelsenkirchen in the early hours of 28 October, Pilot Officer Rogers crashed at Booten, near Reatham, and two of the crew were injured.

In the last week in October 1940 Marham received orders from 3 Group to have six Wellingtons and crews ready to deploy to Malta. Sergeant 'Johnnie' Johnson found himself on a list of fifty names from both flights of 38 Squadron and 115 Squadron, and the Station Commander, 'a remote figure rarely seen', arrived and informed them that they were going on detachment to an undisclosed destination for three weeks or more.[24] Long-range fuel tanks were fitted in the bomb bays of three 115 Squadron aircraft and three Wellingtons of 38 Squadron, and the selected crews were given briefings on routing procedures. On 30 October six 115 and 38 Squadron Wellingtons, led by Squadron Leader Foss, took off from Marham. Pilot Officer A.J.R. Pate DFC, who was flying one of the three 115 Squadron Wellingtons, flew into a balloon cable near Iver, Buckinghamshire, and the aircraft crashed, killing all the crew. A second 115 Squadron Wellington, flown by Sergeant Forrester, developed problems with the fuel feed from the long-range tank and returned to Marham. The four remaining Wellingtons arrived safely in Malta early the following morning. They were joined on the Mediterranean island later by more Wellingtons of 38 Squadron, led by Wing Commander Thomson, which left for Luqa. The squadron never returned and their place at Marham was taken by Wellington ICs of 218 Squadron, which arrived from Oakington in Cambridgeshire.

Marham's Wellington squadrons were operational on only seven nights in November. The night of 14–15 November proved unlucky for Sergeant H.J. Morson of 115 Squadron, whose thirteenth operation it was. Morson's Wellington was hit by flak before reaching Berlin and on the return he ditched in the North Sea. Five of the crew got into the dinghy but Sergeant Dean, the second pilot, emerged from the escape hatch over the cockpit and missed his landing on the wing. He fell between the fuselage and the engine and was not seen again. The rest of the crew were rescued and put ashore at Great Yarmouth by HMS *Pelton*. Morson and his wireless operator, Sergeant D.H.H. Cleverley, were later awarded the DFM for their devotion to duty.

On the night of the 16–17, 127 bombers, the largest number yet dispatched by Bomber Command, set out to raid four targets in Hamburg. Included in the force were eleven Wellingtons of 115 Squadron, which began taking off from Marham at 17:20 hours. Bad weather affected the operation and only sixty aircraft reported bombing Hamburg while twenty-five aircraft bombed alternative targets. Only four of the 115 Squadron Wellingtons found the primary target, as the flak and German fighters caused havoc. Wellington P9286/K, piloted by Sergeant D.E. Larkman, was shot down by Oberleutnant Egmont Prinz zur Lippe-Weissenfeld, Staffelkapitän, IV./NJG1. It was the Austrian Prince's first victory. The aircraft crashed at Winkel, Holland, with the loss of all the crew. Wellington R3213/S, flown by Sergeant D.D. English, also failed to return to Marham. Flight Lieutenant Van landed R1034 at Marham despite the aircraft being badly shot up. T2606, flown by Pilot Officer Tindall, was attacked by four Bf 110s in the target area and the front gunner, Sergeant E. Jarvis, was badly wounded. Tindall got the damaged Wellington home but he was forced to crash-land at Bircham Newton; Jarvis later died of his injuries. P9299, flown by Pilot Officer Roy, crashed at Wittering but there were no injuries to the crew.

Bad weather hampered operations throughout December, and 115 Squadron were on operations on only eight nights while 218 Squadron did not fly its first operation from Marham until 20 December, when two of its Wellingtons attacked Ostend. Three 115 Squadron Wellingtons were lost in December. On 8–9 December Pilot Officer A. Tindall strayed off track on the return from the raid on Bordeaux and he crashed into a hillside near Tredegar in Glamorgan. All the crew died. On the night of 11–12, Sergeant G.W. Hartland failed to return from the attack on Mannheim, and on 29–30 December Pilot Officer P.G.H. Salmon and crew also failed to return. Mannheim on 11–12 December was one of the most notable raids of the war so far. Bomber Command was authorised by the War Cabinet to carry out a general attack on the centre of a German city in retaliation for the recent heavy bombing of cities in England, particularly Coventry and Southampton. A force of 200 bombers was planned under Operation Abigail Rachael, but in the event the numbers were reduced to 134 aircraft, including sixty-one Wellingtons, when it was forecast that weather conditions over the home airfields would deteriorate. Three aircraft were lost and four more crashed in England. Wellington observer Albert E. Robinson in 115 Squadron recalls:

> Bombing by night presented a formidable barrier to the young crews of Bomber Command in
> 1940-41. If groping blindly through the curtain of darkness that had descended over Europe was
> to be overcome, it was crystal clear that in the initial stages an awful lot was going to depend on

the crews themselves. Trial and error mostly only resulted in a high casualty rate. Unfortunately, it was with little result for so great an effort, a pot-pourri of calculated risk, personal skills and circumstances that favoured the more successful crews. The 'X' factor, a quality difficult to define but one that enabled them to take advantage of more than a full share of luck, lifted them high above average. Whatever the mixture, a fierce determination to succeed in spite of the numerous setbacks was a common denominator and it united the crews almost without exception. With such resolution, the crews attempted to face up to their task. It was not made any easier by briefing officers who spoke at length about the necessity for precision bombing. It would not be too critical to suggest that some of these briefings were out of touch with reality. Truthful crews considered it a reasonable effort if the city itself was found, let alone a specific aiming point.

There were many reasons for this but the principal culprit was night navigation. This was based almost entirely on the age-old theory of dead reckoning. There was no problem if all the links in the chain were known but if not, it could turn out to be a hit-or-miss affair, especially with little or no radio assistance to help with the calculations. The basic requirement for success was to establish the wind speed and direction but in order to assess these it was necessary at various times during the flight to define the position of the aircraft in relation to the ground – obtain a 'fix', as it was known to the navigator. Under variable conditions this was not always possible. The flight could be blown well off course, sometimes miles away if there were adverse winds and with it went little chance of finding out the true position of the aircraft. This in turn usually added up to wasted effort, with bombs being brought back or jettisoned in the sea.

Inexperienced crews could end up on the slopes of a mountain or in the grey wastes of the sea. The North Sea in particular was a big enemy to Bomber Command; a heaving predator, menacing in its vastness to any crippled bomber struggling to maintain height over its darkened wilderness. The enemy coast to the hoped-for landfall in England offered little hope if a crippled bomber had to force-land and most certainly so if contact had been lost with any listening post as a result of a damaged radio. A bomber aircraft then was a lonely and desolate figure, struggling against the odds and with the chilling thought that no matter how expertly the aircraft was set down on the sea – turbulent or calm – the bomber would sink within minutes. There was the rubber dinghy, of course. It could be paddled but when exhaustion came and effort faded it would just drift along with the wind and tide, aimlessly and without hope, to a tortured end, unless providence took a hand. God knows how long this would take. Perhaps better not to have taken the dinghy at all.

That's how it went. Such possibilities could only be accepted by crews with a philosophical shrug of the shoulders. It came with a host of other things but even so most crews were optimistic and they set their sights on completing the mandatory, magical number of thirty operations before being taken off for a rest at some training squadron. In comparison to the numbers involved, very few managed to achieve this; the average could have been as low as five missions before the Grim Reaper called the tune. Given the conditions, the chances of survival on any one operation, whether it was the first or thirtieth were not good. Any discerning bookmaker would rate the betting odds low. All aircrew were volunteers to a man but in saying this they needed to be. Each raid was equivalent to 'going over the top' in the 1914-18 war. However, if one were to put the clock back to the briefing room in 1940-41 and peer through the haze of cigarette smoke that hung in swirling clouds, no one would have guessed it. It was more like a gathering at any sports club. We were boisterous, outgoing and extrovert but underneath this cloak there was a quiet confidence and rugged determination. Such an outlook was essential. The effort needed to penetrate Germany, certainly with the out-dated aircraft at the crews' disposal in 1940-41, required a deep-seated motivation and a special quality.

We were lucky to have the Wellington. The Wellington was probably the best of the bunch when compared to the other bombers. A good old war-horse, it was as loyal and forgiving as the crews were to the bomber. But the fact remains that it was outdated, unable to reach much height over the target, poorly armed, had no internal heat and when carrying a full bomb load of 4,000lb had a speed of less than half that of an enemy fighter. Freezing temperatures often coated surfaces with ice and frost, froze controls and radio sets and brought instant ice-burn should metal surfaces be touched without a glove. Engines were often suspect (they invariably coughed and spluttered) and the dials on the instrument panel were constantly watched with anxious eyes, hoping that the readings would not give reasons for concern. Should one engine fail, as they often did, it was a heart-stopping moment with the certain knowledge that the Wellington would not be able to maintain height over a sustainable period. Its flying range would then be determined by irreversible factors such as the state of the aircraft, height at the time, angle and speed of descent and the skill of the pilot to nurse the aircraft along. They were always apprehensive lest the extra workload would cause the remaining engine to overheat – not the least of the problems was the possibility that it too could fail.

If all this sounds gloomy, then add for good measure the fact that from take-off to return the Wellington would be flying in isolation. In many respects the raid would be one of individual effort and self-planning by the crews. Often the route to the target would be varied by crew preference. They normally took into account the known *Flak* areas but defenses could alter their tactics or geographical position, so even the most carefully thought-out plans could go astray and bring the sting of the serpent at an unexpected moment. Strict radio silence did not help but this was essential because of the enemy's rapidly increasing radar detection. To break this silence was to invite trouble, the equivalent to sending a telegram to the Luftwaffe notifying them of intent!

But all these shortcomings were shrugged off with an unflagging optimism. Metaphorically speaking we were all in the same boat and in any case anything bad happened to the other fellow – or at least so said the mind's defence mechanism. The more missions that were flown, the easier it became to believe this. It could also induce a state of mind dubbed by the crews as 'flak happy'. This could loosely be interpreted as over-confidence, a mistake for which many usually paid dearly, joining the list of doomed aircraft. These unfortunate souls just took off and literally vanished, never to be seen again – just like a conjuror's rabbit. The toll under this category became harder to stomach as the casualty list mounted.

Replacement crews to fill the gaps, proud of their newly won wings, keen and enthusiastic, came to the squadron like an endless belt at some factory complex. The crew room became a platform on which the passengers were ever-changing. There was barely time to get to know their names. Sadly, within a month, the fresh young faces who had been so eager to prove their worth would move along up the belt, often within days as crews were called upon to fly operations that were near impossible. Some were lucky, some not, but in all cases there was the same unpredictability as a name drawn at random from a hat. Not all were fresh faces either. The

Grim Reaper was not choosy and some were veterans of many operations. They *always* came back and their demise sent an ice-cold shock through every level in the squadron. The sorrow of their passing gave everyone food for thought.

With Bomber Command heavily committed, in principle any retrograde step was out of the question, and Command was compelled to allow for these losses when planning. It was not a very happy thought for the squadron commanders to lose so many of their valuable, well-trained crews, but it is not possible to make an omelette without breaking eggs, a fait accompli that just about fitted in with a Wellington bomber squadron. Even so, Command intensified its efforts. There would be no respite, no let up, and the battle, if Britain was to keep intact its position as the sole bastion in the struggle against a Nazi Germany, must continue to be fought.

In January 1941 the weather worsened and snow fell. Marham's Wellington's flew only six operations, all without loss, but on 15 January Flying Officer P.F. McLaren of 218 Squadron was killed on his first Wellington solo flight. The bad weather, however, seemed to work to the Luftwaffe's advantage, and on 16 January ten small bombs were dropped on the airfield and some exploded near Lady's Wood and next to a barrack block. Damage was slight and there were no casualties. Despite more bad weather in February, aircraft serviceability remained high and operational bomber raids continued on most nights, with invasion ports at Le Havre, Boulogne, Brest and Rotterdam being frequent targets. On the night of 7–8 February, when thirty-five Wellingtons of Bomber Command attacked Boulogne, 115 Squadron provided ten of the attacking Wimpys. On the night of 10–11 February 1941 3 Group was able to put up more than a hundred Wellingtons for the first time in the war when Hanover and Rotterdam were attacked by 365 bombers. At Marham 115 Squadron contributed eleven aircraft, and 218 Squadron offered ten. Two Wellingtons failed to return from the raid on Hanover. One of them was a 115 Squadron Wellington flown by Sergeant H.H. Rogers, who was returning from the raid and, after almost colliding with another Wellington, decided to turn his navigation lights on. German intruders were over East Anglia and Rogers was attacked over the Swaffham beacon by Hauptmann Rolf Jung of 4./NJG2, who damaged his port engine. Rogers dropped down low to try to avoid further attacks but he was forced to crash-land at Narborough, and the Wellington was soon enveloped in flames. The crew managed to evacuate the Wimpy before it exploded.[25] The intruder was a specially modified Ju 88C of I./NJG2, which had begun flying offensive operations over England from Holland in early September 1940. German intruders returned to the area on the night of 25 February, and a Wellington flown by Sergeant Hoos of 218 Squadron was shot down 4 miles from Marham. The front gunner, Sergeant Stanley, was trapped in the wreckage; he suffered severe burns and his leg had to be amputated later in hospital in King's Lynn.[26]

On the night of 11–12 February, meanwhile, further losses were caused when the bombers returned from Bremen and fog descended on most of the stations. Signals were sent out for aircraft to return as soon as possible and to use airfields in Lossiemouth and Kinloss if sufficient petrol allowed. At Marham visibility was down to just 500 yards and all the returning Wellingtons were advised to head for Wyton, but then this airfield became fogged in. Every available flare was lit at Marham but in the event none of the returning aircraft was able to land. Wing Commander A.C. Evans-Evans and his crew baled out of their 115 Squadron Wellington, which then crashed at Wicken Bonhunt, 4 miles south-south-west of Saffron Walden.[27] Pilot Officer Clarke and his crew abandoned their Wimpy in the vicinity of Cambridge and it crashed on houses in Histon Road, killing three elderly ladies. A fourth lady was badly injured. Three crews managed to put down safely at Wyton and two more at Alconbury, while three more put down at Driffield, Newmarket and Bassingbourn. Sergeant W.S. Adam of 218 Squadron force-landed at Frampton-on-Severn near Stroud, where his plane became stuck in the mud and the incoming tide. Flying Officer Anstey and his crew of 218 Squadron abandoned their Wellington over Tebay, near Kendal in Westmoreland. Five other Wellingtons landed at Gravesend, Finningley, Tangmere, Withernsea and Lindholme. Altogether, twenty-two aircraft, including eleven Wellingtons, crashed in England and five men died.

There was more drama on 22–23 February when twenty-nine Wellingtons were dispatched to Brest to bomb warships there, but only eleven aircraft bombed and four aircraft crashed in England on return. 115 Squadron contributed nine Wellingtons. Pilot Officer Clarke returned early with a technical problem but on landing he swung to starboard to avoid some buildings, and ended up in trees to the west of the airfield. None of the crew was injured and the aircraft was repaired. At 08:25 hours Sergeant E.J. Milton, in *F for Freddie*, called for a bearing and this was acknowledged and orders given to divert to Feltwell, but nothing more was heard. A few minutes later the Wimpy hit a tree and crashed at East Winch near King's Lynn. The aircraft caught fire and all six crew died. R1469/Q was being flown by Sergeant Bright when, about 8 miles north of Morlaix, his rear gunner, Pilot Officer Mills, saw a Bf 110 flying about 500ft below and astern. Mills opened fire with about 300 rounds from each gun into the 110's cockpit. The Messerschmitt was seen to shudder and dip its port wing as it turned to port. Mills asked Bright to turn quickly, and a stall turn and dive brought his guns to bear again on the Bf 110's tail unit, which, after about 200 rounds from each gun, was seen to lose the port fin tail and rudder. The 110's nose came up and stalled into a spin, disappearing through the clouds at about 4,000ft. Later that night L7810/R, which was sent to attack Boulogne, was heard calling for a fix from Hull at around 21.45 hours. Nothing else was heard of Sergeant Lloyd and his crew, who were listed as missing. On 23–24 February Pilot Officer K.N. Arthurs and crew of L7810/R was lost and all the crew killed. On the night of 25–26 February Sergeant Hoos' Wellington of 218 Squadron was badly shot about by Feldwebel Ernst Ziebarth of 1./NJG2, and the Wellington IC crash-landed in a field at Red Lodge, 2 miles south of Swaffham. Three of the crew were injured.

The first bombing raid of March 1941 was flown on the night of the 2–3 when fifty-four aircraft attacked warships at Brest. Wellington 3279, flown by Sergeant G.R. Pike, dived into the sea off Teignmouth. Rescue craft were sent out and they found only the W/T operator alive. Two parachutes and the body of Sergeant Fenwick were also found. A few days later, on the night of 12–13 March, when eighty-six aircraft, including fifty-four Wellingtons, attacked Bremen and other forces attacked Hamburg and Berlin, Flying Officer W.P. Crosse of 218 Squadron failed to return. His Wellington IC was shot down by Oberfeldwebel Hans Rasper of 4./NJG1. Crosse and three of his crew were killed, while two men who survived

Ground crew of Wellington IC F for Freddie at Marham in September 1940. Flight Sergeant E.C. 'Johnnie' Johnson is second from left. F for Freddie was subsequently destroyed on the ground at RAF Luqa, Malta, by Stuka dive bombers. (E.C. Johnson)

were taken prisoner.[28] The following night, 13–14 March, 139 aircraft raided the Blohm & Voss shipyards at Hamburg, and Sergeant Donald returned badly shot up with the W/T operator Sergeant Huffingley dead at his post. Donald crash-landed the badly damaged Wellington at Marham without further casualties. Marham's Wellingtons flew ops on five more nights during March. On 30–31 March the Wellingtons began their campaign against the German battle cruisers *Scharnhorst* and *Gneisenau*, or 'Salmon and Gluckstein' (a famous London department store) as they were known, while the Halifaxes went after the cruiser *Prinz Eugen* at Brest. The warships were visited five times in April and the campaign was to last for more than ten months.

During April Marham's Wellingtons flew eighty-seven sorties for the loss of six aircraft, three of which crashed in England returning from ops. On the night of 3–4 April, when the target was Brest, Wellington IC R1470/H of 115 Squadron, flown by Sergeant C.M. Thompson, was attacked by a Ju 88C of 3./NJG2, piloted by Leutnant Heinz Völker. The Wimpy crashed into the mud banks at Ongar Hill near Terrington St Clements, 5 miles west of King's Lynn, killing all the crew except the rear gunner, Sergeant Russell. He died later of exposure. It was on this night that 4,000lb bombs were used operationally for the first time, when they were dropped on Emden. On the night of 8–9 April, when Kiel was attacked by 160 aircraft, a Wellington of 218 Squadron was badly hit and flew home on one engine where it was landed at Horsham St Faith, near Norwich, after all moveable equipment had been jettisoned over the North Sea. Also, all the maps were thrown out and the fixed aerial had been damaged by enemy action, so the navigator and Sergeant H. Burke, the wireless operator, successfully navigated a course by a combination of guesswork and wireless bearings. Burke was later praised for his 'coolness and skill', which undoubtedly resulted in the safe return of the aircraft.

On 10–11 April fifty-three bombers, comprising thirty-six Wellingtons, twelve Blenheims and five Manchesters, headed for Brest to try and finish off the *Gneisenau* which had been recently damaged by a Coastal Command torpedo bomber. Meanwhile twenty-nine Hampdens and twenty-four Whitleys went to bomb Düsseldorf, and minor operations were flown to Bordeaux/Mérignac airfield and to Rotterdam. Four hits were claimed on the *Gneisenau*. A Wellington flown by Sergeant A.G. Plumb of 218 Squadron failed to return, while five Hampdens were lost on the raid on Düsseldorf. On 12–13 April sixty-six aircraft, including thirty-five Wellingtons, returned to Brest, which was visited again on the night of 22–23 April. On the second raid T2560/E of 115 Squadron, flown by Sergeant Palmer, crashed near Swindon on diversion to Wroughton. Sergeant F. Shaw, the second pilot, was killed. A Wellington of 218 Squadron, flown by Sergeant W.H. Swain RNZAF, failed to return, and another flown by Sergeant W.S. Adams crashed near Clenchwarton station, 2 miles west of King's Lynn. On 24–25 April, when sixty-nine aircraft including thirty-nine Wellingtons attacked Kiel, another 218 Squadron Wellington, flown by Sergeant E.J. Chidgey, crashed near Barton Bendish. All the crew survived. On 25–26 April when sixty-two aircraft including thirty-two Wellingtons were dispatched to Kiel, Flying Officer G.B.S. Agar and his crew of 218 Squadron failed to return. Theirs was the only aircraft lost and none of the crew survived.

During May the Marham Wellington crews divided their attacks, with two raids on the warships in Brest harbour early in the month and raids on German cities in the Ruhr. They took part in three raids on Hamburg and on the second raid, on the night of 10–11, a 115 Squadron Wellington flown by Pilot Officer Saunderson dropped a 4,000lb Minol bomb, which went by the more familiar names of 'Cookie', 'Blockbuster' or 'Dustbin' bomb. In a Wimpy the bomb doors and floor were removed and the bomb attached by a 1in wire hawser and toggle to a metal beam introduced under the main spar. An axe was supplied to cut the hawser in case it hung up. That same night a 115 Squadron crew were shot down by a German night fighter using the Helle Nachtjagd (illuminated night fighting) interception method, whereby German fighters, with the aid of searchlights in northern Germany and in the Rhineland, tried to intercept RAF bombers.[29] Don Bruce, Sergeant Observer in 115 Squadron in 1942, wrote the following account on the shooting down of the Wellington from his squadron:

The weather in the British Isles on Saturday 10 May 1941 was fine with little or no cloud. Visibility was good and similar conditions obtained on the Continent with some high and medium cloud over northwest Germany. There would be a full moon that night. On the bomber squadrons the usual morning routine activities were taking place, Marham was reverberating with the noise of Wellington bombers bearing the code letters 'KO', as 115 Squadron crews lifted off on short cross-country flights to air test machines, equipment and guns. Twenty-six-year-old Sergeant John Anderson touched down on the grass airfield around mid-day in Wellington R1379 KO-B having completed his air test. After taxiing to his dispersal point he and his five-man crew clambered down the ladder to wait for transport back to the Flights. John Anderson, an experienced operational pilot, had recently taken command of this new, combat-inexperienced crew. He had flown three operational flights with them. The second pilot was a twenty-year-old Australian, Sergeant Alex Kerr. Sergeant David Fraser, also aged twenty, was the rear gunner. The observer, who carried out the dual role of navigator and bomb aimer, was Sergeant Bill Legg. Sergeants Geoff Hogg and Bernard Morgan as wireless operator and front gunner respectively completed the crew. Back at the Flights John Anderson noted that instructions were chalked on the boards for the ground crew to fuel and bomb up his aircraft. It signified they would be on operations that night. In the late afternoon in the company of other participating aircrews he and his crew attended briefing and learned that orders had come through from Bomber Command HQ for an attack on Hamburg. 119 bombers were being dispatched to bomb the general city area, Altona rower-station and the shipyards. Sixty of these aircraft would be Wellingtons. Hampdens and Whitleys, plus one Manchester, the forerunner of the Lancaster bomber, would make up the complement. The target for the crew of KO-B was the dock area at Hamburg.

Swinging round to line up with the take-off strip at 22.17 hours the crewmembers of KO-B were very much preoccupied with thoughts of their immediate future. They could not know that the Luftwaffe had already begun a devastating fire-attack on the City of London. This attack, aided by good visibility from a full moon, and an abnormally low tide in the River Thames leaving firemen short of water, would create a 'second' Great Fire of London. They could not know that a lone German fighter was within six minutes' flying time of the British Isles. Bf 110 coded VJ+OQ with Rudolf Hess the Deputy Führer of Germany at its controls was fast approaching its zero hour.

An uneventful outward flight punctuated only with a flak burst from an isolated battery along the route brought them to the port of Hamburg. Homing in on the target at a height of 11,000ft they began to make their bombing run, but fierce opposition from the defences in the form of close proximity flak threw them off course. Sergeant Anderson turned to make another run across the target and this time Sergeant Legg was able to release his bombs. Weaving out of the intense flak barrage they turned onto a predetermined course at full boost. Almost immediately they were picked up by three radar-controlled searchlights and coned in the beams of their attendant searchlight batteries.

The heavy flak now located and started hitting them. Hydraulic pipes in the aircraft were ruptured, releasing hydraulic fluid, which caused the rear turret to jam at an awkward angle. David Fraser also reported over the intercom a fire in his turret. Further, his vision was obscured by hydraulic fluid and oil, which had spread over the perspex windows of the turret. His electric gun-sight had been put out of action. The observer, Bill Legg, made his way towards the rear turret with the cabin fire extinguisher. In the meantime David had stamped out the fire. As Bill made his way back to the cabin he could see Alex Kerr standing in the astrodome watching out for fighters. In the event of an attack Kerr would direct the pilot in his evasive action. Suddenly the flak batteries stopped firing. It signalled the immediate presence of a night fighter.

Twenty-two-year-old Leutnant Eckart-Wilhelm von Bonin of 6./NJG1 piloting a Bf 110 night fighter had been vectored into the vicinity of the enemy aircraft. The searchlights outlining the Wellington bomber had eased his task. He was now manoeuvering into position for an attack from the rear starboard quarter. This was his first operational interception. He was keyed up and very apprehensive of the two guns in the bomber's rear turret. Von Bonin would eventually become a night fighter ace with thirty-seven victories to his credit but he was now to be tested in battle for the very first time. Closing fast on the bomber he could not understand why the rear turret was not swinging in his direction. The enemy gunner must have seen him at this range. Tense, with the adrenaline pumping, he opened fire. As he did so he realized only his machine guns were firing. He had overlooked the firing button for the 20mm cannon. It was a blessing in disguise for the British crew.

Back in the bomber Alex Kerr heard David Fraser's terse voice over the intercom, 'Night-fighter on our tail'. He swung round in the astrodome and saw a dark shape moving rapidly into position on the starboard quarter. As he shouted instructions over the intercom to the pilot he felt Bill Legg brush against him as he returned from the rear turret. The fighter's nose danced with pinpoints of flame as the German pilot opened up. Kerr felt a heavy blow as though he had been punched simultaneously all over his body. He was knocked backwards on to the canvas bed in the aircraft. Before he lost consciousness he noticed a fire had started in the reconnaissance flares which were amidships on the starboard side. They were close to the oxygen bottles. The machine gun bullets had wounded him in ten places including a bullet in his liver. Bill Legg was standing next to Alex Kerr when the fighter attacked. He was off the intercom and didn't know what was happening. A hammer-like blow hit him in the lower part of the back. He twisted involuntarily and received several other hits. With blood oozing from his back and stomach he crumpled and fell unconscious to the floor.

John Anderson, aware of the bright yellow flame burning amidships, began to throw the Wellington about in an effort to blow out the fire. His efforts were unavailing. The bomber continued to burn fiercely. Fearing an explosion would blow the aircraft to pieces, he gave the order to bale out. Although David Fraser's turret was jammed at an angle he managed to squeeze through the narrow aperture left by the partly obscured door and gained access to the fuselage where his parachute was stored. As he made his way to the emergency escape hatch aft of the beam machine gun on the starboard side he saw Alex sitting in front of the hatch. He was obviously badly wounded and very dazed. A quick examination of Bill Legg who was lying further up the fuselage convinced David that he was dead. He returned to Alex, who in the meantime had managed to remove the cover from the escape hatch and was sitting with his legs dangling through the hatch. David placed Alex's hand on the ripcord and pushed him out. He was relieved to see his parachute open. David followed. By now Bernard Morgan and Geoff Hogg had both made good their escape. Having set the automatic pilot, John Anderson scrambled down to the escape hatch and baled out. Unfortunately he landed in the River Elbe and drowned. The aircraft continued on course burning brightly, carrying the badly wounded, unconscious figure of its observer.

The crumpled body of Bill Legg began to stir as he slowly regained his senses. He still wasn't sure what had happened and by an immense effort of will staggered to his feet and climbed over the main spar to get to the cockpit. He was amazed to find the pilot's seat empty. Slowly it dawned on him that he was alone in a burning aircraft 9,000ft above Germany. He had to get out and get out quickly. His parachute was under his table. Having retrieved it he made his way forward to the main escape hatch. Carrying the parachute in his hand instead of immediately clipping it on his harness, he stood over the escape hatch looking down into the night. At that

Above, below and opposite: A smiling twenty-two-year-old Leutnant Eckart-Wilhelm 'Hugo' von Bonin of 6./NJG1 in front of his first night victim, Wellington IC R1379 of 115 Squadron, flown by twenty-six-year-old pilot Sergeant John Anderson. He shot Anderson down near Tönning, Schleswig-Holstein in the Helle Nachtjagd (illuminated night fighting) on 10–11 May 1941, while flying a Bf 110. (Ab A. Jansen via Theo Boiten)

moment his strength seemed to ebb. The chute slipped from his grasp. He watched with dismay as it fell through the escape hatch and into the darkness. His position was now desperate. He had never been officially trained as a pilot and had only taken over the controls of a Wellington briefly for a straight and level flight with one of his pilots.

Weakness brought on by his wounds dulled his senses. He didn't panic. With great difficulty he climbed into the pilot's seat and took over the controls. He released the automatic pilot and switched to manual control. As there was no possibility of surviving he decided to stick the plane down and crash, taking something or someone that was German with him. Losing height rapidly he found he could pick out rivers, fields and buildings in the bright moonlight. He pulled back on the stick and levelled out at about 600ft. One field appeared to be much larger than the rest. He decided to try to crash in it. Easing back on the throttles, unable to employ flap because of the damaged hydraulics, he approached at a speed of 100 knots to avoid stalling. At a height of around 100ft he closed both throttles and braced himself for the crash. About three-quarters of the way along the field the Wellington touched down, bumped along on its belly and stopped. Having released the pilot's escape hatch Bill found he was too weak to pull himself through it. Two German soldiers from a nearby flak battery climbed onto the burning plane and lifted him to safety. [30]

The station's only other loss during May was Wellington R1280 of 115 Squadron, flown by Sergeant Sayers, which lost a propeller and, unable to maintain height, had to be force-landed half a mile short of the runway at Oakington. With the better weather to come, operations were flown from Marham on eleven nights in June with Kiel and Cologne being the most frequently visited targets. On the night of 12–13 June, when eighty-two Wellingtons visited the railway yards at Hamm, Marham dispatched a dozen Wellingtons of 115 Squadron. Shortly after take-off R1805/T, flown by Sergeant Robson, developed engine trouble and he was forced to jettison his bomb load over the Wash and return to Marham. As the Wimpy crossed the airfield boundary the second engine failed and the aircraft crashed, hitting a tree and seriously injuring two of the crew. Sergeant G. Aikenhead died later of his injuries. A few days later, on 17 June, another Wellington was written-off when Pilot Officer A.Y. Evans crashed at Palgrove Farm near Sporle during an air test. Only one man survived. On 20–21 June two 218 Squadron Wellingtons were lost on the raid on Kiel when 115 aircraft, including forty-seven Wellingtons, were dispatched to bomb the *Tirpitz*. Sergeant G.G. Jillett RNZAF and Sergeant M.J. Fraser RNZAF were lost without any survivors. Theirs were the only Wellingtons lost on the raid which failed to find the German ship, and so the aircraft unloaded their bombs on Kiel instead.

On the night of 23–24 June forty-four Wellingtons and eighteen Whitleys made a heavy raid on Cologne. One of the Wellingtons dispatched by 115 Squadron was flown by Pilot Officer Douglas Sharpe. His rear gunner, Sergeant R.F. 'Chan' Chandler, who had been involved in a three PRU Wellington 'prang' the previous month, recalls:

> After bombing Cologne things seemed to go wrong. There was a lot of chatter on the intercom between the pilot and the navigator. There was no doubt whatsoever that we were lost. The crew were repeatedly instructed to keep constant watch for any sign of land through the cloud. Shortly we saw the coastline. There were repeated comments about 'fuel state'. The aircraft was throttled back and a gradual descent was made. I was invited by Pilot Officer Sharpe to bale out over land. I declined, thinking it was best to stay with the aircraft and crew.

Sharpe nursed the ailing bomber back to Suffolk where, almost out of fuel, he decided on a crash-landing. Chandler recalls:

> It so happens that the area around Bredfield, Burgh and Pettistree is very flat and a suitable length of pasture land was selected. Sharpe made a gradual descent and approach. I jettisoned my turret doors and my back was to the starboard side as we dropped to a height of about fifty feet. I lowered my goggles and eased myself out on the edge of the turret. Looking out and down with the ground rushing past at an alarming rate of knots, I thought of rolling out of the turret. Looking along the fuselage I could see trees ahead and slid back into the turret. The next second there was the most tremendous crash and I lost consciousness.

The Wellington had hit the trees and crashed into some council houses at Debach. Incredibly, a man with a child in his arms jumped to safety from the bedroom window of the smashed house. 'Chan' Chandler suffered serious leg, head and arm injuries but would recover. Sergeant Fred Tingley, the second pilot, died later as a result of his injuries. His was the only fatality. Sharpe was unhurt but was killed on his next trip. Another Wellington was written off on 24 June when R1501 crashed on take-off, but Sergeant Skillen and all the crew escaped before the aircraft burned out.

The air war was entering a new phase, with the enemy night defences beginning to inflict heavy losses on Bomber Command. As one Wellington pilot said at the time, 'losses were

On the night of 23–24 June 1941 Wellington T2963 of 115 Squadron, flown by Pilot Officer Douglas Sharpe, crashed into some council houses at Debach. Incredibly, a man with a child in his arms jumped to safety from the bedroom window of the smashed house. Sharpe was unhurt but was killed on his next trip. (Via Bob Collis)

running at approximately 5 per cent so one believed one was living on luck after the 20th trip. One was just as likely to "buy it" on the first as on the last.' During June the German night fighters destroyed sixty-six aircraft. On the night of 29–30 June two Wellingtons of 115 Squadron and one of 218 Squadron, flown by Pilot Officer F.E. Bryant, failed to return from the raid on Bremen. One of the 115 Squadron Wimpys was piloted by Flight Lieutenant A.J. Bailey DFC, who was shot down by Hauptmann Walter Ehle of StII/NJG1.[31] The other was Wellington R1509/P of 115 Squadron, which was flown by Pilot Officer Alan McSweyn RAAF, who also encountered a night fighter. He recalls:

Our first enemy action was heavy flak as we were en route for Bremen. Apparently, although we were not aware of it at the time, we had been hit, because some ten minutes before reaching the target the port engine overheated, the oil pressure dropped and I had to cut the engine just as we reached the target area. We went ahead and bombed the target, dropping from about 13,000ft to 11,000ft after the engine failure and there having difficulty in maintaining height on one engine after leaving the target. As usual we experienced searchlights and flak after leaving Bremen. I had to decide whether to try to stay at 9,000ft, where we seemed able to maintain height, but would have to run the gauntlet of both light and heavy flak. Or whether to take violent evasive action, losing even more height in the process, or dive for the ground to get out of danger at roof-top level. The latter two choices lessened the chance of getting home on one engine, so I elected to stay at 9,000ft, warning the crew to watch for night fighters. Sure enough, the flak ceased while we were still coned by searchlights and then without warning I saw tracer fire passing us and felt the shudder of our rear guns firing. Some days later we were told by other crewmembers that Jimmy Gill, my rear gunner, had shot down a single-engined fighter, probably a Me 109. Almost simultaneously there was another burst of cannon and machine-gun fire, which came straight up the fuselage from rear to front, swathed the right side instrument panel, knocked off the navigator's left earpiece as Wilf Hetherington stood in the cockpit beside me. It hit Bill Wilde, the co-pilot, in the thigh as he stood looking out of the astrodome and seriously wounded Jimmy Gill in the shoulder and chest. Immediately the starboard motor caught fire, and ahead and climbing right in front of us I saw the Me 110, which had caused the damage, but which could not be seen by Ted 'Laddy' Gibbs, the front gunner. Within seconds the whole starboard wing and fuselage was alight; the fire extinguishers were ineffectual and I found the aircraft virtually uncontrollable, so I gave the order to bale out. Wilf Hetherington crawled forward to the front turret to release Teddy Gibbs, while Bill Wilde, though wounded, crawled to the rear escape hatch to warn Jimmy Gill to leave and bale out from there. I saw Laddy Gibbs, Wilf Hetherington and Frank Davidson, the WOP, leave by the forward hatch and, looking back, I could see that Bill Wilde had gone out the rear hatch and Jimmy Gill had gone from the rear turret.[32]

By now the starboard wing had disintegrated and the aircraft was spinning down out of control. With some difficulty I was able to reach the forward hatch and after some effort got it open and baled out. My parachute descent was unsensational, although my flying boots blew off as I left the aircraft and landed in the rear of a farmyard in fairly long grass, landing so quietly among an unconcerned herd of thirty or so cows that I remained on my feet and didn't roll over. I was surprised by the quietness. I had no idea where my aircraft or crew had landed and realised that surrounding wooded areas probably concealed both. I was able to grab a bicycle from the farmhouse nearby and began riding and walking in a vain hope to reach Holland and perhaps help.

Alan McSweyn reached a military aerodrome and managed to get in the cockpit of a Bf 110 but was apprehended while trying to start the engines. Apparently, he motioned from the cockpit to a Luftwaffe ground crewman to assist him with starting the engines. The German fell for it but when McSweyn pressed the starter button the prop nearly took the German's head off. He then spotted McSweyn's dark blue Australian uniform and the game was up! McSweyn concludes:

The rest of the crew all landed in the same area. Jimmy Gill, apparently dazed but not fatally injured, landed in a tree, did not realise how high he was, released his parachute harness and dropped about forty feet to the ground, badly hurting his back. Bill Wilde, meanwhile, could not walk, so rather than leave the two wounded men, the other three alerted some Germans and asked for medical help. Although the wounded were given the best possible medical treatment in hospital, Jimmy Gill died, mainly from a broken back. Wilde fully recovered and the doctors told him that while they regretted being unable to save Gill, his death was really a blessing because had he lived he would have been a paraplegic for life.[33]

Pilot Officer Alan McSweyn RAAF and his crew, taken at 20 OTU Lossiemouth in February 1941, just before he joined 115 Squadron. From left to right: Sergeants Geoff Hogg, Bernard Morgan, David Fraser, Alex Kerr, Pilot Officer McSweyn, Sergeant Bill Legg. All the sergeants in this photo were on the crew of Sergeant John Anderson on the night of 10–11 May 1941, when their Wellington IC (R1379) was shot down by Leutnant Eckart-Wilhelm 'Hugo' von Bonin of 6./NJG1. McSweyn was the pilot of Wellington R1509/P of 115 Squadron, which was shot down on the night of 29–30 June 1942. (David Fraser via Theo Boiten)

In July RAF Bomber Command was operational over enemy targets on six nights, with three targets being hit on three of the nights and two targets being bombed on three other occasions. Wellingtons, and to a lesser degree Hampdens and Whitleys, still constituted the main bombing effort on German cities and the harbour at Brest. With the repeated attacks on German targets enemy night fighters were everywhere.

On the morning of 1 July 115 Squadron dispatched three Wellingtons on a sea search for a dinghy. Sergeant Smith in R1063 was attacked by three Bf 110s. Although the Wimpy was hit three times the aircraft escaped serious damage. None of the Wellington crews sighted the dinghy. On the night of 2–3 July when fifty-two Wellingtons of Bomber Command bombed Brest, Bf 110s appeared again and X9663 returned with cannon holes in the fuselage. On the night of 4–5 July, when the target was Brest, Sergeant Parsons, the rear gunner of Wellington X9671 flown by Sergeant J.T. Wallace, claimed to have shot down a German night fighter. Two nights later when sixty-five Wellingtons and twenty-nine Whitleys attacked Münster, the Wellington flown by Sergeant Wallace was attacked by Bf 110s again, and in the ensuing eight-minute combat the crew co-operated superbly and only very minor damage was suffered. Wellington X9672, flown by Sergeant Berney, could not shake off the fighter and he had to jettison his bombs. During this combat the rear gunner, Sergeant Kerruish, was killed.

A ground crew member paints the words 'Akyem–Abuakwa' below the cockpit of Wellington IC R1448 HA-L of 218 (Gold Coast) Squadron. (RAF Marham)

Wellington IC R1448 'Akyem–Abuakwa' of 218 (Gold Coast) Squadron at Marham in the summer of 1941. (IWM)

The night of 6–7 July was also full of incident. A Wellington of 115 Squadron crash-landed at Marham after being damaged in combat with a Ju 88C intruder of NJG2, and Wellington R1063/D of 115 Squadron, piloted by Sergeant O.A. Mathews RNZAF, crashed in the North Sea with the loss of all the crew, after being attacked by Oberleutnant Helmut Woltersdorf of 4./NJG1. Although an SOS was sent, the subsequent air and sea search failed to locate the crew.[34]

When Bomber Command dispatched fifty-seven Wellingtons to Osnabruck on 9–10 July 115 Squadron contributed four Wimpys. On the return Squadron Leader Sindall had a double engine failure in X9673, and with the aircraft showing no inclination to recover he ordered the crew to bale out. Almost as soon as they had done so and just before he himself was preparing to leave, the engine picked up again and Sindall landed the Wellington at Brackley.

In the summer of 1941 ground trials of the new radar navigational aid Gee[35] were in progress at Marham, Norfolk.[36] Twelve pilots and twelve observers from 115 and 218 Squadrons were involved in the trials and had been informed they would not be undertaking operational flying until these were completed. Understandably they were surprised to be notified of briefing for an attack on Sunday 13 July 1941. It was to be a 'maximum' effort consisting of sixty-nine Wellingtons, forty-seven of which were targeted on Bremen, twenty on Vegesack and two on Emden. All crews would encounter heavy cloud and icing. Sixteen aircraft would claim to have bombed Bremen. Two Wellingtons would fail to return from the Bremen attack.[37] In 115 Squadron the all-sergeant crew of Wellington IC R1502, W.J. Reid, pilot and captain; Geoff T. Buckingham, observer; M.B. Wallis, wireless operator; M.G. Dunne, front gunner; and T.W. Oliver, rear gunner, were short of their regular second pilot. He had been sent to London to attend a Commission Board. Twenty-seven-year-old Sergeant Pilot Frederick Birkett Tipper, who was regarded as a jinx in the squadron, took his place. The crew that he had flown with on his first sortie had suffered a very shaky 'do'. On his second operation the aircraft had crashed on take-off, fortunately with no fatal result. Bremen would be his third operational flight.

The observer's chair in a Wellington moved backwards and forwards in tracks firmly fastened to the floor of the aircraft. When he boarded the aircraft Buckingham found to his intense annoyance that the tracks to his chair were broken, leaving it free to slide all over the place in the event of violent evasive action. Furthermore, the chair cushion was missing. Instead of throwing his parachute pack on the bed as he usually did, he would have to sit on it in lieu of the cushion. Little did he realize that before the night was out, the object of his annoyance would save his life.

The sky was clear in England but over the North Sea thick cloud was encountered. As they approached the enemy coastline there was a partial thinning of the cloud and Sergeant Tipper was able to pass a pinpoint on the Dutch Coast to his observer. Tipper then left the cockpit and made his way aft to the astrodome where he would keep a constant vigil for night fighters. The Wellington was now at 9,000ft. Buckingham had just spotted Texel Beacon and was returning to this station from the cockpit when Sergeant Oliver in the rear turret yelled over the intercom: 'Fighter!' Simultaneously he opened up with his guns, racking the fuselage with vibration and filling it with the fumes of cordite. Oberleutnant Egmont Prinz zur Lippe-Weissenfeld, Staffelkapitän, IV./NJG1, had just made his initial strike, setting the starboard engine of the bomber on fire. He was now somewhere out in the darkness manoeuvring for a second attack. Buckingham rushed forward to the cockpit and pressed the starboard engine fire extinguisher button – this put out the fire. Next he jettisoned the bombs and gave the pilot a reciprocal course to fly. He then returned to the cabin to check his log. At this moment the second attack occurred and it was far more devastating than the first. Cannon fire from beneath the bomber raked the whole length of the fuselage, wounding all members of the crew, some more seriously than others. Buckingham blacked out. When he came round he was lying across the step, adjacent to the forward escape hatch. As the aircraft had gone into a dive the loose seat, which he had cursed so roundly at the beginning of the flight, had slid to the nose and deposited him on the floor by the escape hatch. His parachute pack, which he had used as a cushion, was lying on top of him. He took stock of the situation. The bomber was on fire and he was wounded in the face and arm with cannon shrapnel. There was a hole in the back of his leg, which was bleeding profusely. The door to the front turret was wide open. There was no sign of the pilot. Fastening his parachute pack to the harness he found that one J-clip had been smashed by the cannon fire. He used the remaining clip, then heaved on the edge of the escape hatch. In an instant he was out and away into the night. Hanging awkwardly beneath his parachute, suspended at an angle by one clip only, he made a bad landing, injuring his anklebone. Tipper's body was recovered from the wreckage.[38] It was assumed that Tipper had been killed by the second burst of fire from the night fighter. Later zur Lippe visited the crew in hospital and expressed his regret that a member of the crew had died. He said he was after the bomber not the crew.[39]

On 14–15 July seventy-eight Wellingtons and nineteen Whitleys were dispatched to Bremen where they were given three aiming points: the shipyards, the goods station and the Altstadt. Crews reported that the 'whole town was ablaze'. Four Wellingtons were lost from the Bremen raid.[40] On the night of 15–16 July the Wellington flown by Flight Sergeant N.C. Cook of 115 Squadron was shot down by Hauptmann Werner Streib of StI./NJG1, and the bomber was later reported to have crashed near Nederweert in Holland. None of the crew survived. Streib was also responsible for shooting down a 218 Squadron Wellington flown by Flight Lieutenant J. Stokes with the loss of all the crew.[41] On the night of 21–22 July, when thirty-seven Wellingtons and thirty-four Hampdens visited Frankfurt and thirty-six Wellingtons and eight Halifaxes attacked Mannheim, one Wellington (Z8788/H) failed to return. There were no survivors from the crew under Sergeant N.L. Johnston RCAF of 115 Squadron.

A daylight raid on 24 July certainly made the Wellington crews sit up and take notice. As one of the crew members recalls, 'we just couldn't believe our ears when the CO said that crews were to participate in a daylight operation against the German battleships *Scharnhorst* and *Gneisenau* lying at anchor in the French port of Brest.' A total of 150 aircraft were planned to make the attack in formation, but at the last moment this had to be changed because of the departure of the *Scharnhorst* to La Pallice. The force to Brest was then to be composed of 100 aircraft, of which three were to be Flying Fortresses flying at 30,000ft in the hope of attracting German fighters prematurely. Then eighteen Hampdens escorted by three squadrons of Spitfires with long-range fuel tanks were to attack in anticipation of drawing off more enemy fighters. Finally, the main force of seventy-nine unescorted Wellingtons of 1 and 3 Groups were to attack in the final wave. The Wellingtons, Hampdens and Fortresses made daylight attacks on the *Gneisenau* and the *Prinz Eugen* while Halifaxes attacked the *Scharnhorst* at La Pallice. Marham sent a number of Wellingtons on the major attack at Brest. All three Wellingtons of 115 Squadron were engaged by Bf 109s. During the combats the Wimpys were not hit but their gunners claimed to have shot down three of the enemy fighters. Two of the Wellingtons were damaged by flak but all claimed to have hit the target. Six hits were reported on the *Gneisenau* – two of them by Sergeant Prior – but these could not be confirmed. Ten Wellingtons, including a 218 Squadron Wimpy flown by Pilot Officer M. Jolly RNZAF, and two Hampdens failed to return. Jolly and three of the New Zealander's crew were killed and two survived to be taken prisoner. Five Halifaxes were lost in the attack on the *Scharnhorst*.

Intensive operations continued into early August, seven being flown during the first twelve days. On the night of 3–4 August, when thirty-four Wellingtons were dispatched to bomb Hanover, the Wellington flown by Pilot Officer J.A. Maxwell RCAF of 218 Squadron took off from Marham at 22.28 hours. Cloudy conditions caused severe turbulence and Maxwell's Wellington also suffered a partial instrument failure, and at 23.00 hours, when 7 miles north-east of Norwich, he ordered the crew to bale out. The Wellington crashed at Salhouse and the Canadian pilot was killed. At Hanover the target was cloud covered and one aircraft, a Wellington IC of 218 Squadron flown by Wing Commander J.L.H. Fletcher, was lost. Fletcher and three of his crew were killed and two survived to become prisoners of war. On 5–6 August targets at Mannheim, Karlsruhe and Frankfurt were attacked for the loss of nine aircraft, including four Wellingtons. One of them was flown by Flight Lieutenant F.L. Litchfield of 115 Squadron and all the crew survived to be taken prisoner. On the night of the 11–12, when 115 Squadron dispatched ten Wellingtons to railway targets at Mönchengladbach, none of the twenty-nine Wellingtons that were dispatched by Bomber Command were lost but the target area was completely cloud covered. The operation marked the first service trial over enemy territory of the Gee navigational and identification device, which was carried out successfully by two Wellingtons of 115 Squadron during the raid.

On the night of 12–13 August nine crews, including Gee trials aircraft, took off from Marham for Essen and Hanover. Wellington Z8835, one of the Gee trials aircraft, flown by Sergeant J.T. Wallace of 115 Squadron, was shot down by Feldwebel Ernst Kalinowski of 6./NJG1, crashing 1km south-west of Grafel with the loss of all on-board. Another seventy aircraft, meanwhile, had set out for Berlin and a further thirty Wellingtons, three Stirlings and two Halifaxes went to Essen. Returning to Marham, Pilot Officer Wood of 115 Squadron in T2563/D switched on his navigation lights and almost immediately he was attacked and shot down by Oberfeldwebel Peter Laufs of I./NJG2 flying a Ju 88C intruder. The Wellington caught fire and Wood force-landed at Smith's Farm near Scottow. All of the crew escaped without serious injury except for Sergeant B. Evans, who was sadly killed. Only four operations were flown during the second half of August. On the night of 14–15 August when Bomber Command attacked Hanover, Brunswick and Magdeburg, two more of Marham's Wellingtons were lost when Sergeant C.G. Alway of 115 Squadron and Pilot Officer W.C. Wilson of 218 Squadron failed to return. Alway's crew were all killed and only one man survived on Wilson's aircraft. On the night of 18–19 August two more 218 Squadron Wellington ICs were lost. Sergeant K.C. Shearing and his crew were shot down by Feldwebel Siegfried Ney of 4./NJG1, and the Wimpy flown by Sergeant H.G. Huckle was lost with one man killed and five becoming prisoners of war.

For the operation to Mannheim on the 27–28, ninety-one aircraft of Bomber Command set out for the city and good bombing and many fires were claimed without loss. However, on their return to England, seven Wellingtons and a Whitley crashed. Two of the 115 Squadron crews baled out over Norfolk and the third crashed at West Raynham. The month's operations ended with raids on Mannheim and Frankfurt on 29–30 August when ninety-four Wellingtons were dispatched by Bomber Command. Two Wellingtons failed to return from the Mannheim operation. One of these was flown by Sergeant J.K. Murdoch, which was believed to have been shot down by an intruder near Martlesham Heath. Five men were killed and a sixth died later of his injuries.

In September the high rate of bomber attrition continued as the Nachtjagd increased its capability and bombing operations increased. During the month 115 Squadron alone flew eighty-one sorties on nine operations for the loss of six Wellingtons. On 3–4 September 140 aircraft set off for Brest and all aircraft of 1, 4 and 5 Groups were recalled, probably because of worsening weather at bases, but four aircraft did not hear the signal and, with the 3 Group aircraft, proceeded to the target. Some fifty-three aircraft bombed the estimated position of the German warships through a smoke-screen. No aircraft were lost but two Wellingtons, including one flown by Pilot Officer Scholes, were abandoned near Tavistock, Devon, and a Whitley crashed somewhere in England. On 7–8 September 197 bombers went to three aiming points in Berlin while another fifty-one bombers headed for Kiel. The Berlin force comprised 103 Wellingtons, forty-three Hampdens, thirty-one Whitleys, six Halifaxes and four Manchesters. In all, 137 crews claimed to have bombed their allotted targets in Berlin. Fifteen bombers were missing in action and at least ten, including two Wellington ICs of 115 Squadron, were believed shot down by night fighters.[42] A Wellington II of 218 Squadron, flown by Squadron Leader H.L. Price, crashed in a wheat field at Hall Farm, Barton Bendish, after flying from the Dutch coast with the starboard engine on fire. All the crew survived. On 26–27 September, when 104 aircraft set off for targets at Cologne, Emden, Mannheim and Genoa, all were recalled because of forecasts of fog at bases. The Wellington flown by Sergeant M.E. Farnan of 115 Squadron crashed in the sea off the Friesians with an engine on fire after bombing Emden, and all the crew perished. On the night of 29–30 September when 139 aircraft of Bomber Command were dispatched to four aiming points at Stettin, ninety-five bombers claimed good bombing but eight aircraft were lost and two of them were 115 Squadron Wellingtons that fell victim to night fighters. There were no survivors aboard X9673/B flown by Sergeant L.H. Ellis, which was shot down by Feldwebel Ernst Kalinowski of 6./NJG1. Only the rear gunner aboard Sergeant A.R. Hulls' Wimpy, which was shot down by Oberleutnant Ludwig Becker of 4./NJG1 near Groningen, survived to be taken prisoner.[43] Five more aircraft of Bomber Command crashed in England on return.

So far, Warrant Officer J.W.B. Snowden's crew on 115 Squadron had survived everything the enemy could throw at them, but the constant preparations and flying ops was always a severe test, as Albert E. Robinson, his observer, recalls:

Orders filtered down from high command to the squadrons and in smoke-filled rooms the crews were briefed in detail. If it were a tough target, an unrestrained groan would echo through the briefing room. On the other hand, an easier one would produce a mild cheer, and if the squadron commander even as much as hinted that there was the smallest chance of cancellation, this was met by much stamping of feet and an enthusiastic round of applause. The CO would listen and a faint smile would cross his face. He had heard it all before. He had flown many operations and he understood the crews' outlook. To him this show of humour, usually expressed in an offbeat way best described perhaps as black humour, was quite normal. Whatever it was it covered up quite a lot. This was just as well, since in the few hours following the briefing the adjutant would be reaching for his telegram pad to write out the condolences to loved ones waiting at home. The sight of the telegram boy always caused a chilling premonition and a clutch at the heart.

2

THE NIGHT OFFENSIVE

Albert E. Robinson, observer on Warrant Officer J.W.B. Snowden's crew on 115 Squadron, recalls:

There was much to do before an op. There were maps and charts to prepare, target approach to consider, known fighter bases to ring round in red ink and a whole host of other things to do. It was a busy period, but preparation was vital. Much had to be examined in microscopic detail and the better the grasp of this, the more likely the success of the operation and, in all probability, the chances of survival too. Even so, with all the work and concentration required, somehow it always seemed to be completed with a good hour to spare before take-off time. That hour always took its toll. Irrespective of experience or how many operations had been completed, that hour became the waiting time. It passed with a dreadful slowness. A jumbled-up mass of crews muffled in their flying leathers watched the clock tick over and urged it on, for it gave them time to consider the possibilities that lay ahead and above all offered so much time to think. They were a cheerful, resourceful, happy-go-lucky bunch, mostly in their teens, and in almost hourly touch with death, but on the surface at least, they had an apparent fatalistic acceptance of this role. The mess had an atmosphere of its own. People talked in hushed whispers or on a higher note than usual, and there was an edgy tension. Some wrote letters to a loved one; others thumbed through magazines in a restless way. Some were fidgety, some composed, while others just sat, deep in their own thoughts. Yet, once in the air, with the onset of danger, such thoughts would evaporate completely. The operation would be all that mattered and it called for an authoritative grasp of the nettle. The game would be on.

For the crews that came back, life on the squadron was almost a world on its own, and not only in the world of bombing either. The close-knit relationships were evident in their off-duty times too, and these were celebrated, perhaps not too wisely, at the Red Lion, an old-worldly hotel with a thatched roof and a wealth of oak beams already blackened by the smoke of ages. A much favoured meeting place for the crews, it saw many boisterous, heavy nights with endless frothy pints of beer and a piano banging out bawdy songs with an emphasis that threatened to lift the timbered ceiling that almost brushed our heads. Even when the casualty lists were running at a high level, these carefree times carried on as usual and the frothy pints continued to be hoisted high and drunk with perhaps even more appreciative relish. Callous? Uncaring? Not so. That way some sort of sanity was preserved. Each one had to take his chance. Who would be next? So, live for today, enjoy it while possible. Most crews did just that. Even so, very few left the hotel without a backward glance at its panelled walls and glittering brasses, always with the thought that it could quite likely be for the last time.

That this comradeship, both on the scene of battle and during these relaxed off-duty periods, bore relationship to the atmosphere in which school games were played was no accident. In fact, many squadron commanders actively encouraged this attitude. In a sense, it was a convenient hat and coat hook fixed in some mythical pavilion on which to hang the trauma, a contrivance that also acted on carefully defined lines to help mould the team spirit with which these games were played. To cast this mould was easy. Most of the crews were barely out of school anyway. It was only the setting that was different.

It was apparent right from the very moment on an operational day when the crews strolled over to the mess for breakfast. An early morning mist might be floating over the base in grey wispy patches, a hazy cloak settled over the runways. It became a familiar sight to the crews, and almost a permanent feature of the flat, moisture-filled greenness of the open farmland that surrounded the base and stretched for miles.

At dispersal points the Wellingtons, stark and austere in their camouflage paint, stood waiting – a colossus in their own right with their six Browning machine-guns jutting from their turrets and ominous in their setting. A petrol bowser stood alongside some of the aircraft. Soon it would pump the high-octane fuel into the tanks and a tousled-haired mechanic would peer from the cockpit waiting for the signal. There was always a scene of great activity, as the ground staff fussed around, each to their own job, and a lot would depend on their attention to detail.

The aircrew by now had dispersed, each caught up with the technicalities of their own job. They would not meet again until briefing. As for the navigator, he had a recently introduced system of astro-navigation to study. In reality it was a basic affair, consisting of a sextant, a rather splendid watch for time keeping, and a hooded projector set over the navigator's table. There was illuminated astronomical data on the chart, on which the sextant readings were plotted. It was a brave effort by the boffins to help offset the weakness in night navigation, but under operational conditions it had its limitations. One of the drawbacks was that it was necessary to fly a straight and level course at a constant speed for a protracted period – a gift-wrapped present for German radar. The bumpy, wallowing Wellington could not, by any stretch of the imagination, be described as the ideal platform from which to take hand-held sextant readings. Also there was the question of the stars' visibility themselves, for they were often blotted out by heavy cloud. On the nights when the Plough in Ursa Major could be seen, this was not only useful in the construction of a mental star map, but it was easy to pick out Polaris, the Pole Star. Poised several light years above the North Pole to an accuracy of one degree, it had guided travellers throughout the ages. Now, with its ancient origins and religious connotations, it was to come ironically to the aid of bomber crews.

However, crews at that time gave little significance to such significant or philosophical meanderings. Operations were not the Holy Grail, just a job, which in the interests of their nation they had been called upon to do, and that was their sole object, nothing else. Any personal feelings could not be allowed to swerve or distract. With this in mind and the completion of briefing, it was time to go.

At dispersal points, in the already darkened sky, the crews at their stations, the pilot made ready to start the two Pegasus radial engines. Starter buttons were pressed and there was a cough and a roar as they fired. A column of grey smoke with a sheet of flame shot out from the exhaust. The crews settled down in their positions. Engines were throttled back to tick-over position and, with the pilot's thumb-up signal to the waiting ground staff, the chocks were hauled away from the wheels. Throttles were pushed forward and the engines answered with a roar. Guided by twinkling lights, the Wellingtons, gorged with the bomb loads tucked in their bellies, trundled slowly to take-off position. It was all systems go.

The training manual made it look so simple. Throttles were manipulated to gain full power. The aircraft responded with gathering speed and if all else was carried out correctly, the Wellington took off. But, sitting at the end of the runway, waiting for the green flashing light that was cleared for take-off, it did not seem so simple. In fact, there was a sense of disbelief that nagged at the stomach that the lumbering, heavy Wellington, laden to the maximum with bombs and petrol, would ever leave the ground at all. But it did – well, usually – but if there was ice or frozen snow on the grass airstrip and this affected lift, or there was a significant splutter from either of the engines at the critical point of lift-off, then either of these could threaten disaster. The normal load of 650 gallons of petrol for an average run, plus the 4,000lb bomb load usually carried, could make quite a hole in the ground. Tense moments these, broken only by a sense of relief when the bomber left the ground and began to make its circuit of the airfield ready to set course for far-off Germany.

The Wellington gained height slowly, very slowly. High above on a clear night a myriad of stars pin-pricked the sky with their brilliance. The black nose of the Wellington tilted towards them and the defiant roar of the two engines filled the air with vibrating noise. A lot would depend on those engines. They would have to blast effortlessly away for a good many hours, and more than one aircrew said a silent prayer as they listened to the roar. But there were many other items to consider, and the list was compounded with problems that seemed endless.

Weather could be problematical. Accurate forecasts, with the scant information available to the meteorology officers, were rare. It was more successful to wet a finger, hold it up, and hope. Since all operations were dictated by requirements of war, often this meant flying in appalling conditions. High gusty winds, fog with thick cloud up to high levels, and particularly ice, were common enemies. Ice could layer itself over the wings, and create drag to the point of stalling as the Wellington lurched and sagged in a series of sickening movements. Adverse conditions could make themselves known in the space of a short time, sometimes before leaving the English coast. Then it became a lonely trek flying through the murk until the Dutch coast was reached.

Flak, either from the coastal guns or the numerous flak ships anchored off the Friesian Islands, would come up. An umbrella barrage and dotted tracer like a giant firework display were joined by the probing searchlights spreading their light like some huge, luminous spider's web trying to lure the victim into its mesh. Ahead, blips bobbing and dancing on electronic screens indicated our position to the controller. Then the night fighter bases were alerted. We hoped with some measure of callousness that the blips would be caused by another aircraft. Since it was an invisible thread that connected the Wellington to the night fighter, the gunners in our aircraft did not know until the actual moment of interception. So we, the crew, sat, tensed, waiting for the sight of the Messerschmitt night fighter From now on the Wellington was in grave danger.

This was never more true than on a moonlit, cloudless night. The art of crossing the Dutch coast was by concealment in the clouds. But this too had its drawbacks since it was necessary for navigational purposes to 'fix' the exact crossing point, and naturally this meant emerging from the cloud cover. This we hoped would be over the Friesian Islands or, to be more specific, the island of Schiermonnikoog. Mere hiccups on the chart maybe, but an area with which we had become familiar, especially Schiermonnikoog. If we were correct when we broke cloud cover, it boiled down to a quick movement, 'fix' the position as soon as possible, then head back to the concealment of the cloud with full boost and airspeed. It sounds reasonably simple, but even so it may have been just the moment for which the night fighter crew was waiting. Individual aircraft flying in isolation – and that's how it was for us in 1940-41 – were comparatively easy meat. German radar used the time that this early warning afforded to put the night fighter in a position to suit themselves, usually from astern and below, and always it seemed when the Wellington broke cloud for the 'fix'. The Me 110 night fighters were only too pleased to take advantage of this and were quick to exploit these favourable circumstances. Then the bomber would break into a stomach-heaving routine of carefully rehearsed evasion – not so much to shoot down the fighter, but purely as an evasive tactic. A fighter claimed might be exciting news in the mess, but the successful completion of the operation took precedence. Anything else was a bonus.

Of course, this assumes that the fighter had been spotted before the attack. If not, the first indication would come with a staccato crackle as the red tracer streaked across, and the cannon fire of the Messerschmitt was vicious, both in range and effectiveness, far more than the .303 machine-gun fire of the Wellington. An unexpected attack usually spelled disaster, but it must be said that given an early sight of the enemy fighter, he did not have it all his own way. The Wellington, with alert gunners, could give a reasonable account of itself, and facing aggressive, accurate fire the enemy fighter would often break away and seek easier meat. Even so, it was an apprehensive moment for the crews, and as the gun turrets rotated in the sky, searching with an intensity for the fighter, it was essentially a moment of quick reaction. An off-guard, dreamy relaxation or a split-second delay would quickly decide the issue.

Even with this risk of interception it was of paramount importance to get a 'fix' as the Dutch coast was crossed. This enabled the ground speed and track over the territory to be calculated and made it easier to pick out the landmarks as we flew over Holland. It was a strange, eerie feeling as we did so. To us, Holland was a territory of friendly people and there was a sense of outrage that the Nazis occupied it. We liked to think that when the Dutch people heard the drone of our Wellingtons they recognised it as a gesture of hope. This was confirmed on numerous occasions when flashing lights from down below spelled out a welcome in no uncertain terms. Such a sight made our flight more personal and acted as a strong fillip to morale.

Naturally the German defences did not see it that way, and the inevitable flak came up. If this flak was widespread and heavy, it sometimes made diversion necessary, and this, in many instances, could take the Wellington far away from the calculated track. This caused a period of frustration, since it was not always easy in the darkness to refix the aircraft's position. At such moments of indecisiveness the poor navigation facilities came into question. As one crew member put it succinctly, as we strode out to our Wellington for take-off: 'Here we go again with a map, pencil and rubber. Oh well, the target is only 600 miles away and as for the return, well, just forget it.' It was not quite like that of course, but in the early days of the bombing campaign it just seemed like that. Certainly the loss of compass course and a confused meander over hostile territory provoked high irritation when the search turned out to be fruitless. But it was not all failure. Success came along too, and then the flush of achievement took on a positive and welcome role. It made all the effort and sacrifice worthwhile.

At such times, Essen, Cologne and Bremen were not cities, they were targets – seething holocausts with a glowing spread of a spitting shambles down below. Skies were made colourful by different shades of flak – greens and red predominated – and they were filled with a blinding light that dazzled and compelled the pilot to bank steeply as the searchlights wavered and probed in their systematic search for the raider. Often a whole series of searchlights positioned in a wide circle would take their cue from a master searchlight set in the centre of this circle. This vertical shaft in the sky stood quite still, until the operators felt that they had accurately calculated the height and speed of a particular aircraft. Then it would switch from the vertical with the swiftness of a striking snake in its attempt to centre its beam on the unfortunate aircraft. If this happened, then the other searchlights would simultaneously and instantly converge at an apex above the Wellington and in effect form a giant cone with the bomber trapped in a flood of light. Slowly they would bring the nose of the cone down forcing the bomber lower and lower and then, at a given signal, massed guns would fire up the cone with a fierce intensity that lit up the sky with its menace. When coned it was an almost impossible situation for any aircraft and the only escape lay in violent evasion, sometimes to the point where it put the aircraft's structure at risk, threatened catastrophe and gave the unfortunate souls nightmares. Most such endeavours were fruitless. Like a flickering moth trapped by light, the bomber was rendered impotent as it was pounded by the guns.

Often, other crews over the target saw a blinding flash in the sky as a coned aircraft was blown into fragmentary pieces by a direct hit. It was not a very pleasant sight, or indeed one to inspire confidence, but whatever the feeling it could not be allowed to distract. It made sense to take all necessary precautions of course. But the task to seek out the aiming point was mandatory and still an issue to be solved – not easy for the bomb-aimer as he strained his eyes through the perspex panel let in the floor near the front gun turret and looked down at the blazing inferno. Often blinded by the glare of searchlights and the target obscured by smoke, it was difficult for him to pick out detail. The panoramic display by the entire pyrotechnics in full view was not the most reassuring sight. It needed strong nerves and a calm disposition, since at that moment, having established the aiming point, the bomb-aimer was virtually in charge of the aircraft. He guided the pilot by calling out steering instructions over the intercom. It was a big responsibility, and it decided the success or failure of the operation.

All bomb-aimers hoped to get it right with the first run over the target. Any repeat performance that he deemed necessary did not go down well with the crew, and it was an unhappy voice that came over the intercom when the bomb-aimer decided to abort the run-up for some particular reason and requested the pilot to go around again. To use a bomb sight effectively meant that a

Wellington III X3662 KO-P of 115 Squadron. (IWM)

straight and level course had to be flown through the thick spread of flak, not a happy thought, especially since this usually meant fleeing through the centre of its seething core. It was an effort that stretched nerves to the full. It brought on a pulsating trepidation and caused butterflies in the stomach. The stark reality was that the outcome would only rate as high as the chance spin at a roulette table, with always the disquiet that out of the hundreds of shells layered in the sky, just one hit in the right place would be enough. So, given all this, it was a welcome moment when the bomb aimer, satisfied with his sighting, pressed the bomb release button and yelled over the intercom 'Bombs gone!'

This was the signal to get the hell out of it, and the Wellington was dived, twisted and turned in its dash to break clear of the flak-infested area. Full boost, full airspeed, full everything was applied and the bomber shuddered and creaked under the strain. It was an apprehensive feeling for the crews, since the next few moments would be decisive and all eyes looked for some sort of opening in the fierce barrage set up by the guns. Anywhere would do. Direction was unimportant. Just an opening that could offer some sort of chance. The decision was made – the crew held their breath – and the bomber hurtled through the chosen path. The flak – vivid orange splotches and fragments of hot metal – burst around, rattling the fabric of the bomber. Then, as the Wellington screamed away, there was a numbed realisation that the sky had cleared as if by magic. The iron curtain had been breached. With composure gained, and clear of the danger zone, there was a compelling fascination to bank the Wellington steeply and take a look at the holocaust as it receded. It was an awesome sight, truly a Dantean inferno, as the illuminated tracer streaked up forming an illusion of the wires of a giant birdcage covering the area. Set in its midst was the dull red glow of the stricken city. For the crews it was not the moment for reflection. The raid must be viewed in context and judged as a success.

Now all efforts had to be centred on the struggle to get home. This was tempered by the thought that the long trip to base would be a virtual repeat of the perils that had loomed getting to the target. It was always a sobering thought, but not one without some advantage, with the comforting knowledge that radio locations in England would be listening out for any message, however faint, to give what help they could. This would include a QDM, a radio bearing for the aircraft to home base, a navigator's dream, but with one vital snag – the aircraft had to be within a short range of the English coast before the beam became effective. For the Wellington crew flying in the remote depths of Germany it had to remain a wistful dream for the time being. Even so, the feeling as the course was set for base was simplicity itself: 'We'd made it coming in and we'd make it going back.'

Even the Wellington seemed to enter into the spirit of things. Shorn of its burden of bombs, all 4,000lb of them, it became buoyant again, easier to handle, much faster and able to reach greater heights. These factors gave the crew a feeling of superiority, as the light flak was unable to reach us. The heavy stuff was still there of course, but with some knowledge of their position and the evasive courses we flew, it was possible to avoid the brunt of their fire.

The Wellington droned on, each minute bringing it nearer to home. Crew morale grew higher with every mile. Then at length the Dutch coast came up and so did the flak and searchlights. It was the usual reception, but down below there was the familiar sight of the Friesian Islands, and from now on, if the night fighters left us alone, it was a straight run over the North Sea – a happy thought if all went well. There was the added reassurance that the radio people would be listening, ready to give the all-important heading that would bring us over the red flashing light – with its coded letter of the day, and its proximity to base. That is if all did go well, but it would be unwise to rely on this. Often, with success within grasp. The roulette wheel could throw up the wrong numbers. If it did, the perils were by no means over. A pea-soup fog or densely packed mist – common enemies to the returning bomber – could shroud the home airfield, close down the base and make diversion necessary, sometimes quite a distance away. Often other areas had conditions almost as bad, so a weary aircrew, after many hours in the air, had an unwelcome trek as the aircraft flew on its long tiresome path through the murky half light of a breaking dawn. It was a journey with petrol gauges mostly running at danger level, which in the long run usually meant little alternative but to put down wherever possible. This was a risky business, especially on an airstrip ill-equipped to receive a heavy bomber.

Even when the home base was fully operational, the dangers had not yet passed. An enemy aircraft, usually a Ju 88, could be prowling around the base ready to pick off the unwary – and their proficiency at this was never to be doubted. Sometimes, to achieve an easier kill, it was not unknown for the more audacious German pilots to enter the circuit, navigation lights full on, hoping that their bluff would work as they intermingled with the bombers circling the airfield. If this ploy did succeed, they would then wait until a bomber prepared to land, and attack. This was when the Wellington was at its most vulnerable, with braking flaps down, landing speed adjusted and all attention being paid to touchdown. It was a hapless situation for the bomber, which had no chance at all of surviving this attack; a sad ending on the very last lap of a gruelling operation. Such a disaster was a stark reminder that with the hazards of operational flying nothing was finally settled until the Wellington was safely down, had taxied to dispersal and the exhausted crew had clambered out.

Emotions ran high at this point. At de-briefing most crews were over-stimulated, excited and shaken up, but at least the kitchen staff on the squadron were down to earth and many bomber crews will recall the tempting smell of the bacon and egg breakfast served in the mess on return.

With the crews reasonably calm now, it was a pleasant, relaxing moment. Not only did the food titillate the palate, but it was also an opportunity to reflect on the reprieve – temporary or not – swim with the sweetness of life, and with the not unwelcome thought that the crew would be stood down for a possible two days. Not a lot in terms of time, but enough to prepare mentally for the next operation, and psychologically this was important if the composure to face the future was to be achieved.

Traumatic days, grave days, and the responsibility that had been thrust upon Bomber Command in the years 1940-41 had become not so much a battle but a crusade to hold the fort until the nation gathered strength. This carried with it a vital significance, not only to Britain but also to the whole of Europe, perhaps even to the whole world.

As for myself, a Me 110 [piloted by Oberleutnant Oberfeldwebel Paul Gildner of 4./NJG1] operating from the German base at Leeuwarden, made a copybook attack from astern and below on our Wellington at 19.30 hours on the night of 31 October/1 November 1941 when the target was Bremen. We never saw him until it was too late. We were never in with the chance of a shot. He just loomed out of the murk with a startling suddenness and opened up with a prolonged and devastating burst of cannon fire. It was all over in a matter of seconds. No time to consider. One minute we were happily on course and the next we were plunging down and about to crash, ironically, on Schiermonnikoog itself. Fate decreed that I should survive this, plus some enlightening, even if somewhat dreary years in German prison camps before liberation by Russian troops in May 1945.[44]

October 1941 had begun badly for 218 Squadron at Marham. On the night of the 10–11, when twenty-two Wellingtons were dispatched to Bordeaux, the Wellington flown by Sergeant V.G. Haley failed to return. Haley evaded capture and four crew were taken prisoner while one man was killed. Sergeant McClean's Wellington, meanwhile, came down in the sea off St Alban's Head on the Dorset coast. Two crew died despite an extensive search by the St Ives lifeboat. On the 13–14 when fifty-three Wellingtons and seven Stirlings were dispatched to bomb Düsseldorf, the one aircraft lost was the Wellington flown by Sergeant F.H.E. Deardon of 115 Squadron. All the crew were lost. On the night following, 14–15 October, when eighty aircraft, including fifty-eight Wellingtons, were sent to Nuremberg, the Wellington flown by Sergeant K.G. Fisher took off from Marham at 23.10 hours only for the port engine to fail, and he made an early return. The aircraft collided with trees and Fisher was injured. For those aircraft that flew the operation, conditions were very bad with icing and thick cloud and most of the bombers hit alternative targets. On 16–17 October eight-seven aircraft, including forty-seven Wellingtons, set out for Duisburg. The target was cloud covered and only estimated positions were bombed. The Wellington IC flown by Flight Lieutenant Dunham, which was the first time a 218 Squadron Wellington had taken off with a 4,000lb bomb, was abandoned after the port engine failed crossing the coast outbound; the aircraft crashed at Cantley, 10 miles south-east of Norwich.

If October had begun badly for 218 Squadron then November was to prove an equally tragic beginning for 115 Squadron. On 11 November the Wellington III piloted by Sergeant G.D.H. Dutton crashed at Carol House Farm near Swaffham during fuel consumption tests and a cross-country flying practice. Dutton and his crew and Flight

Wellington III lies wrecked in a field near Marham in 1942. (Via Don Bruce)

Bombing up a 115 Squadron Wellington IC. (RAF Marham)

Lieutenant H.S. Mellows, the Medical Officer, all died in the crash. Two weeks later, on 24 November, the Wellington flown by Sergeant G.R. Bruce crashed 2 miles south-west of March in Cambridgeshire during a training flight, and the six crew and three ground crew aboard for the ride were killed. It appears that during low flying Bruce collided with a line of railway trucks on the March to Spalding railway line. Meanwhile, early in November Sir Richard Peirse, C-in-C RAF Bomber Command, decided to mount a major effort against Berlin. The operation went ahead on the night of 7–8 November despite a late weather forecast, which showed that there was a large area of bad weather with storms; thick cloud, icing and hail would cover the North Sea routes to the German capital. No. 5 Group objected to the plan and they were allowed to attack Cologne instead but 169 bombers were sent to the Big City as ordered. Twenty-one aircraft including ten Wellingtons were lost. One of these was a 218 Squadron aircraft flown by Sergeant J.R.C. McGlashan, whose entire crew survived to be taken prisoner. A few nights later, on 15–16 November, forty-nine Wellingtons were sent to bomb Emden while another forty-seven aircraft attacked Kiel. On the Emden operation four Wellingtons including the one piloted by Sergeant A.C. Homes of 115 Squadron were lost. All of Homes' crew were killed. Pilot Officer Stock of 115 Squadron ditched in the sea off Whitby and, luckily, he and his crew were rescued by a destroyer crewed by Norwegian sailors. At Kiel, four Wellingtons including the one flown by Sergeant A. Cook RAAF of 115 Squadron were lost. All of Cook's crew perished in the North Sea after the Wellington was ditched. On the night of 26–27 November, when eighty Wellingtons and twenty Hampdens went to Emden, only fifty-five aircraft bombed in cloudy conditions and three bombers were lost. One of the two Wimpys that were lost was the one flown by Sergeant Helfer, which had taken off at 17.15 hours and was ditched in the sea off Wells at 23.06 hours. Helfer had considered that the beach might be mined, and the RAF ASR launch that rescued him and his crew told him that his assumption was correct!

By the end of November–December 1941, mainly because of the weather, Marham's Wellingtons had been operational on just eleven nights. There were only two losses and both the 218 Squadron Wellington ICs crashed over England returning from sorties to Brest. One of them was put down at Upavon on 11–12 December and the other was crash-landed, on 16–17 December, at Holme Farm near Powerstock, 4 miles north-east of Bridport, Dorset. The crew baled out and one member suffered a broken leg on landing. At the end of the year Wing Commander Trevor Freeman, CO of 115 Squadron, was awarded the DSO. Mention was made in his citation for his many sorties over a long period. One of these was an attack on Cologne in September when, in spite of fierce opposition, he descended to Low Level, flying above the sea for over an hour searching for the objective. He eventually found the target and he and his squadron bombed it. Also mentioned was the attack on Turin on 10–11 September when Freeman made a successful attack from Low Level despite heavy opposition. In December also, Squadron Leader Foster and Pilot Officer Miller were awarded the DFC and Sergeants Berney and Gilpin received the DFM.

From 1942 onward mass raids were the order of the day, or rather the night, with little attention paid to precision raids on military targets. On 22 February Air Marshal Sir Arthur Harris was appointed C-in-C RAF Bomber Command. He said, 'The Germans entered this war under the rather childish delusion that they were going to bomb everybody else and nobody was going to bomb them. At Rotterdam, London, Warsaw, and half a hundred other places, they put that rather naive theory into operation. They sowed the wind, and now they are going to reap the whirlwind …' A new British directive calling for 'area bombing' of German cities had been sent to Bomber Command seven days before Harris' appointment. The Air Ministry decided that bombing the most densely built-up areas would produce such dislocation and breakdown in civilian morale that the German home front would collapse. With the new directive bomber operations at night entered a new phase that was not restricted to one side of the divide. Harris saw the need to deprive the German factories of its workers and therefore its ability to manufacture weapons for war. To wage the all-out offensive Harris could call upon the Handley Page Halifax and Short Stirling and the new four-engined bomber, the Avro Lancaster. During 1942 eleven Wellington squadrons in Bomber Command re-equipped with four-engined bombers and one was transferred to Coastal Command. The first to re-equip was 218 Squadron, which began conversion to Stirlings, the fourth squadron in 3 Group to do so. No.218 Conversion Flight was formed on 28 February and most of the unit's work was carried out at Barton Bendish. Although the available runway area at Marham had been extended since the original airfield had been built, it was still a grass airfield and not really suitable for bombers requiring a 900-yard take-off run when fully loaded. As a consequence, 218 Squadron's sojourn would be short, with the unit moving to Marham's satellite station at Downham Market, which had hardened runways, in July 1942. A few weeks later 115 Squadron would also leave Marham for Mildenhall. No.218 Conversion Flight joined 1657 Conversion Unit at Stradishall in October.

Meanwhile 3 Group bomber operations continued from Marham. The weather and the need to convert 218 Squadron largely reduced operations during January–February 1942. In March, despite an increase in foggy nights, there was an upsurge in operations and the Wellingtons at Marham operated on eleven nights from 3–4 March onwards. That night Marham was the scene of a disaster when a 218 Squadron Stirling I flown by Flying Officer D.W. Allen landed at 22.55 hours after the raid on Billancourt, and a bomb, which hung up over the target, fell from the aircraft and exploded. Sergeant Laidlaw and Pilot Officer Gales, despite their own injuries, re-entered the burning aircraft and helped free their trapped colleagues. Sergeant W.R. Gregory and Sergeant K.B. Harvey died from their wounds. On the night of 8–9 March Pilot Officer R.P. Runagall DFC and crew of 115 Squadron were lost on the raid on Essen. During March Essen was visited on no less than six nights. On the night of 25–26 March when 254 aircraft were dispatched to the city, which was being attacked for the fourth time that month, it was the largest force sent to one target so far and Marham contributed seventeen Stirlings and ten Wellingtons. The following night, 26–27 March, 104 Wellingtons and eleven Stirlings returned to Essen and ten Wellingtons and a Stirling were lost. Two of the losses were Wellingtons of 115 Squadron.[45] On the night of 28–29 March, when 234 aircraft visited Lübeck, two more Marham aircraft failed to return. A Wellington III of 115 Squadron flown by Sergeant W. Ballard was lost with all the crew, and a battle-damaged Stirling I of 218 Squadron flown by Flight Lieutenant A.G.L. Humphreys was written-off in a crash on return. During fighter attacks on the bomber Sergeant Shannell received a most painful knee wound. Humphreys received the award of an immediate DFC and Sergeant K. Wheeler the DFM. Both men were lost on operations a few weeks later.

Flak defences were a constant thorn in the side of RAF Bomber Command operations. The increase in night bombing raids in the more favourable spring weather (in April 115 Squadron's Wellingtons flew 189 sorties on sixteen nights and Stirlings of 218 Squadron flew 191 sorties) met with a rapid rise in German aerial victories.[46] On the night of 12–13 April Wellington X3596/B, piloted by Sergeant Holder, was shot down by Oberleutnant

Hans-Dieter Frank of 2.NJG1 near Maarheeze in Holland. On the night of 25–26 April, six Stirlings of 218 Squadron carried out a long-range attack on the Skoda armaments factory at Pilsen in Czechoslovakia, while 128 bombers returned to the Baltic port of Rostock which, for two nights running, 23–24 and 24–25 April, the town and the Heinkel factory had been the target for Wellingtons, Stirlings, Whitleys, Hampdens, Manchesters and Lancasters.[47] Pilsen was found to be cloud covered on arrival but at least five Stirlings bombed. W7506 *Y-Yorker*, flown by Pilot Officer Millichamp, failed to return. Although the flak defences at Rostock had been strengthened, no aircraft were lost on the operation, and heavy bombing and many fires were reported.

On 26–27 April, a starry, cold, clear night with a full moon, yet another 115 Squadron Wellington fell victim to a night fighter. At 01.30 in the morning of 27 April only the most inquisitive Danes living in southern Jutland felt able to brave the -3° temperature to look out to see the RAF bombers once again headed for Rostock on the Baltic coast. Just over 100 aircraft were dispatched, and crews were in no doubt that the flak defences would have been strengthened considerably and enemy night fighters would be alerted once more to the possibilities of a 'kill'. Twelve Wellingtons of 115 Squadron took part in the raid. One of them was X3633 *Y-Yorker*, piloted by twenty-three-year-old Sergeant Alfred Fone, a Yorkshireman from Leeds. This was his ninth op, and his rear gunner was Sergeant Albert Edward 'Sim' Simmans, who was flying his fifth operation. This was Sim's second crew. He had been forced to part company with the first, in 40 Squadron at Alconbury, when he developed problems with his ears. No doubt this was caused by the combined effect of a swimming accident as a youngster when he had hit his head on the bottom of the pool, exacerbated by the pressure changes associated with flying. After hospitalisation at Halton, 'Sim' was able to resume his flying career, despite a warning that flying could have an adverse effect on his hearing in later life. He crewed up with Fone and an all-Sergeant crew consisting of Irvine Rollinson, second pilot, Alexander Saint, observer from Bonavista, Newfoundland, and two Scots, William Smith, wireless operator and James Small Grieve, front gunner. 'Sim' had also become engaged to Ann Wynn, a WAAF, and they had made plans for a June wedding. On his last leave home to Barking, Essex, on 2 April Sim's aunt had repaired his silk flying gloves, which he was wearing now to help protect his 'trigger' fingers from freezing at altitude over Jutland. On 13 April Fone's crew had flown a '*Gardening*' sortie and on the 17th had taken part in a raid on Le Havre. On their third operation on 23–24 April they had been part of a bombing raid on Dunkirk.

Everything seemed to be going well. They had taken off in KO-Y at 22.23 hours and had crossed Norfolk and the North Sea without incident. Any thoughts Sim might have had concerning lingering mess bills and a paltry pay-slip of only £2 10s had to be put to one side. As the bomber stream of incoming aircraft approached Sylt at around 01.00 hours, young and older Danes alike followed the sounds of the RAF bombers' engines and those of the German night fighters as they tried to seek them out. Bomber after bomber crossed from west to east. North-west of Toftlund at 02.00 hours a searchlight suddenly coned Fone's Wellington and machine-gun fire could be heard as a Bf 110 of II./NJG3, which arrived from the south-west, made several passes at the aircraft, which caught fire. No one aboard the Wellington bomber stood a chance. Still carrying its bomb load, *Y-Yorker* crashed and exploded at a crossroads

Sergeant Albert Edward 'Sim' Simmans, rear
gunner on X3633 *Y-Yorker*. The plane was
piloted by Sergeant Alfred Fone, KIA, on
26–27 April 1942. (Mike Lewis)

west of Neder Jerstal, a tiny hamlet of twenty-two houses. Windows and doors of buildings
nearby were blown out. The German Wehrmacht and Field Gendarmerie and the Danish
civil police immediately blocked off the roads surrounding the crash site. Wreckage from the
burning Wellington was scattered over a wide area and a large fire started and burned for
hours despite attempts by firemen from Toftlund and Agerskov to put it out.

On 27–28 April Wellington III X3639/K of 115 Squadron, piloted by Sergeant L.G. Harris,
was lost on the raid on Cologne when ninety-seven aircraft were dispatched by Bomber
Command. Altogether, the raid cost six Wellingtons and a Halifax. In Cologne over 1,500
houses were hit or damaged and nineteen other premises were affected, and over 1,680
people were bombed out. The following night eighty-eight aircraft of Bomber Command
attacked Kiel in bright moonlight. The German defences shot down five Wellingtons and a
Hampden. On the night of 29–30 April, when eighty-eight aircraft were dispatched to the
Gnome & Rhône factory at Gennevilliers in Paris, three Wellingtons failed to return. One
of the losses was X3593/C of 115 Squadron, piloted by Sergeant Reynolds, which was shot
down near the French capital.

In a portend of things to come, on 3–4 May 1942, the 100th anniversary of a great
fire, Hamburg was visited by eighty-one bombers. Hamburg was found to be completely
cloud-covered but, while only fifty-four aircraft bombed on to its estimated position,

113 fires were started in the city of which fifty-seven were classed as large and over 1,600 people were bombed out. On 4–5 May, when 121 aircraft were dispatched to Stuttgart, five Stirlings of 218 Squadron returned to Pilsen. One of them was piloted by Flight Sergeant W.H. Gregg, who was shot down with the loss of all the crew, which included Sergeant K. Wheeler who had received the DFM for his actions on 28–29 March. Sergeant G. McAuley's Stirling failed to return from the raid on Stuttgart. A Havoc and Hurricane combination of 1455 Flight at Tangmere shot down a 218 Squadron Stirling flown by Sergeant H.J.V. Ashworth, which was returning from dropping leaflets in the Laon area. The Stirling crashed at Horsham, Sussex. All the crew got out and no one was badly hurt. On 6–7 May ninety-seven aircraft were sent to Stuttgart and nineteen bombers visited Nantes. A Wellington III of 115 Squadron flown by Flight Lieutenant J.A. Sword DFC AFC was shot down on the raid on Stuttgart. All six of the crew baled out, but Sword and Sergeant H.W. Batty died due to insecure parachute webbing and they fell to their deaths. A second Wellington III of 115 Squadron was lost at 16.00 hours when it hit a 240ft wooden radio mast in poor visibility during a training sortie over Norfolk, and crashed at West Beckham, 3 miles south-west of Sheringham. All three sergeant pilots who were on-board were killed. On 17–18 May thirty-two Stirlings and twenty-eight Wellingtons of 3 Group carried out mine-laying in the Friesians and the Heligoland areas. German night fighters were active and five Stirlings and two Wellingtons were shot down. A further twenty-seven aircraft went to Boulogne and one Stirling flew a night leaflet raid to France. Wellington III X3644/A of 115 Squadron, flown by Sergeant F.N. Butterworth, failed to return from a *Gardening* sortie and all five crew were killed. Stirling I N6071, flown by Flight Lieutenant A.G.L. Humphreys DFC, which was also on a *Gardening* sortie, was hit by flak and abandoned over Denmark. Humphreys and five others survived to be taken prisoner. Flying Officer E.R. Barnfather RAAF, a barrister in civilian life, was killed when he was struck in the stomach. Two nights later, on 19–20 May when 197 aircraft set out for Mannheim, eleven aircraft including four Stirlings and three Wellingtons of Bomber Command failed to return. When seventy-seven aircraft including thirty-one Wellingtons and nine Stirlings were sent to bomb the Gnome & Rhône factory at Gennevilliers near Paris on 29–30 May, little or no damage was done to the factory. Four Wellingtons and a Stirling piloted by Flight Lieutenant A.W.I Jones were lost. All eight crew members of the Stirling were killed.

Meanwhile, top-level consultations between Air Marshal Sir Arthur Harris and his subordinate commanders had revealed that the raids on Rostock had achieved total disruption. Whole areas of the city had been wiped out and 100,000 people had been forced to evacuate the city. The capacity of its workers to produce war materials had therefore been severely diminished. Harris had, for some time, nurtured the desire to send 1,000 bombers to a German city and reproduce the same results with incendiaries. Although RAF losses would be on a large scale, Churchill approved the plan. Harris gave the order 'Operation Plan Cologne' to his Group Commanders just after midday on 30 May, so that 1,000 bombers would be unleashed on the 770,000 inhabitants. However, Harris could only accomplish this by using untried crews from the Operational Training Units (OTUs), many of them flying Wellingtons and even Blenheims and Hudsons.[48] All bomber bases throughout England were at a high state of readiness to get all available aircraft airborne for the raid. At Marham, 115 Squadron contributed eighteen Wellingtons, and 218 Squadron offered seventeen Stirlings. Five of the Wimpys carried a 4,000lb HC bomb. Two Wellingtons carried a single 1,000lb GP plus five 500lb GP bombs, and eleven aircraft each carried nine SBCs. Flying in the second seat of Wing Commander Holder's Stirling of 218 Squadron was the 3 Group commander, Air Vice-Marshal J.E.A. 'Jackie' Baldwin. He wrote:

> The weather forecast made it uncertain almost up to the last moment whether we should start. We had not been flying very long before we met much low cloud and this depressed me. The front gunner got a pinpoint on an island off the Dutch coast but the weather was still somewhat thick and there was an alpine range of cloud to starboard. Suddenly, 30 or forty miles from Cologne, I saw the ground and then the flak. It grew clearer and clearer until, near the city, visibility was perfect. First I saw a lake, gleaming in the moonlight, then I could see fires beginning to glow and then searchlights which wavered and flak coming up in a haphazard manner. The sky was full of aircraft all heading for Cologne. I made out Wellingtons, Hampdens, a Whitley and other Stirlings. We sheered off the city for a moment, while the captain decided what would be the best way into the target. It was then that I caught sight of the twin towers of Cologne cathedral, silhouetted against the light of three huge fires that looked as though they were streaming from open blast furnaces. We went in to bomb, having for company a Wellington to starboard and another Stirling to port. Coming out we circled the flak barrage and it was eight minutes after bombing that we set course for home. Looking back, the fires seemed like rising suns and this effect became more pronounced as we drew further away. Then, with the searchlights rising from the fires, it seemed that we were leaving behind us a huge representation of the Japanese banner. Within nine minutes of the coast, we circled to take a last look. The fires then resembled distant volcanoes.

For 98 minutes a procession of bombers passed over Cologne. Stick after stick of incendiaries rained down from the bomb bays of the Wellingtons, adding to the conflagration. Almost all aircraft bombed their aiming point as briefed. The defences, because of the attacking force's size, were relatively ineffective and flak was described variously as 'sporadic' and spasmodic'. In all, 898 crews claimed to have hit their targets. They dropped 1,455 tons of bombs, two-thirds of them incendiaries. Post-bombing reconnaissance certainly showed that more than 600 acres of Cologne had been razed to the ground. The fires burned for days and 59,100 people had been made homeless. The German defences were locally swamped by the mass of bombers and of the forty-three RAF losses. (Another 116 aircraft were damaged, twelve so badly that they were written-off). It is estimated that night fighters shot down thirty. These were mainly achieved on the return journey when the bomber stream had been more dispersed than on the way in.

Marham lost a Wellington and a Stirling. Wellington Z614, flown by Flight Sergeant W. Crampton, was shot down by Oberleutnant Walter Barte of 4/NJG1, and it crashed near Wijchmal in Holland with the loss of all the crew.[49] Stirling I W7502/N, flown by Pilot Officer A.W. Davis, was badly shot up by flak and later crashed at Huppenbroich, 6km north-east of Monschau. Flight Sergeant J.L. Borrowdale baled out, clinging to the back of Sergeant

L. Tate RCAF, but tragically he slipped to his death when Tate's parachute deployed. Davis and three others were also killed. Tate and Sergeant A.J. Smith survived to be made prisoners of war. Stirling I R9311/L, flown by Sergeant S.G. Falconer, had taken off at 23.50 hours and as the huge bomber gained height the port wheel clipped some high ground and was ripped away. Falconer maintained control and continued on course. On his return at 05.55 hours he made a wheels-up landing at Marham. Falconer gained an immediate DFM for his efforts and he was later commissioned.[50]

Squadrons repaired and patched their damaged bombers and within 48 hours they were preparing for a second 'Thousand Bomber Raid', this time against Essen on the night of 1–2 June. A force of 956 bombers was ready. Again the numbers had to be made up by using 347 OTU crews and aircraft. At Marham 115 Squadron contributed eighteen Wellingtons and 218 Squadron gave fourteen Stirlings. Of the thirty-seven bombers lost on the second 1,000-bomber raid on Essen, twenty were claimed by night fighters. Two of the missing aircraft were from the Marham squadrons, Wellington X3721/F flown by Flying Officer Williams and Stirling N3753 of 218 Squadron flown by Sergeant G. McAuley, both failing to return.

On the night of 3–4 June 170 bombers were dispatched on the first large raid to Bremen since October 1941. Eleven aircraft failed to return – eight of them had been shot down by night fighters. Three Marham aircraft were among the casualties. There were no survivors aboard Wellington X3724 piloted by Flight Sergeant J.L. Hutchison RCAF, and only one man survived from X3625/J flown by Flying Officer T.R.R. Wood. Wellington X3749/D, flown by Pilot Officer H.G. A'Court force-landed at Marham on return. Stirling I W7474/K of 218 Squadron, flown by twenty-nine-year-old Pilot Officer James Garscadden and Pilot Officer John Richard Webber, aged nineteen, one of seven Stirlings dispatched from Marham, was the third aircraft lost. Oberleutnant Ludwig Becker of 6./NJG2 shot down the Stirling south of Den Helder at 00.27 hours and all the crew were killed.[51] On 5–6 June 180 aircraft raided Essen.[52] On the night of 6–7 June three more Manchesters, three Wellingtons, two Stirlings and one Halifax were lost from the 233 aircraft dispatched to Emden.

As the RAF night bombing offensive gained momentum the stark obituaries began to fill the newspaper columns. More often they read 'Dead, MIA - believed killed.' Replacements for the losses came from the same OTUs that had contributed many hundreds of young aircrew for the Thousand Bomber raids. Canadian Flight Sergeant Delmer Mooney skippered one crew, which arrived at Marham on 25 May 1942 to join 'A' Flight in 115 Squadron. His front-gunner/bomb aimer was Sergeant Joe Richardson, and his tail-gunner was Sergeant Bill Margerison. Sergeant Eddie Killilea, the wireless operator/air-gunner (WOP/AG) was quite a womaniser and could sing and dance as well. His easy rhythm on the dance floor had helped him during Morse training and he had finished top of his course. Sergeant Don Bruce, a twenty-one-year-old Londoner, was the observer and fifth member of the Wellington crew. He had already escaped serious injury in an Anson crash at Air Navigation School. Bruce recalls:

> Most of the aircrew I met were just mad-keen to fly. They were imbued with the spirit of
> flying during the late twenties and early thirties when momentous events were taking place in
> the development of flight. During our training period I don't think many of us really thought
> seriously about the tasks we would be asked to carry out later on operations. I know I never

gave any deep thought to it, I just loved the job I was doing in the air. When I was posted to 115 Squadron, the first five ops I flew were really exciting because it was all new and the dangers were not fully appreciated. It was wonderful to have dated and returned safely. After debriefing and breakfast it was marvellous to sink mentally and physically exhausted into cool sheets and with the noise the aircraft engines still singing in your ears drift into a deep sleep. The novelty disappeared after this when I realized things could go wrong. I firmly believed that everyone was frightened on ops but you covered up and hid it from your fellow crewmembers. I think the dividing line between those who came off flying through Lack of Moral Fibre (LMF) and those who didn't was extremely thin.[53] When we were being shot at by flak and the aircraft w being lifted by the blast and pieces of shrapnel were whining around inside the aircraft, I used to 'freeze'. These were short periods when I was so scared my brain refused to function properly As soon as we were away from the flak I came back to normal, but I always had an underlying feeling of fear when on ops.

There were so many things that could go wrong. When we rook off the bombers were always overloaded and difficult to get off the ground. If you crashed then it was 'curtains' for everybody. I always had on my shoulders the worry and responsibility of not getting the aircraft lost, which could easily cause us to stray across a heavily defended area. There was the risk all the time from night fighter attack and flak over the target. Then there was the difficulty of getting home, particularly if the aircraft was damaged. Landing in the darkness was also a hazard. Because of the risk of intruders aerodromes could nor be lit up. As we made the landing approach the Chance Light would be turned on momentarily so the pilot could see the runway, and as soon as his wheels touched the ground it was switched off and we returned to darkness.

I'm sure no one enjoyed the open bombing of towns and cities which we were being asked to carry out. I had experienced being bombed during the Blitz in 1940 when I lived in London. That was why I felt sick when I did my first bomb dropping on Emden [22–23 June 1942] and saw all the fires and thought of the population below.[54] You had to put all that on one side and just do your task. We flew with Joe Richardson, who eventually came off with LMF. Also, on one trip we rook a front gunner, Sergeant J. B. Smith, who was suspect LMF. When we got near the target he said that his leg was playing him up. He had been wounded in the leg on an earlier occasion. Sergeant Del Mooney RCAF, my pilot, told him to go back on the bed and he cowered there all the time we were in the target area and then went back into the turret later on the return journey. At debriefing he was telling the Intelligence Officer all that he had seen over the target. This was in front of us. It was pathetic and I felt desperately sorry for him. I thought this could well be me if I cracked. Del and I had to make a report to the Group Captain on him and we had to tell the truth. Del said he would refuse to fly with him if he were asked to take him again. He was posted away from the squadron LMF. The poor devils got a rough time; they were demoted and given the most menial of jobs. This happened to NCOs; I think the treatment of LMF officers was more lenient. To sum up, I was very frightened on ops, I swore if I got through a tour I wouldn't do a second tour. When I had parachuted into Holland I heard one of our bombers overhead returning home. At first I thought how lucky they were. Then I thought tomorrow or the next day they will have to go through all that ordeal again and believe it or not I felt relieved that I was out of it.

Main undercarriage of Stirling I W7474 HA-K of 218 Squadron, flown by twenty-nine-year-old Pilot Officer James Garscadden and Pilot Officer John Richard Webber, aged nineteen. This plane was one of eight shot down on the night of 3–4 June 1942. W7474 was claimed by Oberleutnant Ludwig Becker of 6./NJG2, south of Den Helder at 00.27 hours. All seven crew were killed in action. (Karl Fischer)

Oberleutnant Ludwig Becker – 'The Night Fighting Professor' – of 6./NJG2. (Rob de Visser via Theo Boiten)

It was the practice for 'green' crews to fly their first op with an experienced pilot. Thus, Sergeant W.C. 'Norrie' Norrington was to be the crew's pilot for their first op, on 6–7 June. Sergeant Don Bruce recalls:

A bomber operation began in the morning really. After breakfast we reported to the Flights, A and B, for nominal roll call by our Flight Commanders. Approximately eight crews in each Flight plus the reserves. We were allotted our aircraft for local flying or air testing. Our kite was KO-A, a newly delivered machine, which we would write off temporarily in a crash-landing at Exeter aerodrome after having been badly shot up by flak over Brest but that was for the future. Now we were to take it up for air firing, George test – Automatic Pilot, and Homing practice – Gee. After an hour we landed and taxied to dispersal. As we passed through the Flights we saw instructions to the ground crews chalked up on the boards. Six hundred gallons of petrol and a 'standard' high explosive bomb load, six five hundred pounders and a thousand pounder to drop in the middle of the stick, for KO-A. We then knew that we would be on 'stand to' that night. Speculation was rife as to the target. Had it been 450 gallons it could have meant 'Happy Valley', which is the nickname for the heavily defended Ruhr Valley or even a cushy trip to Paris and the Renault factory.

After lunch we spent the time relaxing as far as possible and then around tea time we were briefed and told the target was Emden.[55] From then on I was busy preparing the Flight Plan. At this stage of the war we were still given a certain amount of freedom in choosing our route and the height at which we would bomb. Another tense period of waiting in which time I collected my bag of navigational instruments, a met report, and operational rations for the crew – usually chocolate, oranges or raisins, chewing gum and six thermos flasks, two of black coffee, two of tea and two of Bovril. Finally we were seated outside the Flights complete with flying kit and parachutes ready for the transport to take us to the aircraft at the dispersal points.

As each crew arrived at their dispersal we wished them luck. Then we were seated on the grass by KO-A. It was still light. We had a long wait as we were near the end of the take-off sequence. Some 24 aircraft from 218 and 115 Squadrons would be airborne before it was our turn. I looked over the hedge and saw a farmer ploughing his field. It was all so peaceful. I wished desperately that I could change places with him. Tense and nervous we urinated against the wheels of the aircraft for good luck. This was a standard practice among aircrews, later to be prohibited by Air Ministry order as the subsequent corrosion was causing undercarriage failures. As our take-off time approached [23.35 hours] I climbed into the aircraft and set the detonator and diffuser on Gee and its map container. It was warm inside and strangely quiet compared to the noise of the aircraft outside. I was alone for a moment and I looked around the observer's compartment trying to visualise a burst of cannon fire from a night fighter ripping through the cabin. Now the rest of the crew were climbing aboard. The pilot was starting the engines and I was too busy with my duties to think of anything else.

We taxied along the perimeter track maintaining strict W/T silence. The aircraft ahead of us got the 'green' from the Aldis lamp and then we were swinging round to face the take-off strip. No one spoke to the pilot. He must not be distracted. His aircraft is heavy and would take all his concentration to get it off the ground. He would do an 'operational take-off'. The heavy tail turret complete with gunner must be raised off the ground first so he jammed on the brakes, and pushed the throttles up to the gates. The Wellington shuddered and roared. He pushed the stick forward until it almost touched the instrument panel. Slowly the tail lifted and when the nose was pointing slightly down he released the brakes and we trundled off. Momentum gathered and at 100 mph he was holding her down. At 120 mph we lifted off the ground. As I lifted my hands off the log to note the time we were airborne I saw that the place where they were resting was moist with sweat. Take-off with full petrol and bomb load was extremely dangerous.

We climbed on course. The next hazard would be if we passed over a British convoy sailing down the coast. A convoy would open fire on any aircraft passing directly over it. We were low and vulnerable and although we knew its approximate position this could be quite inaccurate as the convoy maintained strict W/T silence whilst in these waters. Some aircraft had been badly damaged in the past by convoys. We passed out to sea without incident, still climbing. The gunners called up for permission to try out their guns. The whole structure of the aircraft shuddered as the guns opened up and the reek of cordite pervaded the atmosphere in the cabin. We hoped that no patrolling night fighter had spotted our one in five tracer.

Approaching the Dutch coast we unfolded and locked in position the armour plate doors. These doors were protection for the cabin and cockpit from a rear attack. Still climbing on course, the wireless operator in the astrodome assisted the rear gunner in his endless search for night fighters. This is where the area began, the Dutch coast, the beginning of the night fighter belt. The aircraft commenced to weave gently from side to side as the pilot attempted to uncover the blind spot below us for the gunners. Ten thousand feet, cold but not unpleasant, we began to use oxygen. The pilot had difficulty in engaging the S-blower (supercharger). If he failed we would have to stay at 10,000ft. I asked the pilot the outside temperature but he couldn't tell me as the indicator had fallen off the dial. He was worried that the oil temperature on the port engine was too high. He throttled that engine back. The rear gunner was experiencing difficulty with his turret. Would I check the recuperator rams, which indicated the hydraulic pressure? I put my hand out and felt them. They were flat. The turret could only be operated manually. Should we turn back? The pilot decided to carry on. Twelve thousand feet. We could see the glow from the target. Apart from the odd flak gun popping off miles out of range we had experienced little hostility. I worked out the course to bring us out of the target towards the sea.

The gunners were now calling over the intercom warning the pilot of pockets of flak. We started to weave violently. I moved forward to the bomb aimer's position setting the course on the pilot's compass as I went past. Lying prone along the bombing hatch I got a good view of the target which was well alight. It was like a running red sore in the blackness of the night. For a brief moment I felt sick with horror and thought of the human beings below. Then I was too busy to care. I set the rotor arm that would space the stick of bombs and removed the bomb release from its holder. This automatically fused the bombs. I lined the target up in the wires of the bombsight. The flak was heavy and the pilot weaved desperately. Red balls of light flak started lazily from the ground. Gaining in impetus they appeared to come straight for my stomach. I sucked my breath in. They passed like lightning to one side of us and were arcing above us. This confirmed what we have been told that the light flak at Emden reached 14,000 feet. We were menaced by both heavy and light flak. I got a glimpse of the target. No time for standard 'bombing pattern' now. The gunners were yelling for the bombs to be dropped. They wanted to be away. All was noise, confusion, flak, searchlights and roaring, lurching, aircraft. I saw the target again.

Get over to port man. Hold it. BOMBS GONE.

The bomber rose, unburdened and free. We swung round on course and I scrambled back to the cabin. We left the target behind in a Shallow Dive to increase our speed. We were away to the comparative safety of the open sea.

Everyone relaxed. We were flying parallel to the coast and danger was remote. Perhaps a patrolling Ju 88 night fighter but the chance was slight. I was busy with my navigation. The wireless operator poured coffee for us and took an empty milk bottle up to the pilot so that he could relieve himself. GEORGE, the automatic pilot, was u/s so he could not get back to the Elsan toilet. The pilot was still concerned about the oil temperature. It turned out later that the gauge was reading incorrectly. The final stretch of sea and then the English coastline. I switched on the IFF. We didn't want to be intercepted by our own fighters and for the same reason we stayed at a predetermined height. Crossing the coast and moving inland, eyes were peeled for Norwich and its balloon barrage should we be off course. We picked up the aerodrome and started to circle. The pilot tested the undercart and the red light stayed on meaning the wheels would not lock.

We called up the ground. 'Hallo Waggon Control, this is Reveille *A-Apple*'. No reply. We repeated several times, then it dawned on us that the transmitter had packed up. The receiver was working. We heard another aircraft calling. The aerodrome replied. It is not Waggon Control. We were over the wrong aerodrome. Panic for a moment until we found our bearings and arrived over Marham. We crossed the flare path at right angles and fired the distress signal, double green. Then we flew over again flashing 'A' on our downward identity light. They were calling us from Waggon Control and telling other aircraft to get out of the circuit. To cheer us up they told us that the ambulance or 'blood wagon' and the fire tender were standing by. They didn't know we were receiving them so they flashed a green from the Aldis lamp. We made a pass but the pilot overshot. We were braced ready for a crash-landing. Second time round we made it. A perfect landing. The undercart locking light wasn't working. We climbed out. Suddenly my parachute harness weighed a ton. A quick debriefing with Intelligence and then cool, smooth sheets and wonderful, deep sleep.

In between 'ops' air crews let their hair down when they could. On 12 June Don Bruce, Eddie Killilea and Bill Margerison visited nearby King's Lynn. Killilea, attracted by a tall blonde in the doorway of the Eagle pub in Norfolk Street, suggested they pay it a visit. Bruce and Margerison were hungry and declined and they went their own way to a café. A short time later, a Dornier Do 217, exploiting a hole in the clouds to excellent advantage, made a hit-and-run attack on the town. Bruce and Margerison finished up under the table. Further down the road the Eagle was flattened by one of the four bombs dropped by the raider. Killilea and four other RAF men were among the forty-two bodies pulled from the wreckage. Jack Goad replaced Killilea and Flight Sergeant Del Mooney returned to captain the crew.

Wellington III Z1657/R (formerly *A-Apple*, as retained on the nose) near Lady Wood, Marham, in August–September 1942. (Jack Goad)

On the night of 17–18 June the crew of KO-A Z1648 were part of a small force of twenty-seven Stirlings and Wellingtons which flew an operation to St Nazaire, while another forty-six aircraft carried out mine-laying off the French port and in the Friesians.[56] Aboard Mooney's Wellington were sixteen 250lb bombs, but the target could not be identified in poor weather and only six aircraft bombed. (RAF crews were not allowed to release bombs over France if the target could not be determined). Bruce had trouble with his compass and the ETA for landfall in England came and went:

> When Bruce finally got his pinpoint worked out he nearly had a baby on the spot! He shouted over the intercom, 'We're right over Brest!' Just at that moment the searchlights came on and coned us. Del started to weave the Wellington but the flak was already bursting closer. He climbed 500 feet and then dived 500 feet. It was rather sickening for us and as we dived the gravity sucked the fuel from the engines and they cut out. We did not know if we had been hit only Del knew that. I was absolutely paralyzed with fear and what with the table going up and down I could not plot a thing.

Suddenly, Del Mooney snarled over the intercom, 'Give them a stick!' Eight 250-pounders whistled down into the night and as they exploded the searchlights went out. However, the port engine, which ran the hydraulics and the radio, had been put out of action. Mooney turned and limped away from Brest in a northerly direction. Over the sea the remaining 250-pounders were jettisoned. White managed to get his transmitter working off batteries and sent out a 'Mayday' distress call, which was acknowledged. Bruce was so dejected that he swore if they got back, he would never fly again; they did get back. Mooney suggested they crash-land but the Englishmen aboard warned how hilly the West Country is. Mooney thought they should crash-land on the beach

Sergeant Don Bruce, observer on Flight Sergeant Del Mooney RCAF's crew in 115 Squadron at Marham, in July 1942. (Don Bruce)

but the crew was worried about mines. Bruce, now standing in the second pilot's position, saw runways passing below the bomb panel. He exclaimed, 'Hey! We're over an aerodrome'.

It was Exeter aerodrome. Mooney banked carefully and the aerodrome put its light on. As they made their approach a searchlight was swung onto the Wimpy, almost blinding the swearing Canadian. Exeter was a fighter airfield and had a different system of lights, which no one understood. Mooney ended up going downwind at 110mph. Bruce looked back at the undercarriage and could see the wheels hanging down. Grimly, he gripped Mooney's seat and as they touched the concrete runway, the wheels folded and the Wimpy collapsed onto its belly. Great streaks of sparks shot back from the fuselage. Fortunately, the starboard engine was still operating and it slewed the bomber around in a 180° arc as 'blood wagons' chased them along the runway. They finished up facing the opposite direction. Everyone got out safely but KO-A was a write-off. No one was sad to see the end of it, for the gun turrets had never worked! In the afternoon Squadron Leader Cousens flew down from RAF Marham to take the crew home. By the next day Bruce had got over the Brest episode.

On the night of 19–20 June the RAF raided Emden and 194 aircraft took part, including 112 Wellingtons. Of these 131 crews claimed to have bombed Emden but bombing photographs revealed that part of the flare force started a raid on Osnabrück, 80 miles from Emden, in which twenty-nine aircraft eventually joined. Emden reported only five HE bombs and 200–300 incendiaries with no damage or casualties. The RAF lost nine bombers including six Wellingtons. On 20–21 June 185 RAF bombers made a return raid on Emden. Mooney's Wellington carried a 4,000-pounder in the bomb bay. The crew returned safely once again but eight aircraft were lost, including three Wellingtons and two Stirlings; among them was W7530 of 218 Squadron. Two nights later, on 22–23 June, the RAF hammered Emden again when a force of 227 aircraft was dispatched, comprising 144 Wellingtons, thirty-eight Stirlings, twenty-six Halifaxes, eleven Lancasters and eight Hampdens. Some 196 crews claimed good bombing results but decoy fires are believed to have drawn-off many bombs. Emden reported that fifty houses had been destroyed, 100 damaged and some damage caused to the harbour. Six people were killed and forty injured. Bomber Command lost six aircraft, including Stirling N6078 of 218 Squadron, and four Wellington ICs, one of which was X3555/W flown by Pilot Officer Malcolm Freegard of 115 Squadron, which was damaged over the target. Freegard recalled:

> We came back on one engine and I struggled to reach home. Then the second engine went and I was obliged to ditch in the sea some 70 miles due east of Cromer. After twelve hours in a dinghy an ASR Walrus amphibian picked up my four crew and me. The ASR crew who had been guided to their dinghy by a Wellington and a Hudson and which took three attempts to take-off was pleased, as we were the first crew they had rescued. After patching us up we were taken back to Marham, where all except one of us recovered to go back on ops.

On the night of 25–26 June the RAF mounted the third and final 1,000-bomber raid, when 1,067 aircraft were dispatched to Bremen. Again, the force was mainly comprised of Wellingtons and Halifaxes, and included 102 Wellingtons and Hudsons of Coastal Command. Although the raid was not as successful as the first 1,000-raid on Cologne on 30–31 May, large parts of Bremen were destroyed, especially in the southern and eastern districts. The price Bomber Command paid for this raid was very high – no less than forty-eight aircraft were lost, the highest casualty rate in the war so far. Marham lost two aircraft: Wellington Ic X3554 flown by Sergeant H. Abbott was lost over the target, and Stirling W7503 also failed to return.[58]

On the night of 27–28 June Del Mooney's crew were one of fifty-five Wellington bombers among the 144 aircraft that re-visited Bremen. Of these, 119 aircraft bombed blindly through cloud after obtaining Gee fixes. Nine aircraft failed to return including Stirling DJ974 of 218 Squadron, but Mooney's crew landed back a Marham safely. Flight Sergeant McCann of 115 Squadron returned with a dead rear gunner when his Wellington (BJ589) was attacked by a night fighter. Two nights later, on 29–30 June, when 253 aircraft were directed to bomb Bremen again, BJ796 flown by Pilot Officer Stanford suffered an engine failure and he was forced to jettison his bombs. The aircraft, however, continued to lose height and Stanford had to ditch in the sea 40 miles off Lowestoft. All the crew except for Flight Sergeant Linwood made it back safely in a dinghy. That same night Sergeant W. Ken Dunn and his crew of a 115 Squadron Wellington, who were on their thirty-first operation, encountered enemy fighters. Dunn recalls:

We had been routed to the target along the coast and advised to return the same way but as we turned for home I saw two aircraft shot down within a minute and I decided to take a more direct route some forty miles inland, hoping to avoid the fighters. We set course for Texel, the most western island of the Friesians, at 10,000ft. Visibility was good. There was low stratus at 2,000ft and some medium at 12,000ft. We were flying on a course of 335 degrees just west of Groningen when the attack came as a complete surprise. Normally one of the crew, usually the rear gunner, saw or 'sensed' the approach of a fighter and so warned the pilot. But on this occasion the first intimation I had was the sight of tracer shells and bullets shooting past me on both sides of the cabin and the noise of explosions as some of them hit parts of the aircraft. The enemy aircraft was first observed by the rear gunner diving out of a patch of cloud on to our stern, but before he had a chance to report the enemy aircraft opened fire. The rear gunner returned fire and registered hits on the fighter's port wing. I was skidding and sideslipping the aircraft to present as difficult a target as possible.

The enemy aircraft, identified as a Me 110, then dived away to port and the front gunner gave it a short burst, with no visible result. The wireless operator, now in the astrodome, reported that the Messerschmitt had worked its way round to the port quarter and lined up for a second attack, but before he could get within range we had turned on him and he skimmed over the top. Again he came round on the port quarter and again we turned. He stayed with us for quite a time and followed us as we spiralled to practically ground level and making for the stratus cloud at 2,000ft where we eventually lost him. In his subsequent attacks I don't think he hit us again, but his first attack was so successful – from his point of view – that he probably registered us as a 'highly probable?'

We flew back to Holland very low and I remember seeing the lights of houses, which should have been blacked out, I suppose. The cloud cleared as we crossed the coast at about 1,000ft. Just west of the Friesians we flew over a convoy which sent up red and green tracer. Over the North Sea we climbed up to 7,000ft, with some difficulty, and began to check. We had sustained considerable damage. The flying instrument panel was unserviceable. The trailing aerial fairway had been shot away. Petrol seemed all right at first sight but the hydraulic oil tank was empty. There was a large hole in the fabric by the wireless operator's cabin and a strip nearly three feet wide had been torn off to the tail. I put in the automatic pilot and went down the catwalk and there was the North Sea clearly visible through the geodetic construction.

It soon became clear that the port petrol tank had been hit and was leaking. We switched the balance cock to use up what remained before running both engines off the starboard tank. Although the hydraulic system was not working the turrets could be operated manually. The undercarriage had fallen but did not lock. However, we managed to lock it later by using the emergency hand pump. It was not possible to use any flap on landing. As we landed at base the port main wheel burst. As we lost flying speed on landing the port wing sagged when gravity took over – a cannon shell had struck the main spar. Bullets had holed the nacelle tanks and the reserve petrol had leaked away. When the engineering officer came over to inspect the aircraft he declared it was a 'write-off'. Obviously, the officer's opinion on the state of the aircraft was revised on closer inspection; the badly shot-up Wimpy was repaired and flew on Ops again a few months later.

Mooney's crew's run of operational bombing sorties were interrupted towards the end of the month. On 30 June they made two search operations over the North Sea for a missing aircrew. Bill Margerison moved from the rear turret to the front and a new rear gunner, Sergeant Ron Esling, joined the crew as WOP/AG and flew with the crew on the night of 2–3 July when Bremen was bombed again, this time by 265 of the 325 bombers dispatched. Thirteen aircraft were lost, including Stirling N3718/A of 218 Squadron, which was shot down by a German night fighter on the final Stirling operation from Marham. All of Pilot Officer G.G. Jeary's crew were killed. Another Stirling had to fight off three other night fighters but returned safely to Marham. On 7 July the Stirlings left the station for Downham Market.[59]

Mooney's crew's next operation was to Duisburg, Germany, on the night of 13–14 July when 194 aircraft, including 139 Wellingtons, were dispatched in what was the first of a series of raids on this industrial city on the edge of the Ruhr. Mooney and his crew were given a new Wellington Mk.III, KO-K, to replace KO-A. By now Mooney's crew were old hands on the squadron, with six weeks' operational experience. This operation would be Don Bruce's eleventh trip; unlucky thirteenth if he counted the two search sweeps over the North Sea. All throughout the briefing Bruce's mind was on the bomb load they would be carrying deep into Germany. It was a lightly cased 4,000lb 'dustbin-shaped' bomb studded with detonators. For maximum blast effect it had a protruding rim to prevent it penetrating too far into the ground. The Wellington had to be stripped of its bomb-bay doors and flotation bags to accommodate the sinister weapon, and that meant the bomber would not be able to fly on one engine or float for long if they had to ditch. Mooney's crew was to follow in the wake of a main bomber stream. There would be a lull after the main force had finished bombing and the Germans would assume that the raid was over. Their rescue services would be in full swing and the KO-K would arrive over Duisburg to drop its maximum blast bomb, effectively wiping out any rescue services.

The briefing room was crowded and hot. Thirty-one-year-old Frank W. Dixon-Wright DFC, the CO popular with his crews and who had already completed a tour of operations, addressed his crews: 'Go for the centre of the town, boys. Plenty of old dry timber there. It will burn well … after all they do it to our towns so we do it to theirs.' Mooney's crew left the briefing and prepared to take-off for Duisburg. Bruce recalls:

Prior to take-off I was busy preparing the Flight Plan. I collected my bag of navigational instruments, a met report and operational rations for the crew.. Finally, we were seated outside the Flights; complete with flying kit and parachutes, ready for transportation to the dispersal point. As each crew dropped off at their dispersal point we wished them luck. We sat on the grass by KO-K. It was still sunlight and we had a long wait. Forty aircraft from two squadrons were getting airborne at approximately two-minute intervals. Tense and nervous, we urinated against the wheels of the aircraft for good luck. As take-off time approached I climbed into the aircraft and set the detonators on Gee and its map containers. It was warm inside the aircraft and strangely quiet compared to the noise of the engines outside. Alone for a moment, I looked around the Observer's compartment and wondered what it would be like with a hail of cannon shells from a night fighter ripping through the cabin. Then the rest of the crew began climbing aboard and Del started the engines. Slowly, the tail lifted and when the nose pointed slightly downwards he released the brakes and we trundled off. s.

We climbed on course, passing out to sea without incident. Still climbing, the gunners asked permission to test-fire their guns. The whole structure shuddered as their .303 in calibre guns opened up and the reek of cordite filtered through into the cabin. We hoped that no patrolling night fighter spotted the one in five tracer shells. Approaching the Dutch coast we unfolded and locked into position the armour plate doors. They were supposed to protect the cabin and pilot's position from rear attack. Still climbing on course, the WOP/AG in the astrodome assisted Ron Esling in his search for night fighters. This was their area. Del started to weave the Wimpy gently from side to side to uncover the blind spot below us for the gunners. At 10,000ft, cold but not unpleasant, we started to use oxygen.

Approaching Duisburg and running in at 13,000ft, Mooney became cautious, steering the bomber around the town. Suddenly, he spotted what he had been seeking, another Wellington about 500ft below and making its run across the target. It was attracting the flak and the searchlights. KO-K followed unmolested. When things became too hot for the crew, the other Wimpy banked away in a dive. KO-K maintained its position, right in the centre of the target. The Wellington bucked as the 4,000lb bomb was released. The defences tried to bring them down. All Hell was let loose and the blue 'radar' searchlight on them was joined immediately by other searchlights, which formed a cone around them. Mooney had forgotten to put his goggles on and was blinded by the glare. Esling, who had been wounded by flak once before, was shouting over the intercom for Mooney to get out of the beams. Bruce thought, 'We have very little time before our height and course are predicted. Can't shake them off. They are hitting us. A sound like a stick rattling on corrugated iron. The port engine is hit.' In desperation the pilot pulled the nose up and up. There was an inert sensation throughout before the stall, and then Mooney swung the bomber over in a stall turn. The Wimpy was now diving in the opposite direction. The searchlights lost the bomber in its exacting gyrations but would the Wellington stand up to the great stresses Mooney was imposing upon it? The bomber plunged to 9,000ft. Inside, the crew was floating in space. Only the navigation table held Bruce down where it pinned his knees. Maps, stray nuts, bolts and pencils floated past his face. All this time his eyes remained glued to the Observer's airspeed indicator. The needle had started on the inner circle: 320, 330, 340, 350 mph. He read the ever-increasing airspeed indicator with alarm, thinking of the red warning plate mounted on the pilot's control panel, which said, 'THIS AIRCRAFT MUST NOT BE DIVED AT SPEEDS OF 300 MPH'. Down and down the Wellington dived. Gravitational force pressed on the hands and arms of the crew, making them feel as heavy as lead and forcing Bruce down into his seat and onto the navigational table. His eyelids began to close involuntarily.

Before the 'final squashing process' Mooney somehow managed to pull the Wimpy out of its near fatal dive. The crew could hear him, panting with exertion through his microphone. They were as one with this terrible load that was wrenching at every rivet in the aircraft. As suddenly as it had begun it was over, and incredibly the bomber was back on the straight and level. All manner of debris littered the table and floor. The case containing the rations had burst open showering the observer's table with raisins. In the dim light Don Bruce watched an earwig emerge from the sticky heap.

Bruce gathered his maps from the floor near the bed while Mooney was still fully employed with the control column and rudder, desperately trying to keep the port wing, with its dead engine, on an even keel. He climbed 500ft but the starboard engine could not do the work of two and began overheating. As the aircraft levelled out it dropped back to 500ft. It lost height so rapidly that the crew realised that they would not make the coast. A hurried consultation between Mooney and Bruce resulted in the immediate order of 'Jump, jump, rear-gunner!' There was no reply from Esling. Bruce was about to investigate when Mooney cried out. 'Don't bother – he's gone.' The Canadian could tell from the trim of the aircraft, which was flying light in the tail, that he had baled out. If Bruce had been required to turn the turret using the 'dead man's handle' it is doubtful whether he and Mooney would have got out in time.

The forward escape hatch in the Wellington was for use by the pilot, wireless operator, front gunner and the observer. Bill Margerison went through the forward escape hatch first after taking some time to find his parachute, which had been dislodged during the stall turn. Bill Hancock started but almost at once returned to his position to retrieve his gloves! Bruce removed his intercom to prevent strangulation during the parachute descent, loosened his tie (the RAF dressed for war!) and fastened his parachute to his harness. Mooney grinned and gave Bruce the thumbs up. 'Good old Delmer, he's a great guy', thought Bruce.

The Wellington had a diamond-shaped escape hatch on the starboard side, near the bed. It was cut away in the geodetics and either covered with fabric or a trapdoor. This was to be used only in extreme emergency but Bruce doubted whether anyone could exit through it with a parachute pack. He was not about to try. He moved to the forward escape hatch and gingerly, he lowered his legs through the hole. The slipstream caught them like chaff in the wind and he was swept along the underside of the fuselage, his parachute pack jamming against the hatch in the process. Finally, Bruce was away – down into the night.

'THE RIPCORD! Pull the ripcord you fool!' Bruce shouted to himself. There was a sharp slither of fabric as the pilot 'chute tugged at the main fabric, and then a crack like a pistol as the chords holding the harness across his chest broke free. There was a terrific jolt and the umbrella of silk opened. He felt sick and hung limply in his harness. Dim shapes began to form. He got into a sitting position. The parachute trailing ahead in a light wind caught in a tree. Bruce swung into soft earth and grazed his elbow. He had, in fact, landed near a farm at Nijnsel in Saint-Oedenrode, owned by Mr Van Dijk. The Wellington had been shot down at approximately 03.30 hours. Ron Esling, the first man to bale out, had landed in a farmyard. One by one the entire crew were apprehended by the Germans and placed under arrest. After four days at Eindhoven they were put on a train for Amsterdam. There they were put in cells below ground for two days. Hancock was retained for more questioning and then sent to Stalag Luft III. Mooney, Margerison, Bruce and Esling were sent to the Dulag Luft Interrogation Centre outside Frankfurt. At Dulag Luft, they signed the visitors' book,

WIRELESS OPERATOR   PILOT AND CAPTAIN   FRONT GUNNER

P/O BILL HANCOCK   F/SGT DEL MOONEY   SGT BILL MARGERISON

BASE – 115 SQUADRON MARHAM

SGT DON BRUCE   SGT RON ESLING

DUISBURG
NIGHT 13/14ᵀᴴ JULY 1942
BAILED OUT NIJNSEL / SON

OBSERVER   REAR GUNNER

Flight Sergeant Del Mooney RCAF's crew, who were shot down on 13–14 July 1942. (Don Bruce)

checking to see if there were any other crews that had been shot down on the Duisburg raid. It was not until after the war that Bruce discovered that they were one of five crews shot down on the raid and, according to the visitors' book, the only survivors. The four airmen were marched away to solitary confinement, interrogation and eventual processing for onward transmission to POW camps. On 19 July they were dispatched to Stalag Luft VIIIB at Lamsdorf to begin almost three years of tedious and sometimes painful internment behind barbed wire. Ironically, their route took them past Duisburg. Much to the amusement of the escorting German Officer, Bruce and his fellow crewmembers were surprised at the lack of bomb damage around the city.

Pilot Officer Malcolm Freegard of 115 Squadron had returned to ops on 11 July, with a mine-laying trip and then it was off to Duisburg on the 13th:

Mine-laying trips were fairly cushy unless you saw a flak ship and people could and did get shot down. Duisburg was particularly well defended. It put the wind up you to see the old night fighters creeping around. I hated bombing cities, I really did. I was happier when I was given military targets. Saturation bombing of German cities was awful. Waging war on children and old people and historic cities is not what I wanted to do. I was 20 years old. I had wanted to be a fighter pilot where the war was one on one. When I joined 115 Squadron I was as patriotic as the next man. Then I began to think about all the energy and human ingenuity used to wage war that could have been employed in better ways. This war was an expensive spirit and a waste of shame.

My seventh op, on the night of 21/22 July, we set out at 23.49 hours to bomb Duisburg again. Shortly after bombing we were attacked from underneath by a Me 110 night fighter close to Düsseldorf and my faithful Wellington caught fire and was damaged beyond any hope of recovery. Fortunately, I was again carrying no second pilot that night. As it was three of my five crew were killed in the aircraft. (One of the lads had been married only three months).[60] After checking them to make sure they were dead, Sergeant Bill Rogers the front gunner and I escaped with some difficulty. I had been wounded slightly in the thigh by an exploding cannon shell and I had a hell of a job getting out through the front hatch. When I finally opened my parachute I was well under a 1,000ft from the ground. I thought, this is it – I've had it. It's what I joined up for. But to my great relief, the chute opened and I landed in open countryside in a sodden wet field, breaking an ankle in the process. Guns were going off in the distance. Aircraft continued to fly overhead. I went to sleep wrapped up in my chute. When it started getting light I began walking along a road but I did not get far. A car with three Luftwaffe officers in it drew up and I was captured, Eventually, I ended up at the Dulag Luft interrogation centre in Frankfurt. There the kommandant came to see me. He showed me a book and pointed out a photo of a group of people. One of them was my father! The book was about the Chiswick Convention, which my father and apparently the kommandant, had attended every year. The kommandant was genuinely pleased that my father was his friend.

I was to be put on a train under guard for PoW camp. While we waited at Frankfurt railway station, a tiny, wizened, old lady, who was almost certainly Jewish, approached me. She was so small her head reached only as a far as my waist. She said to me, 'Got bless you.' I patted her

Pilot Officer Malcolm Freegard of 115
Squadron, who enjoyed only a brief career as an
operational Wellington pilot at Marham, until he
was shot down on 21–22-July 1942. (Malcolm
Freegard)

gently on the cheek. There was uproar all around me. I was put on a train and finally taken away
to captivity. 'For you the war is over', the Germans would say. Some of them said it crowingly.
Others said it with envy in their voices. They must have thought, 'Ruddy war. Sodding Hitler.
We're all in the same boat.' To them, 'For you the war is over' meant 'you lucky bugger'. They
thought that for me the war was over. It wasn't. The next three years were spent in Stalag
Luft III, notorious as the setting of *The Great Escape*, following which, 50 allied officers were
executed on the orders of the Führer himself.[61] I was one of those responsible for getting rid
of soil from the tunnels. I was in the same hut as Tom Lees and two of the officers who were
among the 50 who were executed. It was terrible. There were even one or two Germans who
were as upset by the murders as we were. Now I look back on the whole experience like it
was a book you read about someone else. Sometimes, suddenly, I am there again. An expensive
spirit, a waste of shame …

On 26–27 July 1942, in full moonlight, the target was Hamburg. In all, 403 bombers were
dispatched. Twin-engined types like the Wellington and, to a lesser extent, the Hampden
still formed the backbone of Bomber Command. Air Marshal Harris was gradually
building up his numbers of four-engined types and the 181 Wellingtons and thirty-three
Hampdens were joined on the raid by seventy-seven Lancasters, seventy-three Halifaxes
and thirty-nine Stirlings. The plan was to make a long sea crossing wide of Heligoland, as
though bound for the Baltic via Jutland, before turning south-east below Rendsburg to

Sergeant Jim Burtt-Smith and his crew at 11 OTU Bassingbourn, before they were posted to 115 Squadron at RAF Marham in June 1942. From left to right: Pilot Officer Barney D'Ath-Weston RNZAF, navigator; Sergeant W. 'Frizzo' Frizzell RNZAF, rear gunner; Sergeant Lionel 'Len' Harcus, bomb aimer; Sergeant Jim Burtt-Smith, pilot; Sergeant Jack French, WOP/AG. On the night of 26–27 July 1942 Burtt-Smith and his crew of Wellington III BJ723 KO-B were hit on the way home from Hamburg and the crew ditched. Picked up by a German seaplane from Nordeney, they finished the war as POWs. (Burtt-Smith)

fly down the Elbe estuary to the target. At Marham at around 22.00 hours 115 Squadron put up fourteen Wellingtons and crews. Wing Commander Frank W. Dixon-Wright DFC led the briefing. Some members of his crew of Wellington BJ615 were second tour men. They too were well respected. Normally this crew would fly with Squadron Leader Cousens, OC 'A' Flight, but Cousens was on stand down. Twenty-year-old Sergeant Baden B. Feredey, an experienced pilot with fifteen operational flights, captained another 'A' Flight crew.[62] Not every crew flying to Hamburg was as well experienced as these. Sergeant Jim Howells RNZAF had completed five operations as a second pilot with other crews, and he was given captaincy of a new crew in 'A' Flight.[63] There had been recent criticism of the squadron for failing to obtain suitable photographs of the target, so the New Zealander decided that his crew would bring back a superb photograph. Sergeant Jim Burtt-Smith and crew had been with the squadron for just over a month. They had been allocated to 'A' Flight. Having overcome their operational teething problems, including writing-off a Wellington when returning from a raid, they were now settled in to completing a tour of thirty operations flying Wellington B3723 B-Bear. Hamburg would be their ninth operational flight.

Howells, the novice captain, had managed to coax his Wellington up to 14,000ft by the time he reached Hamburg. He was carrying a mixed load of high explosive and incendiary bombs. Despite the opposition from the defences he was still determined to obtain a good photograph of his bomb bursts. Reaching the aiming point his bomb aimer released the bombs. This action automatically opened the shutter on the fixed camera and released the flash bomb. All the pilot had to do was fly a straight and level course until the flash functioned. The photograph would then be taken. More experienced, perhaps more prudent pilots would have had greater concern for the immediate safety of their aircraft than bringing back a photograph for the planners at base to study. The flak at Hamburg was accurate and intense. In such situations following the release of the bombs it was usual to stick the nose down in a Shallow Dive, build up speed and corkscrew like Hell away from the target, but Howells was resolute. Following a straight and level course he flew blissfully on. It was a golden opportunity for the flak batteries and one they could not ignore.

Almost immediately the Wellington was ranged, and flak hit the port engine. It may have damaged the propeller as well as the engine. Intense vibration began to rack the airframe. Howells quickly feathered the propeller and switched off the engine. To his dismay the aircraft began to lose height. He managed to weave away from the target with no further damage to the bomber. Rapidly losing height he crossed the German coastline in an attempt to fly back over the comparative safety of the North Sea. It was all to no avail. The Wellington would not stay in the air. Below he could clearly see the tops of the breaking waves. He issued orders for ditching. The observer collected all the survival apparatus including the Verey pistol and cartridges and placed them in a bag. As the bomber hit the sea, a wall of water cascaded through the fuselage. It tore the bag from the observer's hand. When they clambered into the dinghy they found the marine signals stowed aboard had perished. They were adrift in the North Sea with no Verey pistol or any means of attracting the attention of a passing ship or aircraft. They were to drift like this for three days. On the first day a Beaufighter came close to them but did not see them. That night they drifted within earshot of a fierce naval battle presumably between German E-boats and a convoy. On the second day two Spitfires flew over without seeing them. On the third day a German seaplane from Nordeney rescued them and took them off to captivity.

B-Bear and Sergeant Burtt-Smith's crew arrived in the target area about the same time as Howells. Fortunately for them the defences were preoccupied with another aircraft and they quickly made their way to the aiming point, released their bombs and set course for the German coastline. Jim Burtt-Smith continues:

We were on course, homeward bound and flying between Bremerhaven and Wilhelmshaven, when New Zealander 'Frizzo' Frizzell piped up from the rear turret, 'What about a bloody drink? I'm gasping.' Sergeant Jack French, the WOP/AG was just about to hand me a cup of coffee when, BANG! We were hit in the port engine. The smoke and havoc was appalling. I feathered the port engine and managed to bring her head round. Fortunately, no one was hurt. The bomb aimer, Sergeant Lionel 'Len' Harcus, came out of the front turret to hang on to the rudder bar to try to help counter the violent swing to port. I took stock of the situation and tried to increase boost and revs on the starboard engine, but to no avail. By this time we were losing height. I got Barney D'Ath-Weston, my New Zealander navigator to give me a new course for home. Heavy ack-ack was still pounding away. We were heading for the open sea and try as I might, I could not gain any height. As we headed over the coast the searchlights pointed our way to the fighters. We were now down to 1,000ft. I told Jack to let out the 60-foot trailing aerial. We were having a terrible time trying to keep the aircraft straight and level. The drag of the dead engine was pulling us to port. I applied full rudder bias and Len hung onto the rudder for dear life. It was impossible to set a straight course. I gave instructions, 90 miles out over the North Sea, to take positions and prepare for ditching. It was as black as a November fog; no moon, no nothing.

As Jack and Len left the cockpit I jettisoned the fuel, shut off the remaining engine and turned towards England. I had no idea of height because when the port engine failed, so did the lights and instruments. Jack clamped the Morse key down so our people could get a fix on us.[64] I told him to give me a shout when the aerial touched the water so I knew I had 60 feet of height left. I had to keep playing with the stick to keep her airborne, letting the nose go down then pulling her up a bit, just like a bloody glider. I prayed for a moon, knowing full well that if I couldn't see to judge which way to land we would plunge straight in and down. (One had to land towards the oncoming waves; any other way would be disastrous.) [The bomb aimer and the wireless operator retreated to their ditching stations. Jim Burtt-Smith shut off the starboard engine and began to glide, repeatedly dropping the nose and then pulling up gently].

'Jack shouted out, 'Sixty feet!' and there we were, wallowing about like a sick cow. I shouted to the lads to hold tight, we were going in. 'Frizzo' turned his turret to starboard so that he could get out when we crashed. This was it! Prepare to meet thy doom. Suddenly, the moon shone and, thank God, I could see the sea. The moonbeams were like a gigantic flarepath. We actually flew down them. We were practically down in the drink when I saw we were flying the wrong way. I lugged B-Bear around, head-on to the waves. I hauled back on the stick and there was one almighty crash. We were down! It was 03.00 hours.

The water closed over my head and my Mae West brought me to the top. I got my head out of the escape hatch and there we were, wallowing in the sea. Then the moon went in! It was again as black as it could be. Len helped me out of the cockpit. Jack popped out of the astro hatch carrying the emergency kit, followed by D'Ath, who had stayed to destroy the Gee box and papers. 'Frizzo' scuttled along the fuselage and we all scrambled into the dinghy, which had popped out of the engine nacelle and was inflating in the water, still attached to the Wimpy, which was sinking fast. D'Ath slashed the rope and we pulled away as best we could before we got sucked under.

At 09.30 hours a German seaplane from Nordeney picked up the crew of B-Bear and they all finished the war as POWs.

Sergeant Baden B. Feredey and the crew of KO-K, meanwhile, reached Hamburg without incident. The outward journey was relatively calm and there were no interceptions from night fighters. The inward flight was near Borkum and Feredey flew down the side of the river to Hamburg. Sergeant Frank Skelley, the youngest member of the crew at nineteen, jokingly remarked that his skipper wouldn't be able to find the aiming point, as the only part of Hamburg he knew from his Merchant Navy days was the red light district. He had joined the

Merchant Navy as a boy; after war broke out he had transferred to the RAF to train as aircrew. Skelley acted as bomb aimer and he manned the front turret. KO-K carried a 4,000lb bomb. This huge bomb was not designed for delivery by a Wellington aircraft, and so modifications to the bomb bays were necessary. Most of the flotation bags had to be removed. These were the bags which gave the aircraft buoyancy in the event of a ditching. As the perimeter of the bomb canister protruded below the bomb doors these had to be removed also. When the bomb was dropped the open space of the bomb bays would cause considerable drag. Feredey continues:

I approached Hamburg at about 13,000ft. The place was well alight and the bombing was causing plenty of havoc on the ground and many searchlights illuminated the darkness. I bombed and flew around to take photographs. (There was some rivalry amongst the crews on the squadron to get good photos of our attacks. On a previous raid on Duisburg I had a photo of my bomb hitting the target and the photo was put on display on the Squadron for all to see). I flew over Hamburg taking pictures with the aid of other flash bombs exploding and then asked my navigator [Sergeant G. 'Harry' Lindley] for a course to fly home on. He told me that in two minutes we should be crossing the German coast. Suddenly all hell broke out. North of Bremen a blue master searchlight pinpointed me and 20-30 other white searchlights coned me. At the same time ack-ack poured through to the aircraft and the first shell burst a few inches away from my face. I could smell the cordite from the explosion, which blew the fuel lines to the instruments, causing them all to go to zero. The oil from the burst pipes came down on the compass, blanking it out and making it impossible to use. The only thing working was the altimeter; I was at 12,000ft. Both turrets were u/s and the guns were of no use. I was in this situation for three-quarters of an hour, diving and turning to try to get out of the glare of the searchlights. At the same time the guns were giving me hell from the ground. I went down to 8,000ft. Later the crew told me the aircraft was peppered with holes, through which you could map-read below. I gave instructions to Sergeant Glafkos Clerides [the wireless operator, who was in the astrodome] to come forward to destroy the paperwork and secret codings. At this point a piece of shrapnel caught him in the leg and caused him to collapse on the floor. His intercom plug came out of its socket. When he came to he was talking into a dead mike. He thought we had baled out so he decided to jump out through the rear escape hatch. Two searchlights followed him down to the ground. The Germans must have thought we were going to follow him or we were all dead as all the lights went out and the ack-ack guns were silent.[65]

When I got out of the searchlights I found I was heading back to Hamburg so I decided to go home the same way I had entered Germany. The wheels and flaps had come down causing drag. I climbed to 14,000ft and re-crossed the coast over Borkum where again the Germans shot at me. Then all was quiet. I checked the fuel gauge and found I had lost 200 gallons in 20 minutes. The rear gunner [Sergeant Kelvin Hewer Shoesmith, a 21-year-old Australian] had to tell me if and when I was turning, as I had no instruments to fly on. (While we had been in the dilemma of ack-ack and searchlights the rear gunner had been shot in his side. However badly I never knew but subsequently it hastened his death). I instructed Skelley to radio our troubles to base. (As my wireless operator had baled out, it meant that the front gunner was now sending out radio messages to warn the Squadron what was happening to us). All the time I was losing height and I went down to 1,500ft. Lindley put the nacelle tanks on so I estimated I had about one hour's fuel left. I was down to 500ft by this time. Then the starboard engine started to cough and splutter. I sent out a Mayday on the radio. This was becoming the final phase in the drama. I told the crew to prepare for ditching. First the starboard engine and then the port engine stopped. I suddenly realized that the escape hatch over my head was still closed but I managed to get it open. As all this was going on I had turned away from the moonlight and was heading into total blackness for a ditching. My speed was about 140 mph. I had to land tail first to help slow the speed down.

Finally we went into the sea. I wasn't strapped in so my head went through the windscreen. I may have been temporarily knocked out but the cold water soon brought my senses back. I was up to my waist in water with water pouring in through the escape hatch over my head. I wrenched my helmet off to release me to get out; I also lost one flying boot as I got out of the aircraft, which was already going under with the tail in the air. After getting onto the port wing I was chest deep in water. By this time the front gunner and navigator had made their escape via the astrodome. Sergeant Kelvin Shoesmith RAAF jumped out of the rear turret but he got entangled with the trailing aerial and he shouted that the rapidly sinking bomber was dragging him under. [Frank Skelley and Harry Lindley swam over and released him. They all worked hard on the dinghy to inflate it but it was riddled with shrapnel holes. Their task was impossible]. The four of us managed to get hold of a loose wooden box, which one stood on to look out of the astrodome, that had floated out of the open hatch just before the aircraft sank. We each grabbed a corner with one hand and the other hand held on to the adjacent crewmember. We drifted with the waves breaking over us continually. All we had to keep us afloat were our Mae Wests. We were able to talk to each other and we tried to estimate how far from land we were. Shoesmith told us he had been wounded in his side but we were unable to ascertain his injuries. His Mae West was deflating so Harry Lindley had to blow it up with his mouth to keep him afloat. [The shrapnel, which had pierced his side, had also penetrated his Mae West]. At times we were up to our lips in water, this was causing us to swallow some of the salt water. The harrowing part of this tale was when Lindley began to pray and asked God to save us. When I tried to reassure him that we would be saved, he rubbed his hand down the back of my head and said that he was grateful for cheering him up. It seemed pretty hopeless at the time, as the water was up to our mouths as we floated around.

After a few hours Shoesmith, who was directly opposite me, suddenly went quiet. He opened his eyes and they seemed to turn around. Some white foam came from his nose and mouth. At this point Skelley was unconscious. I tried to lift him on to the box to keep his head out of the water but minutes later he too died very quietly, again with white foam coming from his nose and mouth. He hadn't been injured but later I realized that he was pretty near to death. When the front and rear gunners died we let them go but they continued to drift near us. After six hours in the sea only two of us were alive. Then in the distance I saw a German seaplane flying towards us. I tried to attract the attention of the crew and Lindley started blowing his whistle. I kept telling him they couldn't hear him but his mind had gone blank. They circled around and the chap in the gun turret turned his gun towards us. I honestly thought he was going to shoot us. However he lifted his hand and saluted. Thank God, what a relief that we weren't going to die in this way. The seaplane landed and taxied towards us with its two engines ticking over but they were too fast to grab us as they passed. They returned on just one engine with crew on the floats holding boat hooks. I managed to grab hold but they had to hook Lindley by his jacket to stop him going past. They lifted me on to the float and tied a rope around my waist to lift me into the aircraft where I was laid on the floor and a blanket placed over me. Lindley was then brought in. Although they must have seen that the two gunners were dead the Germans did not stop to pick them up and they allowed them to continue floating in the sea. Shivering with cold I motioned to one of the crew for a drink but instead of a hot drink or a brandy they gave me soda water! I fell asleep as we took off for Nordeney where we landed and were lifted out of the water onto the beach. I was helped to my feet and out of the plane into the daylight where an ambulance waited to take us to hospital. The German crew came with us. At the hospital I thanked the crew for picking us up and I asked the pilot what time he had started searching for us. He told me it was 03.40 hours; the exact time I crashed in the sea. Lindley remembered nothing of the rescue or his journey to hospital and it was six pm that evening when he recovered sufficiently to be taken into custody.[66]

In all, 115 Squadron lost four Wellingtons on the night of 26–27 July. At 02.35 hours Hauptmann Helmut 'Bubi' ('Boy') Lent of II./NJG1 was patrolling over the North Sea north-west of Vlieland in a Bf 110 night fighter, when he brought down a Halifax.[67] His victim crashed in the North Sea, and four minutes later a dark shape loomed into his line of sight. Quickly closing the gap between himself and the other aircraft he perceived the unmistakable bulky outline to be a Wellington bomber. Not wishing to overshoot and lose the enemy aircraft in the darkness, Lent eased back on his throttles. Wing Commander Dixon-Wright and his crew of Wellington BJ615 were doomed. Their aircraft crashed into the sea north-west of Vlieland, near the crash position of Lent's Halifax victim at 02.39. The only body recovered from the water was that of twenty-five-year-old WOP/AG Pilot Officer J. Whittaker DFM.[68]

Night fighters were active on 26–27 July because of the clear moonlight conditions along most of the route, and over the target flak was accurate. 115 Squadron's four missing Wellingtons were among twenty-nine bombers shot down[69], eight of them by night fighters of II/NJG1 at Leeuwarden. Hamburg suffered its most severe air raid to date and widespread damage was caused, mostly in the housing and semi-commercial districts. The Fire Department was overwhelmed and forced to seek outside assistance for the first time. 337 people lost their lives, 1,027 were injured and 14,000 people were made homeless. Damage amounted to the equivalent of £25,000,000.[70]

In August 115 Squadron's Wellingtons flew seventy-four sorties without loss until the 20th–21st, when ten Wimpys at Marham were among fifty-seven aircraft dispatched on *Gardening* operations from Brest to Danzig. Three Stirlings and three Wellingtons were lost, including X3989/V flown by Flight Sergeant Newman. Pilot Officer Grimston was forced to crash-land BJ660/H at Exeter. On the night of 27–28 August, when just over 300 aircraft were dispatched to Kassel, thirty-one aircraft including twenty-one Wellingtons failed to return. One of the Wimpys that were lost was BJ710/L flown by Flying Officer Skelton. The WOP/AG, Flight Sergeant Middleton, was the only one to escape from the doomed Wellington. The following night, 28–29 August, 159 aircraft including ten Wellingtons of 115 Squadron were dispatched to Nuremberg. Bomber Command suffered the loss of twenty-three aircraft including fourteen Wellingtons, though none of the losses were from Marham. A smaller force of 113 bombers visited Saarbrücken and the force was made up largely of

Hauptman Helmut 'Bubi' ('Boy') Lent, a Ritterkreuzträger and Kommandeur of II./NJG2 in early June 1942, when his score stood at thirty-four night and eight day victories. Lent had become a national hero after the air battle of 18 December 1939; when flying a Bf 110C-1 *Zerstörer* in 3./ZG76 he had claimed three Wellingtons IA destroyed. (Anneliese Autenrieth)

Wellingtons, with five of them from 115 Squadron. Seven aircraft were lost, but although one of 115 Squadron's Wellingtons was forced to land at Manston and two others aborted with malfunctions, none of 115's aircraft were lost.

Throughout the first half of September 115 Squadron flew on fourteen nights, up to the 21st–22nd, when targets in Germany and *Gardening* operations were the main objectives. On 1–2 September, when 231 aircraft were dispatched to Saarbrücken again, four aircraft failed to return, including Wellington BJ895/C flown by Pilot Officer Shires. On 4–5 September, when 251 aircraft visited Bremen, ninety-eight Wellingtons comprised the major part of the force, which was led by new pathfinding techniques. Seven Wimpys failed to return, including BJ771/L flown by Sergeant Keith and BJ663/N flown by Pilot Officer Davies. In addition the force lost five other aircraft, three of them Lancasters. With 115 Squadron's days at Marham numbered (signals received on 19 and 21 September outlined plans for the station to transfer to 2 Group), four more Wellingtons were lost on five more raids during the month. The first of these was on the night of 6–7 September when BJ724/P, flown by Flight Sergeant Lanceley, was one of five Wellingtons lost on the raid on Duisburg. Three other aircraft out of the 207 dispatched also failed to return. A week later, on the night of 14–15 September, BJ693/J flown by Sergeant Boaden was one of only two Wellingtons

Sir Alan Burns, Governor-General Designate of the Gold Coast, visiting 218 (Gold Coast) Squadron in 1942. (RAF Marham)

lost from the force of 202 aircraft (of five different types) that were dispatched to bomb Wilhelmshaven. Three nights later, on 18–19 September, when 115 aircraft were dispatched on *Gardening* operations between Lorient and Danzig, X3718/Q flown by Pilot Officer Owen failed to return. Another 115 Squadron Wellington was lost on mine-laying operations on the night of 21–22 September, when BJ962/D flown by Sergeant Evans was one of three Wellingtons that went missing.

The final Wellington lost flying from Marham occurred on 28 September when six Wellingtons attacked Lingen on the Dortmund-Ems Canal. A Bomber Command directive was issued, whereby crews stood down from night flying would be employed on daylight intruder sorties to keep the German sirens wailing and disrupt industry by driving the workers into air-raid shelters. The RAF crews' only protection was cloud cover and it was essential that there was sufficient cloud to hide in. A Wellington was no match for a German fighter and all aircraft captains had strict orders to return to base if the cloud cover broke up. On Monday 28 September three Wellingtons of 115 Squadron were detailed for such a 'cloud cover' daylight bombing attack on Lingen, and as the aircraft made their way east the cover thinned out rapidly to a scattering of isolated clouds. Sergeant Crimmin in BJ695 decided to turn back. Squadron Leader Sandes in BK272 made a similar decision. Squadron Leader

Left to right: Bill Berry, Ken Bryant, Pat Wallace and Jack Goad at Marham in August or September 1942. (Jack Goad)

Robert James Sealer Parsons in Z1663 decided to press home the attack but, 8km south-west of Urk over the Zuider Zee, he was attacked by Unteroffizier Kurt Knespel of 10./JG1 in a Fw 190. As his cannon shells tore through the fuselage Flight Sergeant John Austin Parker, the Canadian WOP/AG, was hit and died instantly. Flames from the ruptured wing gasoline tanks spread rapidly, fanned by the slipstream. Parsons shouted over the intercom that he would try to ditch the bomber. The front gunner, Sergeant Gilmour, entered the cockpit from his turret and saw Flight Sergeant William Leonard Clough, the thirty-one-year-old observer, with the cabin fire extinguisher in his hand, vainly trying to subdue the raging furnace. The aircraft hit the sea and only the Canadian gunners, Sergeants Gilmour and Stansell, emerged.

On 23 September 115 Squadron began the move to Mildenhall to end a three-year occupation at Marham, which awaited the imminent arrival of two Mosquito squadrons.

3

LOW LEVELLERS AND THE SHALLOW RAIDERS

In September 1942 Marham was transferred to 2 Group, Bomber Command, and on the 13th 105 and 139 Squadrons received orders to vacate Horsham St Faith by 28 September, as the Americans were due to arrive to base medium bombers there. The Mosquito Conversion Unit also moved to Marham with the two first-line squadrons. 105 Squadron were equipped with Mosquito Mk.IV bombers and 139 were then converting to this type from Blenheim V (Bisleys), while the Mosquito CU flew a mixture of Blenheims and Mosquitoes. (On 18 October the CU was renamed the Mosquito Training Unit.) On 19 September 105 Squadron attempted the first daylight Mosquito raid on Berlin. Amid the changeover, on 19 September, six crews in 105 Squadron attempted the first daylight Mosquito raid on Berlin. Two pilots – Sergeant Norman Booth[71] and Flight Sergeant K.L. Monaghan – were both forced to return early. Flight Lieutenant Roy Ralston and Flying Officer Sydney Clayton bombed Hamburg after finding Berlin covered by cloud. George Parry and 'Robbie' Robson were intercepted on two occasions by Fw 190s but managed to evade them. Parry jettisoned his bombs near Hamburg and turned for home, heading back across the north coast of Germany and into Holland. At 1,000ft just off the Dutch coast, two 109s attacked but although one of them scored hits, Parry dived down to sea level and soon outran them. Squadron Leader Norman Henry Edward Messervy DFC, an Australian from Point Cook, and his navigator, Pilot Officer Frank Holland, in *M-Mother* were shot down by a Fw 190, piloted by Schwarmführer Oberfeldwebel Anton-Rudolf 'Toni' Piffer of 2nd Staffel/JG1.[72] The Mosquito crashed 30km north-north-west of Osnabrück with the loss of both crew. Messervy was a second tour man, having flown on sixty-eight operations on Blenheims and PR Spitfires on 3 PRU in 1941. Only Warrant Officer Charles R.K. Bools MiD and Sergeant George Jackson succeeded in bombing the 'Big City'.

A few days later the expert low-level raiders in 105 Squadron were told to prepare for a long overwater operation, which would be flown at heights of just 50–100ft. George Parry, now a squadron leader, would lead, with 'Robbie' Robson as his navigator. The three other crews were Pilot Officer Pete W.T. Rowland and Pilot Officer Richard 'Dick' Reilly, Parry's No.2; Flying Officer Alec Bristow and Pilot Officer Bernard Marshall; and Flight Sergeant Gordon K. Carter

Flight Lieutenant Victor 'Robbie' Robson DFC★ and Squadron Leader D.A.G. 'George' Parry DSO DFC★ of 105 Squadron in front of their Mosquito B.IV *G-George*. This image was taken soon after the Oslo raid on 25 September 1942. (George Parry)

and Sergeant William S. Young. Their target was the Gestapo HQ in Oslo. The Norwegian Government in exile in London had been made aware by reports from the Norwegian Underground that morale in their Nazi-subjugated homeland was at a low ebb. They also learned that a rally of Hirdsmen (Norwegian Fascists) and Quislings would take place in the Norwegian capital between 25–27 September, and it therefore seemed an ideal opportunity for the Mosquitoes to help restore national pride. As well as disrupting the parade, they were to bomb the Gestapo HQ between the Town Hall and the Royal Palace, which stands on a hill.

On 25 September the four Mosquitoes, their bomb bays empty, taxied out at Marham and took off for Leuchars in Scotland, where the operation came under the control of Wing Commander Hughie Edwards VC DFC. The raid involved a round-trip of 1,100 miles with an air time of 4 hours 45 minutes, the longest Mosquito mission thus far, the crews using dead reckoning along the entire route. The Mosquitoes were refuelled and bombed-up with four 11-second delayed-action 500lb bombs, and they set off at low-level to Norway, 50ft all the way. They went through the Skaggerak, made landfall at the southern end of Oslo Fjord and flew up the eastern side. As they flew up to a police radio station perched on a hill, Parry hit the flexible 45ft-high radio antenna, although it did no damage to his Mosquito. Crews had been briefed that there would be 10/10ths cloud at 2,000ft over Oslo, but it was a lovely day with blue sky. They had also been told that there were no fighters to worry about, but the Germans had brought a squadron of Fw 190s south from Stavanger for a fly-past during the parade. They had landed at Fornebu and had only been on the ground a short time when the Mosquitoes swooped out of brilliant autumn sunshine over the centre of Oslo at 3 p.m. A lookout at the southern end of Oslo Fjord reported the bombers and two Focke Wulfs got into the action although, fortunately, the rest did not get off in time. The pilot of the leading fighter was twenty-two-year-old Unteroffizier Rudolf 'Rudi' Fenten, who had temporarily left his unit to train on and pick up the new Fw 190 at Sola/Stavanger. Flying the other Fw 190 was twenty-four-year-old Feldwebel Erich Klein of 3./JG5 based at Herdla near Bergen. Both pilots were very experienced. Fenten had been in the Luftwaffe since 1940, while Klein had joined it in 1937. At first Fenten thought that the twin-engined aircraft flying ahead of him in two pairs were part of the fly-past. Then he realized they were too low and he chased after Carter's Mosquito. Fenten set his port engine on fire and he followed until the Mosquito exploded in front of him and crashed into Lake Engervannet near Sandvika.

Parry, meanwhile, was concentrating on 'buzzing' the parade and taking a line south-west over the centre of Oslo for the bomb run. Pinpointing the Gestapo headquarters was simple enough. Parry was flying at 280–300mph when he dropped his bombs. Erich Klein, meanwhile, went after Pete Rowland and Dick Reilly. The two aircraft chased around the fir trees north of Oslo for many minutes, until Klein struck a tree with his wing and he was forced to return to Fornebu.[73] Some of the Mosquitoes' bombs did not explode but everyone thought that it was a remarkably successful raid, especially since it was the first long-distance raid the Mosquitoes had carried out. All three crews were debriefed and they flew back to Norfolk the next morning to rejoin the squadron at Marham. The post-mortem and camera pictures taken on the raid revealed that at least four bombs had entered the roof of the Gestapo HQ; one had remained inside and failed to detonate and the other three had crashed through the opposite wall before exploding.

Squadron Leader D.A.G. 'George' Parry DFC and Flying Officer Victor Robson of 105 Squadron flew B.Mk.IV Series II DK296 on the Oslo Gestapo raid of 25 September 1942. *G-George* passed to Squadron Leader Bill Blessing DSO DFC RAAF, who crash-landed DK296 at Marham and broke its back. The aircraft was repaired and on 24 August 1943 was placed into store with 10 MU at Hullavington. In September 1943 it was issued to 305 Ferry Training Unit at Errol, Scotland, where it was given Russian markings and trained Russian crews who were convening to Albemarles. On 20 April 1944 DK296 was ferried to the Soviet Union by a Russian crew, being officially accepted there on 31 August 1944, and subsequently went on to serve with the Red Air Force. (Via Graham M. Simons)

Mosquito B.IV DZ464 C for Charlie of 139 Squadron, the only one of four to escape unharmed after a chase by two Fw 190s following an attack on Malines on 11 April 1943. This aircraft later FTR on 21 May 1943 during an operation to the locomotive sheds at Orleans, its 17th trip. Squadron Leader V. R. G. Harcourt DFC RCAF and Warrant Officer J. Friendly DFM, a South African, were killed in action. (RAF Marham)

Mosquito B.Mk.IV DK338 of 105 Squadron. On 1 May 1943 DK338 was launching for an operation to Eindhoven, when an engine failed just after take-off and the aircraft crashed near Marham, killing Flying Officer Onslow W. Thompson DFM RNZAF and Flying Officer Wallace J. Horne DFC. (Via Shuttleworth Collection)

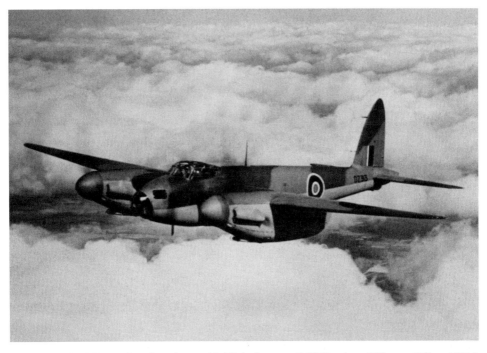

Mosquito B.IV DZ313 of 105 Squadron, with Flight Sergeant L.W. Deeth and Warrant Officer F.E.M. Hicks on-board, failed to return from the raid on Hanover on 20 October 1942. (Via Shuttleworth Collection)

October ushered in new tactics as two distinct types of low-level attack eventually came to be developed by 105 and 139 Squadrons. These were the low-level proper and the 'Shallow Dive', and they were frequently used together on the same target, starting at Liège on 2 October. Six to eight low-level raiders went in at the lowest level, carrying bombs that exploded eleven seconds after impact, and they would be followed by the second formation of 'Shallow Divers' who climbed up to about 2,000ft just before the target was reached. When over the target they peeled off and dived straight down on the target and released their bombs fitted with instantaneous fuses at about 1,500ft. Only a very restricted number of Mosquitoes could cross the target at Low Level before the leaders' bombs exploded but a 'Shallow Dive' formation enabled a target to be hit by a far larger number of Mosquitoes. October was a mix of low-level shallow-dive raids at dusk on targets in Belgium and Holland and high-level attacks on German cities. It was also a month when several crews were lost to the 'Butcher Birds' of JG1 and JG 26. On 9 October Wing Commander Edwards and 'Tubby' Cairns, and another Mosquito crewed by Warrant Officer Charles R.K. Bools MiD and Sergeant George Jackson, set out to bomb Duisburg. Feldwebel Fritz Timm of 12./JG1 shot down Bools and Jackson over Belgium.[74]

At dusk on Sunday 11 October three pairs of Mosquitoes were dispatched to bomb Hanover but two of the Mosquitoes were intercepted by Fw 190As of II./JG26 while en route over Holland. Unteroffizier Günter Kirchner of the 5th Staffel took off from Katwijk and intercepted Pilot Officer Jim Lang and Flying Officer Robin P. 'Tommy' Thomas 2km from Utrecht and shot them down. Unteroffizier Kolschek of the 4th Staffel was credited with shooting down Squadron Leader James G.L. 'Jimmy' Knowles DFC and Flight Sergeant Charles Gartside. Lang and Thomas survived to be taken prisoner but no trace was ever found of Knowles and Gartside.

Night Intruders were flown against targets on the continent. On 30 October Sergeant Reginald Levy, Sergeant Les Hogan, Flying Officer William 'Bill' Blessing RAAF and Sergeant J. Lawson in 105 Squadron attacked the Luftwaffe night fighter aerodrome at Leeuwarden in Holland. They attacked successfully but Levy was hit by flak from the ground defences coming across the boundary of the airfield. The port engine was set on fire and the instrument panel and windscreen disappeared with the nose of the aircraft. Levy and his observer, Les Hogan, who was wounded in the arm, got back to Marham but the Mosquito was completely demolished on landing. After three weeks in Ely Hospital both men were back at Marham and operating again.

In November 139 Squadron ceased all operational work while the squadron was being fully equipped with Mosquitoes; the whole month and the first few days of December were spent in bombing practice and formation flying. On 7 November Squadron Leader Roy Ralston led six Mosquitoes at wave top height across the Bay of Biscay and the Gironde estuary to attack two large German blockade-running motor vessels loaded with rubber. The operation had been mounted at short notice and preparation had been minimal, but the ships' crews were taken completely by surprise as the 500lb bombs fell full on them. Things only got hectic afterwards, but no one stayed around for long. The Mosquito flown by Flight Lieutenant Alec Bristow and Pilot Officer Bernard Marshall was shot down by flak and they

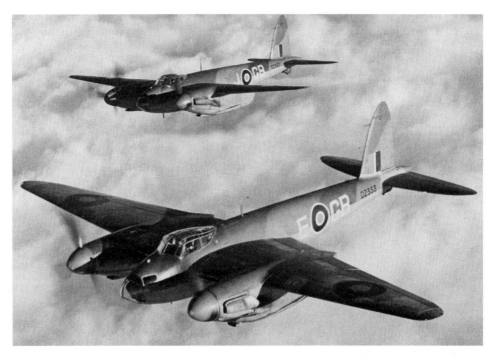

Mosquito B.IV DZ353/E and DZ367/J of 105 Squadron in formation from Marham. DZ353 later served with 139 and 627 Squadrons in 8 Group (PFF), but failed to return from a raid on the marshalling yards at Rennes on 8 June 1944. Flight Lieutenant Harry 'Bill' Steere DFM and Flying Officer K.W.'Windy' Gale DFC RAAF were killed. Squadron Leader D.F.W. Darling DFC and Flying Officer W. Wright were also killed in action when flying DZ367/J FTR over Berlin on 30 January 1943. (RAF Marham)

survived to be taken prisoner. Ralston was to become one of the most accomplished and skillful low-level bomber pilots of the war. A raid on 9 December demonstrates his quick thinking and rapid response to a given situation. He spotted a German troop train about to enter a tunnel on the Paris to Soissons railway line and immediately decided on a plan of action. Unlike the more conventional thinking of the 'average' pilot he did not attack the train itself but decided to create more havoc with an unconventional attack. He dropped down to tree top height behind the train and dropped a bomb into the mouth of the tunnel. He then quickly orbited the tunnel and bombed it at the other end before it emerged, thus effectively entombing the train, its crew and cargo in the tunnel.[75]

Meanwhile, plans were well advanced for mounting 2 Group's biggest operation of the war, an attack on the Philips works in Eindhoven, Holland, from Low Level. Although some industrial processes had been dispersed to other sites, Eindhoven was still the main centre, especially for research into electronic counter-measures and radar. Preparations for Operation Oyster, the most ambitious daylight raid conceived by 2 Group, had been given the green light on 9 November. Originally plans called for the Strijp Group main works to be bombed by twenty-four Venturas, twelve Mitchells and twelve Mosquitoes, while twelve Venturas and thirty-six Bostons would at the same time attack the Emmasingel

105 Squadron line up at Marham on 11 December 1942. DZ360/A failed to return from Termonde just eleven days later and Flight Sergeant Joseph Edward Cloutier RCAF and Sergeant Albert Cecil Foxley, who were on their first 105 Squadron operation, were killed when they were shot down by intense light flak as they crossed the coast near Dunkirk. DZ353/E was lost on 9 June 1944. DZ367/J was shot down on the raid to Berlin on 30 January 1943. DK336/P lost its starboard engine returning from a raid on Copenhagen on 27 January 1943, then struck a balloon cable and a tree and crashed at Yaxham, Norfolk, killing Sergeant Richard Clare and Flying Officer Edward Doyle of 139 Squadron. DZ378/K was withdrawn from service after only two sorties following damage sustained on 20 December 1942. DZ379/H was shot down by a night fighter on 17 August 1943 while flying with 139 Squadron on a diversionary sortie to Berlin for the Peenemünde raid. Flying Officer A.S. Cook (an American pilot from Wichita Falls, Texas) and his navigator, Sergeant D.A.H. Dixon, were killed.

Lamp and valve works half a mile to the east. The slower Venturas would lead the way at Low Level with HE and 30lb incendiaries before surprise was lost. On 17 November a full-scale practice was held on a route similar to the one to be used, with the St Neots power station as the 'target'. Many basic lessons were learned, while other problems associated with a mixed force, such as the differences in bombing techniques and cruising speeds, were exposed. Rain was falling in East Anglia on the morning of Sunday 6 December 1942 when ninety-three light bombers prepared to take-off to attack the Philips works. At Marham Wing Commander Hughie Edwards VC DFC carried out the briefings. Eight Mosquitoes of 105 Squadron and two of 139 Squadron, led by Edwards, rendezvoused with the other bombers at a point over the North Sea. Then they trailed the Bostons and Venturas to the target despite the Mosquitoes' cruising speed of 270mph, about 100mph faster. The Mosquitoes were to make a shallow diving attack on the Strijp works, while the other bombers bombed from Low Level. Unfortunately, the timings went wrong and instead of being 60 miles behind, the Mosquitoes caught up with the other bombers. As the

Mosquitoes flew in over the Scheldt at 50ft they began to 'wobble' flying along at 160mph, trying to maintain the speed of the leading bombers. They flew through a flock of ducks and one went through George Parry's windscreen, split his leather flying-helmet and cut his head. He did not feel a thing but his head went ice cold. Robbie Robson was cut by flying glass and, thinking his pilot was 'out', he grabbed the stick. Parry recovered and headed inland. Fw 190 fighters came up and Parry and Flight Lieutenant Bill Blessing, his No.2, broke away to decoy them away from the Venturas coming in over the coast behind. Parry went underneath a Fw 190 whose pilot did not see him, and he and Blessing deliberately drew the 190s on themselves, then let them go chasing as they opened the throttles to full speed. The Mosquito IV was not quite as fast as the 190 at 20,000ft, but at deck level it was about 5mph faster. Parry was later able to rejoin the formation. Blessing, who turned into the fighter attacks and circled for ten minutes at 50ft, decided to abandon the flight and made for home chased by the Fw 190, which only abandoned the pursuit about 8 miles east of Vlissingen. Pilot Officers Jimmy Bruce DFM and Mike Carreck had an equally close encounter with another Fw 190 until the enemy fighter ran out of ammunition, and they also headed back to Marham after first jettisoning their bombs.

The Mosquito flown by Pilot Officer John Earl O'Grady, who was on his first trip, was hit by flak and streamed smoke as they left the target area. O'Grady and his navigator Sergeant George Lewis died when their aircraft hit the sea. Nine Venturas and four Bostons also failed to return. The Philips works was devastated, essential supplies destroyed and the rail network disrupted.[76]

After Eindhoven the Mosquitoes' targets were small-in-number raids on railway lines and yards in France, Belgium and Germany. On 20 December eleven Mosquitoes of 105 and 139 Squadrons, led by Squadron Leader Reggie Reynolds with Ted Sismore, attacked railway targets in the Oldenburg-Bremen area in north-west Germany. One Mosquito came down so low that the crew read the name *Fritz* on a river tug. The bombers swept over men working on a new barracks and one pilot reported later that 'They were near the end of the work and we finished it off for them'. Near Delmenhorst Reynolds planed off to attack a gasholder and his four 500lb GP bombs set the gasometer on fire. The Mosquito took a 40mm cannon shell in the port engine, which made the aircraft lurch drunkenly but Reynolds managed to get the Mosquito on an even keel again. However, the anti-freeze mixture was pouring from the radiator and the cockpit filled with cordite fumes. His No.2, Warrant Officer Arthur Raymond Noesda, moved in closer to Reynolds. Together the pilot from Western Australia and his CO re-crossed the German coast over Wilhelmshaven Bay. Coastal batteries opened up on them and the guns of a warship joined in. Fountains of water rose on each side of the aircraft, which were down on the deck, but Reynolds got his crippled Mosquito back to Marham where he landed wheels up. Squadron Leader Jack Houlston DFC AFC and his observer, Warrant Officer James Lloyd Armitage DFC, failed to return. They were buried in the Reichswald Forest war cemetery. Luck finally ran out for Noseda, who had flown Blenheims on suicidal anti-shipping strikes from Malta, and his observer, Sergeant John Watson Urquhart, on 3 January when they were hit and killed by anti-aircraft fire in the attack on engine sheds at Rouen.

In January 1943 attacks were maintained on rail targets on the continent. Of course, with no armament the Mosquitoes relied on speed and hedgehopping tactics. Sergeant Reginald Levy recalls that:

> … at that time the Focke Wulf 190 was appearing and they could get in one attack on us if they saw us first. The main casualties came from flying into the ground or sea, bird strikes and even from our own bombs. These were fitted with an 11-seconds delay but sometimes this didn't work or else you were unlucky enough to get the blast from someone else's bomb. I watched with apprehension, a bomb, from the machine in front of me, bounce high over my wing whilst attacking the marshalling yards at Terquier, France on 3 January. Just before that, on New Year's Eve 1942, I had been on another marshalling yard attack to Mouceau-sur-Chambres in Belgium. It was dusk and we ran into a snow storm and I flew between two huge slag heaps, only seeing them as they flashed past high above each wing. We then hit a bird, which smashed through the windscreen, covering my observer, Les Hogan and myself with feathers and blood. It was bitterly cold all the way back and although we bathed, scrubbed again the bird smell hung around and we were not the most popular partners at the New Year's dance.[77]

In January a fortnight's work went into low-level formation training, in preparation for a raid on the Burmeister and Wain U-boat diesel engine works in Copenhagen in occupied Denmark. Wing Commander Hughie Edwards VC DSO DFC and Flying Officer 'Tubby' Cairns DFC would lead nine Mosquitoes of 105 and 139 Squadrons in a round trip of more than 1,200 miles to the target. Edwards was to recall that on the 26th the weather 'gave every promise of being satisfactory.' After much speculation about the target the crews assembled in the briefing room at 09.30 hours to see the tracking strings stretching right across the North Sea and Denmark to Copenhagen. Edwards thought that everyone 'felt that here at last was a man-sized war-winning job'. Unfortunately, the briefing was almost over when the trip had to be cancelled because of a sudden change in conditions over the target. They were promised that the weather conditions were almost certain to be perfect on the 27th, which they were, and in the early afternoon Edwards led nine Mosquitoes to Denmark. The Mosquitoes' war paint of dull silvery grey and green blended well with the cold, grey-green wave-tops and Danish countryside, as they flew at Low Level in close formation to avoid attacks from enemy fighters. If it had been summer visibility would have been impaired by dust and squashed insects splattering their windscreens but Edwards' only concern was that they were too far south and fuel consumption was a vital consideration. When the coast was eventually sighted the lighthouse on Braavardo Point showed up clearly. Edwards said that 'this made it evident that we were 20 miles north of track. Then no sooner were we across the coast than we went straight over the top of Bröndurn aerodrome. This was a bad start, for we had hoped to get well across Denmark before the alarm went up. Near the coast light flak from ships opened up on the formation. Flight Lieutenant John 'Flash' Gordon and Flying Officer Ralph Gamble Hayes thought their aircraft had been hit when the trailing edge of the starboard wing became enveloped in puffs of blue smoke. Thinking he had been hit by flak Gordon carried out evasive action but he had caught the port wing in telegraph wires and damaged the aileron.

1. Mosquito B.IV DZ476 XD- *S for Scottie* (note the dog and the black spinners) of 139 Squadron normally flown by Flying Officer G.S.W. Rennie RCAF and Pilot Officer W. Embry RCAF. (DH)

2. Mosquito B.IVs of 139 Squadron in formation in February 1943. (RAF Museum)

3. 139 Squadron at Marham with Wing Commander Peter Shand DSO DFC in the white jacket (right). Shand and his navigator were shot down and killed on the night of 20/21 April 1943.

4. Wing Commander Hughie Idwal Edwards VC DFC.

5. Valiant B(K)I XD870 of 214 Squadron taking-off from Khormaksar, Aden, for Marham in 1964. (Ray Deacon)

6. Valiant B(K)I XD812 of 214 Squadron taking-off at Khormaksar, Aden, for Marham in 1964. (Ray Deacon)

7. Lightning F.3 XP756/E of 29 Squadron moves in to refuel from Victor K.1 XA938 of 214 Squadron. (Dick Bell)

8. A Victor K.IA refuels a Lightning from the centreline tank during a tanking exercise in the summer of 1972. (Dick Bell)

9. On 25 August 1971 74 'Tiger' Squadron disbanded at Tengah and 56 Squadron in Cyprus acquired all of the remaining F.6 Lightnings. Starting on 2 September the F.6s were flown over the 6,000-mile route to Akrotiri, a thirteen-hour trip, staging through Gan and Muharraq and completing seven air-to-air refuellings with Victor tankers of 55 Squadron. (Mike Rigg)

10. Victor K.IA XH650 of 55 Squadron refuelling Lightning F.3 XF700/K of 29 Squadron. XF700 was lost after a take-off accident at RAF Wattisham on 7 August 1972. The pilot ejected safely. (BAE SYSTEMS)

11. Three Victor tankers, with two of them air refuelling. (Dick Bell)

12. Tornado GR.I ZA491/N *Nikki* (formerly *Nora Batty*).

13. Starboard side of Tornado GR.I ZA491/N *Snoopy Airways* riding a LGB.

14. Tornado GR.I ZD890/O *Hello Kuwait G'bye Iraq*.

15. Tornado GR.I ZA456/M *Hello Kuwait G'bye Iraq*.

16. Tornado GR.I ZD790/D *Debbie*.

17. Starboard side of Tornado GR.I ZD790/D *Snoopy Airways* riding a JP233.

18. Tornado GR.I ZA399/G 'G–Gran'/*Hello Kuwait G'bye Iraq*.

19. Tornado GR.I ZD892/H *Helen*.

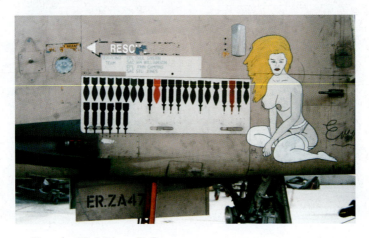

20. Tornado GR.I ZA471/E *Emma*.

21. Victor K.Mk.2 with brake chute trailing, taxiing in at Marham in October 1993. (Author)

22. Canberra T.4 'AV' of 39 (I PRU) Squadron at Marham in June 1997. (Author)

23 – 28 *This page:* Victor K.Mk.2s XH671 *Sweet Sue* (formerly *Slinky Sue*) of 55 Squadron, XL164 *Saucy Sal*, XM715 *Teasin Tina*, XM717 *Lucky Lou*, *Lusty Lindy* and XH672 *Maid Marian* of 55 Squadron. (Author)

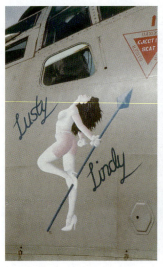

29. Tornado protoype aircraft carrying two underwing 330-gallon drop tanks and two *Sky Shadow* dummies. (BAe)

30. Tornado GR.I 'FB' of 617 Squadron in Desert Pink scheme for Operation *Jural*. (RAF Marham)

31. The forlorn remains of Victor K.Mk.2 XM717 *Lucky Lou* after the Victors were cut up for scrap. (Author)

32. Line up of Luftwaffe Tornadoes at Marham in July 1996. Nearest aircraft is G-71 43+13 GS002. (Author)

33. Tornado GR.IA 'FB' of 13 Squadron in a HAS at Marham in July 1993. (RAF Marham)

34. Canberra PR.9 'AA' of 39 (I PRU) Squadron at Marham in June 1997. (Author)

35. Tornado GR.Is taking off from a snow-covered Marham. (Author)

This, together with the fact that the rest of the formation had gained a considerable lead, caused Gordon to decide to abandon and he jettisoned his bombs at 16.09 hours and headed home. Edwards continues:

> Cairns did a fine piece of work by steering a little north of east until we were across the neck of Denmark. This must have led the Germans to suppose that we were going for a target in the Baltic coast of Germany. We passed just south of the great bridge over Star Strom, then turned slowly north and ran up past Cliff Lighthouse. It was rather a thrill to look away to starboard and see Sweden. By the time we were halfway across Köge Bay we could see the outline of Copenhagen on the horizon. We flew up the east coast of Amagen and could clearly see ships in the canal separating it from the mainland. Then the Wing Commander opened his bomb doors and we packed in tight for the bombing run. The buildings of Burmeister & Wain came up just as we had seen them in the photographs and as we swept low over the roofs the bombs could be seen showering down – skidding, bouncing and crashing into the factory. Then, as we turned away across the spires of the city, the flak came streaming up from the ships in the harbour to the north. Only one aircraft was slightly damaged [Edwards' Mosquito received two holes in the starboard nacelle] but five minutes later a Mosquito went smack into a set of high-tension cables and blew up. [Sergeant James G. Dawson and Sergeant Ronald H. Cox were killed]. This was the worst of misfortune but the rest of us got safely away without further incident.

Sergeant pilot H.C. 'Gary' Herbert RAAF of 105 Squadron and his navigator, Sergeant C. 'Jakey' Jacques, flew number two to Wing Commander Edwards. Herbert wrote:

> Quite a long trip. When we eventually found the target it was getting dark but we hit it good and proper. We attacked between two big chimneys and hit the machine shops and power station. Our bombs were delayed half-hour, three hours, six hours and 36 hours to disorganise the place for a while. Other kites had eleven second delay bombs as well as long delay. We got quite a lot of light flak as we left the target but kept on the housetops and nobody was hit. When we got well away it was pretty dark and one of the kites was hit and crashed in flames. Petrol was getting short so we throttled back to 230 mph and as we passed the last island on the west of Denmark we went straight over a machine gun post at 200ft. It threw up a lot of flak but I jinked and dodged it OK. We came back quietly and landed in the dark at 8pm. One kite ran out of juice and crashed about twenty miles away killing [Sergeant Richard Clare and Flying Officer Edward Doyle of 139 Squadron, who hit a balloon cable and tree at East Dereham after the starboard engine failed]. Got a scare, on the way back we were struck by lightning twice and each time a ball of fire appeared on the wing and gradually died out. I looked at the wing but there wasn't a mark on it. Seems queer to me but the weather man said it had happened before so I couldn't have had the DTs. [Edwards landed with only fifteen gallons of fuel in his tanks; enough for about another six and a half miles.] Invited the Officers over to the mess in the evening to have a few drinks and fight the battle again. Nice evening. At the time for the bombs to go off we drank a toast to them. On Friday 30th some news came in from Sweden of our raid on Copenhagen. Apparently it was a huge success and the Diesel works were flattened.

The navigator of a B.IV Mosquito demonstrates how the Mk.IV bomb sight was used, just as in heavy bombers. (Shuttleworth Collection)

A sugar factory and another six-storey building burned to the ground. They thought our delay bombs were duds but they all went off OK on time.[78]

On 30 January there was some trepidation among Mosquito crews at Marham, who were due to raid Berlin to disrupt speeches in the city's main broadcasting station on what was the tenth anniversary of Hitler's seizure of power. Three crews in 105 Squadron, led by Squadron Leader 'Reggie' W. Reynolds DFC and Pilot Officer E.B. 'Ted' Sismore, would bomb Berlin that morning when Reichsmarschall Hermann Göering was due to speak. In the afternoon, three Mosquitoes of 139 Squadron would arrive over Berlin at the time Dr Joseph Göebbels, Hitler's propaganda minister, was due to address the German nation at the Sports Palast. Reynolds had flown a tour on Hampdens and a tour on Manchesters. Sismore had flown on Blenheims on 110 Squadron and, while at the Blenheim OTU at Bicester and the Whitley OTU at Honeybourne, he had flown on two of the 1,000-bomber raids in 1942. Most of the pilots and navigators could not face breakfast. An exception was Flying Officer A.T. 'Tony' Wickham of 105 Squadron who was taking part in the morning raid with his navigator, Pilot Officer W.E.D. Makin. Wickham heartily drank three tins of orange juice and polished off half a dozen fried eggs. A month earlier, as a young pilot officer going on his first trip, a high-level dawn raid on cities in the Ruhr (when casualties were particularly heavy) his reaction during a gloomy five o'clock breakfast had been quite

Mosquito B.IV DZ367/J of 105 Squadron being bombed up at RAF Marham. DZ367/J was shot down on the raid to Berlin on 30 January 1943, and Squadron Leader D.F.W. Darling DFC and Flying Officer W. Wright were killed in action. (*Flight*)

different. Wickham suddenly burst out and said, 'I suppose this is a death or glory effort?' Hughie Edwards lent forward, looked at him and said, 'There is no glory in it and that's what makes it so worthwhile.' Flight Lieutenant John 'Flash' Gordon DFC and Flying Officer Ralph G. Hayes DFC, who three days earlier had returned with a damaged port wing, completed the trio of aircraft due in Berlin for 'elevenses'. The three Mosquitoes arrived over Berlin at exactly 11.00 hours and the explosion of their bombs severely disrupted the Reichsmarschall's speech. Listeners heard a few muffled words followed by confusion of many voices, then another shout or bang, after which the microphone was apparently switched off and martial music played. It was then announced that Göering's speech would be delayed for a few moments. But after three-quarters of an hour, martial music was still being played!

That afternoon the three Mosquitoes of 139 Squadron arrived over Berlin at the time Göebbels was due to speak. They were flown by Squadron Leader Donald F.W. Darling DFC and Flying Officer William Wright, Flight Sergeant Peter John Dixon McGeehan and Flying Officer Reginald Charles Morris and Sergeants Massey and R.C. 'Lofty' Fletcher. The Mosquitoes dropped their bombs right on cue. However, the earlier raid alerted the defences and flak brought down the Mosquito flown by Darling and Wright. Both were buried in Berlin's 1939–45 war cemetery. That night 'Tony' Wickham treated British listeners to the BBC's 9 o'clock news to an account of the action: 'Lord Haw Haw' trying to sound convincing in a German broadcast to any who cared to listen, announced that, 'Thanks to the U-boat campaign Britain is so starved of materials that she has been compelled to build her bombers of wood.' Reynolds was awarded the DSO, while all the other officers received the DFC and the sergeants got DFMs.

On the afternoon of 14 February, in what became known as the 'Great Tours Derby', six Mosquitoes of 139 Squadron and a subsidiary formation of four Mosquitoes, led by Squadron Leader Robert Beck 'Bob' Bagguley DFC, set out to attack the engine sheds in the French city. 'Unfortunately, the weather marred the complete success of the show,' reported Flying Officer William E.G. 'Bill' Humphrey. 'For though the leader and four aircraft of his formation succeeded in bombing their primary – the engine repair shops – from fifty feet, the rest of the formation was split up by cloud right down to the deck. Three of the remainder turned back but Flying Officer Pereira carried on by himself and carried out a Shallow Dive attack on the engine round house to the east of the town. He scored direct hits with at least two of his six bombs, one of which hit the turntable in the middle.[79] Flying Officer Rennie RCAF, having lost the formation, looked around for an alternative target and finally bombed a train with devastating results, hitting the engine with all four bombs in salvo. Everyone returned safely from this operation.' The following evening, twelve Mosquitoes of 105 Squadron attacked the goods depot from Low Level and, on the 18th, twelve Mosquitoes made a Shallow Dive attack. Two aborted and one aircraft failed to return.[80]

On 14 February Hughie Edwards, who had been promoted Group Captain four days earlier, left 105 Squadron to take up a post at HQ Bomber Command prior to taking command of RAF Binbrook on the 18th.[81] Edwards' successor was Wing Commander Geoffrey P. Longfield who, on 26 February, led an attack by twenty Mosquitoes of 105 and 139 Squadrons on the Rennes Naval Arsenal. Ten aircraft were to go in at Low Level, led by Longfield, and ten Mosquitoes of 139 Squadron were to follow just behind, climb to 2,000ft and dive bomb behind the first wave. Longfield's navigator, Flight Lieutenant Roderick Milne, lost his bearings on the final run up to the target, which took the Mosquitoes to an airfield 6 miles south of the target. The airfield defences sent up a hail of light flak as the Mosquitoes turned towards the target. On low-level attacks the Mosquitoes had always flown in echelon starboard and any left-hand turns created no problems, as all members of the formation could keep the aircraft in his left in sight. However, Longfield, who had turned too far to the left, suddenly turned right again. In a sharp turn to the right, as each pilot lifted his left wing, his wing obscured the aircraft on his left because he could not drop down as in higher altitudes. Canadian Flying Officers Spencer Kimmel and Harry Kirkland, who were formatting on Longfield, sliced into their leader's tail and Longfield went up into a loop and dived straight into the ground west of Rennes St Jacques. Kimmel lost height and disappeared below the trees at 300mph. Longfield and Milne and Kimmel and Kirkland all died. (On the way home a 139 Squadron Mosquito flown by Lieutenant T.D.C. Moe and his observer, 2nd Lieutenant O. Smedsaas, both RNAF, crashed and the two Dutchmen were killed).

By the time the others reached the target Warrant Officer 'Gary' Herbert, who before the operation had agreed to change positions with Kimmel, could see the dive bombers already starting their dive. The Australian pilot knew his formation would be blown up by the eleven-second delayed action 500lb bombs carried by some of the Mosquitoes if they went in.

He therefore turned violently to the west and climbed to about 700ft, dived below the other formation and got his bombs on the target. Others in his formation bombed alternative targets. Pilot Officer G.W. 'Mac' McCormick, a young officer on only his fourth operation, did not see the dive bombers until it was too late and he went in at Low Level. (139 Squadron were dropping 500lb MC – medium capacity – bombs with instantaneous fuses). Herbert said, 'God knows how he got through because photographs showed him right in the middle of the bursts. He came back with his radiators full of flock from bombed bedding stores. He used up a lot of luck today.' The next day 'Mac' McCormick and visiting Wing Commander John W. Deacon were killed on a training flight when the wing fairing broke up during a dive from 30,000ft, and they crashed a mile to the south-east of Marham at Brick Kiln Plantation.

On Sunday 28 February six of 105 Squadron's Mosquitoes led by Wing Commander Roy Ralston went to the John Cockerill Steel works at Liège. Four more led by Pilot Officer Onslow Thompson DFM RNZAF and Pilot Officer Wallace J. Horne DFC went to the Stork Diesel Engine Works at Hengelo, in what was the eighth raid on the Dutch town by Mosquitoes.[82] At Liège the Mosquitoes bombed at about 200ft and results were 'good' but at Hengelo very little damage was done to the factories.

On 3 March Wing Commander Peter Shand DFC and Flight Sergeant Christopher D. Handley DFM led ten Mosquitoes of 139 Squadron to the molybdenum mines at Knaben in South Norway. Molybdenum is a metallic element used in the production of high-speed steels. At the target Shand would lead the six Mosquitoes of the Shallow Dive section while Squadron Leader Bob Bagguley led would lead the four Low Level attack aircraft. The formation set course over Marham at 12.10 hours in good formation for Flamborough Head. Shand wrote:

> We were ninety minutes over the sea at Low Level, during which time the 10/10 cloud gave way to a clear sky and brilliant sunshine. Track was maintained accurately by constant drift reading and a landfall was made within a mile of the appointed place. Visibility was exceptional and the snow capped mountains over which we had to climb presented a striking sight.

Flying Officer William S.D. 'Jock' Sutherland, a Scot from Dollar, whose navigator was Flying Officer George Dean, flew No.2 to Wing Commander Shand. They were very impressed by the scenery over Norway. Sutherland recalled how 'Visibility was about 20 miles and there was no cloud. The snow-covered mountains with lakes dotted about made a very pleasant change after the long sea trip. We reached the target after climbing up and started our attack straight away.' The six Shallow Divers led by Shand commenced their climb and the remaining four Mosquitoes kept as low as possible on Sirdale Lake, overtaking them. They were seen to pass underneath the Shallow Divers just before reaching the northern end of the lake and then turn east, climbing steeply over the surrounding hills in line astern and stepped down. The Shallow Dive formation then turned east on to course. Bagguley's formation climbed up the rather steep crevice and the much studied pinpoint of Risones was picked up. 'From then onwards' said Bagguley, 'it was a piece of cake. The target appeared just as per illustrations and was cleanly silhouetted against the snow of the surrounding mountains. We made a perfect run on and dropped our bobs from roof-top height.' Flight Sergeant Peter McGeehan DFM and Flying Officer Reginald Morris DFC, flying at the rear of the Low Level formation, were not

Flying Officer William S.D. 'Jock' Sutherland, a Scot from Dollar, whose navigator was Flying Officer George Dean. Returning from Jena on 27 May 1943, they flew into high voltage overhead electric cables when attempting to land at RAF Coltishall. They crashed at Wroxham railway station – both were killed. (RAF)

in a suitable position for an attack so they peeled off and took another run at it. McGeehan remarked that 'During this time we saw the Low Level bombs going off, the Shallow Divers making their attack and Massey attacking the gun positions. It looked good and the stuff was still going off as we ran over, successfully this time.'

As the Shallow Divers approached the target they saw brown and white smoke rising from the Low Level formation's bombs, and only the roof of the target building was still visible. They commenced their attack immediately. Sutherland continues:

I followed the Winco in rather low and the debris from his bombs flew up at least 300ft above us. After bombing we headed straight for home and could see smoke from the target rising to a very

105 and 139 Squadron aircrew at RAF Marham after returning from Berlin on 31 January 1943. Seated left to right: Flying Officer Ralph Gamble Hayes, Squadron Leader Reggie W. Reynolds and Pilot Officer E.D. Makin. Standing: Flying Officer Reginald Charles Morris, Flight Sergeant Peter John Dixon McGeehan; Sergeant Massey, Flight Lieutenant John Gordon; Flying Officer J.T.Wickham; Sergeant R.C. 'Lofty' Fletcher; Pilot Officer E.B. 'Ted' Sismore. Morris and McGeehan were KIA on 16 March 1943 and are buried at Den Burg, Texel. Either Morris or McGeehan carried this photo at the time of their death and it was found by German troops searching the wreckage of their Mosquito (DZ497). (Via Theo Boiten)

considerable height. Crossing the Norwegian coast going out we saw a Mossie being attacked by two 190s. We didn't wait to see the result.[83] We made a landfall at Hunstanton and landed at base at 1630. Altogether a very enjoyable and satisfactory trip.

Bomb bursts accompanied by orange flashes and a red glow were seen on and around the target, which resulted in the plant being enveloped in clouds of white and brown smoke and debris being blown to a height of 1,000ft. AOC Air Vice-Marshal J.H. d'Albiac sent his congratulations for a 'well planned and splendidly executed attack ... Mosquito stings judiciously placed are very painful.' On 4 March Squadron Leader Reggie Reynolds DSO DFC led a successful attack by six Mosquitoes at Low Level from 50–200ft on engine sheds and repair workshops at Le Mans. On 4 and 8 March 139 Squadron made two extremely successful attacks on Aulnoye. The first of these, directed against the railway engine sheds and a bomb manufacturing factory, was led by Squadron Leader Bob Bagguley DFC. Three Mosquitoes were employed on the Low Level attack on the railway target and three on the Shallow Dive. Bagguley's navigator, Flight Lieutenant Charles Hayden DFC, recalled: 'A most pleasant trip. We made good landfall thanks to J. C. and my pilot and met no opposition the whole way to the target. The bombs made a wizard sight as they went up, making a sheer column of flame about 200ft high. No opposition was encountered on the way out except some machine-gun tracer, which was seen going up at another Mossie. We landed in semi-daylight.' Sergeant Robert Pace and Pilot Officer George Cook, who were part of the Shallow Dive formation on the bomb factory, were flying their first raid. Cook recalled that it was 'A most enjoyable first op. Good to see bombs from two aircraft in front hitting the roof of the target and 300 foot columns of smoke after leaving target. Our photographs show direct hits from our own bombs.'

On the second raid on Aulnoye on 8 March against the railway repair shops, the six Mosquitoes of the Shallow Dive attack was led by Wing Commander Shand and the four in the Low Level section by Squadron Leader Bob Bagguley. One of the Shallow Divers was the Mosquito flown by Flying Officer Jock Sutherland and Flying Officer George Dean. Sutherland recalled:

> We took off in good order, setting course for the enemy coast from North Foreland. Crossing the French coast slight A/A fire came up at the rear part of the formation. At le Cateau we turned on to a North-East heading for the target climbing up to 4,000ft. The Low Level formation continued at 50ft. As we were about to attack our target we saw a huge sheet of flame and black smoke where the Low Level boys' bombs were going off. Our target was bombed at 1855. There was no flak from the target area, which was covered with a slight industrial haze. We did not see our own bombs burst for once but got good photographs and saw a very thick cloud of smoke as we left the target. We came out at Termonds. Coming out of the coast there was a great deal of flak aimed in our direction from the shore on one side and ships on the other. I think we caught them with their trousers down, for they were too late. We landed away from base owing to bad weather and returned the following morning.

Another of the Shallow Divers was the Mosquito flown by Flight Sergeant Peter McGeehan DFM and Flying Officer Reginald Morris DFC. They were so engrossed in looking at the large sheet of flame and quantities of black and brown smoke coming from the engine sheds, which had been bombed with excellent results by the Low Level formation that they overshot. They had to peel off to starboard and come in last before dropping their bombs on the target. Looking back after they had reached ground level again they could see a column of smoke 1,000ft high.

That same day three Mosquitoes of 105 Squadron bombed rail targets at Tergnier, 12 miles south of St Quentin in France from Low Level, and Flight Lieutenant Gordon led another pair of Mosquitoes in an attack on the railway shops at Lingen in Germany. The Mosquito flown by Sergeant W.W. Austin and Pilot Officer P.E. Thomas was hit by flak and crashed on the return trip at Den Ham in Holland. Both men survived and were taken prisoner.

On 9 March the Renault Aero Engine Works at Le Mans was the target of fifteen of Marham's Mosquitoes. The whole formation was led by Squadron Leader J.R.G. Ralston DSO DFM and his navigator, Flight Lieutenant Syd Clayton DFC DFM, at the head of five Mosquitoes from 105 Squadron, who carried out the Low Level attack. A Shallow Dive section was led by Squadron Leader Bob Bagguley DFC at the head of ten aircraft of 139

Squadron. One of the Shallow Diver teams was Flying Officer Sutherland and Flying Officer Dean. Sutherland wrote:

> Rather a ropey take-off. Squadron Leader Bagguley had trouble with his port engine and turned back. I took over the lead but Bob caught us up on the circuit and regained the lead. From then on it was a normal trip. Visibility was bad, but we spotted the target wreathed in smoke from 105's Low Level attack. We were greeted by plenty of accurate flak over the target, but managed to avoid same as we were diving fast. Coming out over the coast, we found an enemy convoy of twenty ships dead ahead. Big moment. We altered course to port, and the escort ship challenged us by lamp. We gave her a long series of garbled 'dits' and 'dahs' on our recognition lights and nipped smartly off. Base was reached without further incident.

'Bob' Bagguley and Flight Lieutenant Charles Hayden DFC were seen to bomb the target and when last observed, 'appeared to be sailing home in fine style' but they failed to return. No trace of the crew was ever found.

On 12 March twelve Mosquitoes of 105 and 139 Squadrons, led by Squadron Leader Reggie Reynolds and Pilot Officer Ted Sismore, were briefed to attack the John Cockerill steel and armament works in the centre of Liège. The briefing officer stated that two crack fighter units had recently been moved to Woensdrecht, south of Rotterdam, and that they had recently been re-equipped with Fw 190s. (II./JG1 at Woensdrecht was equipped with 35 Fw 190A-4s of which twenty were serviceable.) Allowing for several doglegs flight time to target was between 2 and 2½ hours. Attacks of this nature were normally planned for dusk or just before dark so that the Mosquitoes could return to England individually under the cover of half-light or darkness. Bombing had to be carried out very accurately to keep losses to a minimum, and this task was given to the Shallow Dive section, led by Squadron Leader John V. Berggren of 139 Squadron with his observer Flying Officer Peter Wright DFC. At 15.40 hours all twelve Mosquitoes took off. They headed south before flying across the Channel to France and up and over the cliffs to the west of Cap Gris Nez, then on across the heavily defended Pas de Calais at nought feet. Finally, the Mosquitoes seldom flying at more than 100ft and keeping echelon formation on the leader, picked up the River Meuse which led straight in to the target. At around 5 miles from the target 105 Squadron split from the rest of the formation and went straight in at Low Level to each drop their four 500lb eleven-second delayed action bombs. These burst in the target area as Berggren and his six Mosquitoes hurriedly climbed to 3,000ft and then dived onto the target to release their four 500lb bombs with instantaneous fuses. Turning away to the north the crews could see a huge mushroom of smoke building up over the main target area. Leaving the target the formation broke into individual aircraft and raced for the Scheldt Estuary at 280mph in gathering dusk. The Mosquitoes had to climb to 200ft to avoid HT cables, which criss-crossed Belgium and France. The Mosquito flown by Sergeant Robert Pace and Pilot Officer George Cook was hit by flak and caught fire, before it crashed on the runway of Woensdrecht airfield and was smashed to smithereens on impact, leaving a stream of burning debris in its wake.[84]

On 16 March sixteen Mosquitoes of 105 and 139 Squadrons, led by Squadron Leader John Berggren DFC, made Low Level and Shallow Dive attacks on roundhouses and engine

Wreckage of BIV DZ497/Q of 139 Squadron, which was shot down by Kriegsmarine flak on the squadron's operation to Paderborn on 16 March 1943, and subsequently crashed in Holland in dunes near Den Hoovn, Texel. Pilot Officer Peter John Dixon McGeehan DFM and Flying Officer Reginald Charles Morris DFC were KIA. (Via Theo Boiten)

sheds at Paderborn. Flight Lieutenant Bill Blessing DFC of 105 Squadron led the Low Level section. Berggren's navigator, Flying Officer Peter Wright DFC, recalled:

Paderborn is quite a few miles east of the Ruhr, and it looked an alarmingly long way into Germany when we studied the route on the large-scale map in the briefing room. There were to be sixteen aircraft, which by our standards is a big formation. The target consisted of engine sheds, and they were to be attacked in two waves, first by six aircraft at Low Level and then by ten from about 1,300ft in a Shallow Dive. Apart from the bombing run, we were to fly at Low Level all the way. We, in our aircraft, were to lead the formation to a point about twenty-five miles short of the target, and then to climb to 3,000ft with nine others behind us, while the last six raced in ahead to bomb first from Low Level. The rest of us were to dive down to thirteen hundred feet before bombing. It was hoped that our bombs would begin falling just as the last of the low-level aircraft had got clear of the target. It would be too bad for him if we bombed a bit early. You can't see Mosquitoes when you are directly above them; their camouflage is too good. So, good timing would be needed if we were going to make a concentrated attack, and yet give that last man a chance.

All went well till we were over the Zuider Zee, when we were intercepted by a formation of low-flying ducks. They attacked strongly, but inflicted only one casualty. Their leader crashed through the perspex of Sergeant Cummings' aircraft, and landed as a heap of blood and feathers on his observer's stomach. Two others hit his starboard engine nacelle. It was very draughty in that aeroplane (and messy, too), so it turned back for home. The rest of us managed to take the effective evasive action. We are better at avoiding birds than we used to be.

We carried on very smoothly over the flat lands of Holland and North-West Germany. Occasionally we would lift a wing to avoid a church steeple. Visibility was just right – enough to map read by, and no more. Between Minster and Osnabruck the country became hilly and the formation inevitably got more ragged. But everything was still very quiet. We crossed a big autobahn and began to climb, while the last six Mosquitoes stayed down. It's an uncomfortable feeling to be up at 3,000ft after a spell of low flying. You feel naked and motionless and a sitting target for the gunners. But it gets better when you dive on to the target and the earth comes close again and you recapture the feeling of speed.

There was a lot of industrial haze drifting over from the Ruhr, and the target was difficult to see. Perhaps it was the haze that made the flak gunners so slow off the mark. They allowed half of us to bomb before they opened up. When they did open up, they were pretty good, and the boys at the back had a nasty few minutes. Flight Sergeant McGeehan was hit and did not return.[85] Sergeant Massey came back on one engine and did very well to make a crash-landing at an aerodrome close to base.[86] We, personally, were lucky and were out of the target area in time. When we looked back the target was going up into the air, and above it the Mosquitoes were bucking like broncos to avoid the streams of orange balls thrown up at them from all angles by the Bofors guns.

On the way home over Germany the mist got thicker and thicker and we all felt safer and safer. We saw two Junkers 52's and wished we had some guns. Nothing else happened, and we sneaked quietly out over the Dutch island, which we thought would give us the least trouble. I doubt if they could have seen us, anyway.

On 17 March Acting Wing Commander John 'Jack' de Lacey Wooldridge DFC* DFM RAFVR took command of 105 Squadron. Wooldridge was born in Yokohama, Japan, on 18 July 1919 and was educated at St Paul's School, London. As a composer he studied with Sibelius. Wooldridge had joined the RAF in 1938 and he flew two tours (seventy-three operations) on heavy bombers prior to taking command of 105 Squadron, including thirty-two ops on Manchesters. For the last three months he had been attached to the tri-service PWD, working on the FIDO fog dispersal system.[87]

On the 20th six Mosquitoes of 105 Squadron carried out low-level attacks on the engine sheds and repair shops at Louvain in Belgium. Six Mosquitoes of 139 Squadron, led by Flight Lieutenant Mike Wayman DFC and Flying Officer G.S. 'Pops' Clear, carried out a Low Level dusk attack on the railway workshops at Malines. This raid was unsuccessful as Flying Officer Jock Sutherland recalled:

Everything was OK until we reached the enemy coast [Over Blankenburg]. Mike Wayman was hit in the starboard engine. He tried to carry on, but after a couple of miles he peeled off and feathered his airscrew. We took over the lead. Near the target, the visibility closed in to 500 yards and we were unable to locate our exact position in the industrial haze and general filth. We eventually bombed a goods train. We boobed coming out and went slap across Antwerp aerodrome, where we got plenty of accurate flak. There we ran into trouble good and proper in the Flushing estuary, where everything opened up, including a convoy and escort. Fortunately we were not hit and landed OK at base at 20.30 hours.

Wayman made it back to England and he crashed at Martlesham Heath on overshoot, but Wayman and 'Pops' Clear were killed. Flying Officer Cussens and Sergeant Munro had also experienced 'intense' flak crossing the coast at Blankenburg, which knocked out their hydraulics. They saw the target momentarily but were unable to open the bomb doors. Coming out they had more flak at Antwerp and an 'incredible amount' at Beveland Island, which shot away their rudder controls and port landing edge causing the aircraft to stall at 180mph, eventually landing at Marham. Flying Officer Brown summed up the operation thus:

> Never has the carefree attitude of some aircrews toward operating been more apparent! We stooged almost over Ostend to make a good landfall, pouncing on the target at thirty seconds' notice. A false alarm of 'snappers' after the target – which we missed – resulted in Mosquitoes pulling the plug in every direction and screaming about like a gaggle of alarmed hens; not to mention some cheery optimist who flew for fifty miles or so over enemy territory with his navigation lights on. The visibility was wicked; we went over Antwerp; we went over the mouth of the Scheldt; and back over this country, we went round from aerodrome to aerodrome with our wireless u/s, before base, which had spent a busy evening changing the flarepath about, condescended to receive us. What a life![88]

On 23 March ten Mosquitoes of 139 Squadron, led by Wing Commander Peter Shand DFC, and five of 139 Squadron, led by Flight Lieutenant Bill Blessing DFC, attacked the Compagnie Génèrale de Construction des Locomotives Batigniolles-Chatillon at St Joseph, 2 miles north-east of Nantes at Low Level. The raid had to be timed to perfection for when the French factory workers finished work. Flying Officer J.E. Hay, a South African from Pretoria, who was navigator to Pilot Officer T.M. Mitchell in the Shallow Dive section, recalls:

> The Battle Order was issued early on the morning of the 23rd March and my pilot and I were on the list, which was a long one. All this, and the very long trainload of bombs being pulled along the tarmac, seemed to indicate a big 'do'. We entered the briefing room with more than the usual feeling of excitement that a formation made up of both Squadrons was to attack the St. Joseph Locomotive Works at Nantes – quite a deep penetration into enemy-occupied territory. We were airborne at 1350 and set course across the aerodrome about ten minutes later. The weather was good over base, but it had started to deteriorate before we reached the south coast. People at the seaside that afternoon must have been startled as the large formation went out over the Channel at nought feet. The weather improved for us over the Channel and on schedule the French coast was sighted – a low belt of sand dunes followed by wooded downs. We shot over these in tight formation and for once experienced no flak – we were over the first hurdle. From this point onwards the weather was perfect with excellent visibility and some cloud about 2,000ft above us.

Our route across France lay over a series of hills and valleys. We skimmed over the hilltops, and flew down through the valleys and across the small towns. On one hilltop we saw three Huns make a dash for their machine-gun; we dived straight at them, and they threw themselves flat as we roared over the gunpit. There was nothing very dangerous in this, for we could see the tarpaulin cover still on the gun! Then, after almost thirty minutes of breathless chase across France, we swept into the broad plains of the River Loire to find the sun breaking fitfully through the clouds. At about a quarter to four the town of Nantes appeared ahead and we began to climb up to our bombing height, while Squadron Leader Blessing led 105 Squadron on ahead at Low Level. As we climbed away from the earth, we seemed at first to hover stationary in mid-air. Then we saw the first black puffs of anti-aircraft fire. As we peeled off for our dive, I saw 105 streaking across the target below us and then the vivid flashes of their bombs exploding. Within a few seconds we were diving fast after them and our bombs were following theirs. Then we went across the town and away to the south. Looking back, I could see the old works covered by an immense pall of smoke and I also caught a glimpse of six enemy fighters circling about twenty miles away to the west in the direction of St. Nazaire. They suddenly formed up and flew off north, apparently not having seen us. As we were racing south with a very pretty turn of speed, they were soon lost to sight.

The job completed, we flew out over the Bay of Biscay in brilliant sunshine, heading for home. In every direction there seemed to be Mosquitoes just skimming the wave-tops. It was a grand sight! Shortly afterwards we all lost touch in a heavy bank of fog, and when we at last emerged from this the Cornish coast lay below us.

This raid was an outstanding success; not one bomb missing the target, and no building in the target area failed to be hit. Squadron Leader Berggren added, 'the target … looked a good enough mess even before the second formation dropped their bombs.'

The next day, 24 March, three Mosquitoes of 105 Squadron were sent on a Rover operation to Shallow Dive-bomb trains and railway lines within specified areas in Germany. On 27 March 139 Squadron dispatched six aircraft on another low-level raid on the Stork Diesel Works at Hengelo. The bombing results at debriefing were described as being uncertain, although photographs showed many near misses. On this occasion serious damage was done to the primary target although nearby houses were hit once again. Henk F. van Baaren attended a funeral for the first time in his young life, when a seventeen-year-old boy from his school and a member of the same gymnastic club was killed.[89]

On 28 March seven Mosquitoes, led by Flight Lieutenant 'Flash' Gordon, were dispatched to attack the railway marshalling yards at Liège, but rainstorms reduced the evening visibility to half a mile, and instead he led the aircraft in an attack on a factory north of Valbengit Bridge at Liège. They were spotted by Unteroffizier Wilhelm Mayer of 6th Staffel JG26 heading towards Dunkirk at Low Level, and Oberfeldwebel Adolf 'Addi' Glunz and three other Fw 190s of 4./JG26 were sent off from Vitry immediately. They intercepted the Mosquitoes after they had bombed. Glunz was credited with shooting down, in the space of a minute, the Mosquito flown by Flying Officer George Bruce DFM and Flying Officer Dick Reilly, about 18 miles east of Etaples, and Sergeant George Leighton and Sergeant Thomas Chadwick, south of Lille. All four airmen were later buried in Lille Southern Cemetery. (Glunz finished the war with seventy-one confirmed victories.)

Mosquito crews at RAF Marham, Norfolk, early in 1943. Flight Lieutenant John 'Flash' Gordon, head on one side, unfastening his Mae West, is talking to Flight Lieutenant C.Vernon Pereira, a Trinidadian who flew eighty ops on Mosquitoes on 139 and 105 Squadrons, and was awarded the DFC and Bar. Behind Gordon is Syd Clayton. (RAF Marham)

Wing Commander Hughie Idwal Edwards VC DFC, an Australian of Welsh ancestry, was twenty-six years old when he took command of 105 Squadron in August 1942. He was only the second Australian to receive the VC (the first had been awarded to Lieutenant F. H. McNamara of the RFC in the First World War) for his leadership on 4 July 1941 when he led 9 Blenheims on the operation to Bremen. On 10 February 1943 Edwards was promoted Group Captain and he became station commander of Binbrook. By 1944 he had taken up an appointment in ACSEA, and held the rank of Senior Air Staff Office until the end of 1945. Edwards was awarded the CBE in 1947 and in 1958 he was promoted to Air Commodore before retiring from the RAF in 1963. He returned to Australia, was knighted, and in 1974 became Governor of West Australia. (RAAF)

On 30 March ten Mosquitoes of 139 Squadron, led by Wing Commander Peter Shand DFC, set off to bomb the Philips Works at Eindhoven, which was about ready to begin full production again. One 139 Squadron Mosquito, which was hit by flak while crossing the enemy coast, lost its hydraulics and was unable to open its bomb bay doors and abandoned the strike, leaving four aircraft to attack from Low Level and five in a Shallow Dive. The attackers switched back over Holland, dodging flocks of seagulls over the Zuider Zee and tearing over Eindhoven once more at zero feet. Pilot Officer T.M. Mitchell, who brought up the rear of the formation with his navigator, Flying Officer J.E. Hay, recalls:

We encountered very intense light flak at the coast. This was accurate and followed all the aircraft for about eight miles inland. We saw no further flak until the target was reached. The run-up was beautiful, the building being silhouetted against the sky. On reaching it we found it necessary to climb 50ft in order to get over that blasted chimney, about which we had been warned. I saw the Wing Commander's bombs, which were timed to go off a short time after impact, fall into the buildings as we skimmed over the rooftops. Then I let our own bombs go right into the middle of the factory. As I circled after the attack I saw the whole building become enveloped in smoke with huge red flashes as the bombs exploded. On the way out the weather was very bumpy but we reached base without further incident. My navigator saw V-signs flashing from Dutch homes in the falling light.

Flying Officer Paney and Sergeant Stimson noticed a Dutchman hoeing in a garden. He glanced up once and then went on hoeing!

On 1 April six Mosquitoes of 105 Squadron, led by Wing Commander Roy Ralston DSO DFM and Flight Lieutenant Syd Clayton DFC DFM, whose 100th op this was, set out with four of 139 Squadron led by Squadron Leader John Berggren. Their targets were a power station and railway yards at Trier and engine sheds at Ehrang respectively, which were bombed from 50–400ft. Bombs from the first formation were seen to fall in the middle of the railway workshops, throwing up large quantities of debris followed by showers of green sparks. Bomb bursts were also observed on the power station followed by a sheet of flame, which rose to a height of 100ft. The attack by the second formation on Ehrang resulted in a huge explosion and a red flash from a coal container. One bomb was seen to bounce off railway tracks into a house, which was blown to pieces. On leaving the target area smoke was seen rising to about 1,500ft. No aircraft were lost, although Flying Officer Talbot's and Sergeant Sleeman's Mosquito of 139 Squadron, which was hit by blast from bomb bursts and also by flak, returned on one engine with gyro artificial horizon and turn-and-bank indicator out of action. They crossed the enemy coast 1 mile south of Boulogne harbour, amid flak 'of various assortments' following them up to 5 miles out. Talbot, who landed safely at Manston, concluded 'Ain't life grand!' In the messes that night crews celebrated Syd Clayton's award of an immediate DSO, and wished him luck on his pilot's course. He had been waiting for three weeks to complete his century.

On 3 April Wing Commander Wooldridge led his first 105 Squadron operation, when eight Mosquitoes carried out Rover attacks on railway targets in Belgium and France. All three of 105 Squadron's Mosquitoes returned safely from attacks on locomotive repair sheds shops at Malines and engine sheds at Namur, but a Mosquito of 139 Squadron was lost. Flying Officer W.O. Peacock and his observer, Sergeant R.C. Saunders, were shot down by Oberfeldwebel Wilhelm Mackenstedt of 6./JG26 3km south of Beauvais for the German pilot's sixth and final victory.[90]

On 11 April four Mosquitoes of 105 Squadron, led by Squadron Leader Bill Blessing DFC and his navigator Flight Sergeant A.J.W. 'Jock' Heggie, ventured to Hengelo to bomb the Stork Works. This was the tenth and final Low Level attack by 2 Group Mosquito IVs on the long-suffering town. Light was failing and visibility was about 3 miles with 10/10ths cloud at 3,000ft, when the formation was intercepted at 50ft by two formations of three Fw 190s before reaching the target. One section of Fw 190s fired a burst of two seconds and then they broke off to starboard to attack two of the Mosquitoes. Flying Officer Norman Hull RCAF and Sergeant Philip Brown, No.3 in the formation, were intercepted by four Fw 190s who came in from starboard and opened fire for about fifteen seconds at a range of 350 yards. The Mosquitoes carried out evasive action by turning into the attack, weaving and gaining and losing height between 150–200ft, and increasing speed. After making one attack, the enemy aircraft broke off and wheeled round to attack *Z-Zebra*, flown by Flying Officer David Polgase RNZAF and his observer Flight Sergeant Leslie Lampen, which had been hit by flak at the coast. *Z-Zebra* had one airscrew feathered and with his speed greatly reduced Polgase and Lampen fell behind the rest the formation. Unteroffizier Gerhard Wiegand of 2./JG1 shot them down. The Mosquito crashed in a wood near Bentheim, Germany, and both crew were killed. Flying Officer F.M. 'Bud' Fisher, an American pilot from Pennsylvania, and Flight Sergeant Les Hogan were unable to bomb the primary target and attacked a train in the area instead. Blessing pressed home his attack from 50ft and he dropped his bomb load directly onto the Stork Works, causing severe damage to the plant. The Resistance seems to have signalled London that the Stork and Dikkers factories should no longer be considered targets, as production of war machinery had stopped.[91]

On 19–20 April there were no Main Force operations, and six Mosquitoes of 2 Group failed to locate rail workshops at Namur in bad visibility, returning without loss. On the night of 20–21 April nine Mosquitoes of 105 Squadron and two from 139 Squadron, led by Wing Commander Peter Shand DSO DFC, carried out a bombing attack on Berlin. This was a diversion for 339 heavy bombers attacking Stettin and eighty-six Stirlings bombing the Heinkel factory near Rostock. The Mosquito 'night nuisance' operations were also designed to 'celebrate' Hitler's birthday. Over Berlin it was cloudless with bright moonlight and the Mosquitoes dropped their bombs from 15,000–23,000ft. Flak was moderate and quite accurate but the biggest danger proved to be night fighters. One of these was Oberleutnant Lothar Linke, Staffelkapitän 12./NJG1, who the night before had claimed to be the second Nachtjagd pilot to destroy a Mosquito whilst flying a standard Bf 110G.[92] Linke, again led by his night fighter controller *Eisbär* (*Polar Bear*), overtook Shand's Mosquito at high altitude and at high speed in a power dive, shot the Mosquito down over the northern part of the Ijsselmeer at 02.10 hours. Shand and his navigator, Pilot Officer Christopher Handley DFM, were killed.[93]

On 26 April two Mosquitoes of 105 Squadron, led by Flight Lieutenant John 'Flash' Gordon DFC and his navigator, Flying Officer R. Hayes DFC, were ordered to bomb the railway workshops at Jülich, near Cologne. This had always been looked upon as a particularly difficult target to find, as it had no easily distinguishable landmarks near it to assist the observer. Any errors in navigation would bring the aircraft dangerously near to Cologne to the east or Aachen to the west. Gordon wrote:

Very shortly after briefing we were airborne, and after circling base a couple of times both aircraft set course for the Dutch coast. All the way over the North Sea I did nothing but sweat –' I hope we're not too high. Can any enemy ships see us? Down a bit. Altimeter reads just under nought feet. Hope to Heaven our landfall is OK. Worry! Worry! Worry!'

At last the enemy coast loomed up, the spires of Gravenhage to the left, the Hook of Holland to the right. We were very low. Closer now. A latticed naval beacon went past to the left; we turned four degrees to port and straightened up for our run in. I saw the hummocks on the beach; the white foam breaking on the sands; soldiers running like the Devil for their guns –' Look out for flak ' –we're over! Weaving madly, we shot over the sand-dunes and set a new course, flying as low as we dared over the glass roofs of the bulb nurseries and turning and twisting among the tall thin chimneys of the greenhouses. Soon we left the coastal towns behind us and, altering course southwards, roared across the level plains around the River Maas and past the tall smoking chimney of Eindhoven. Soon we could see rich black fields of ploughed earth, teams of chestnut Belgian horses and sleepy red-roofed hamlets. A quick glance behind showed us that Coyle, our No. 2, was just behind our tail.

Another alteration of twenty degrees to port and we crossed the frontier into Germany, with plenty of dark cloud ahead and green plantations of young Douglas firs below. Then, in the gloom ahead we picked up the gleam of the Roer River, pin-pointed ourselves quickly, and made a slight alteration to bring us directly onto the target. A river and a railway crossing appeared immediately ahead – good show, we were dead on track. The little town of Jülich soon showed up, and in climbing to clear the buildings we saw the big railway sheds lying in a valley running southwards from the town. As I opened the bomb doors we dived straight for the target and waited until the serrated roofs were just in front of the nose. I got a quick impression of tall chimneys on either side, a small engine snorting and grunting on the sidings, stacks of white wood laid on long waggons and a group of workmen scattering in every direction – ' Look out, you blasted Huns! Here they come! Bombs gone!' My navigator slewed round in his seat and, looking back, shouted 'Yes! I can see where they've gone in. Up they go! Number 2's hit it as well!'

No flak. I turned to starboard onto the next course and throttled back a little. Why all the hurry? Then we ran into a sharp rainstorm. I passed the target to starboard again, as I turned back and grey smoke was drifting slowly away. It began to get really dark on the way home, the dusk obscuring the power cables that raced underneath from time to time. A few lighted windows showed through the trees – it was too dark for a fighter interception now. I relaxed slightly. Everything seemed too easy, and there was plenty of cover in this semi-darkness.

'Take care,' came a warning from Hayes. 'We're off track. Keep low - lower still.' Then, before we knew what had happened, we were over the middle of Eindhoven Aerodrome. Everywhere there seemed to be little spurts of fire from machine-guns and great gobs of flame from the Bofors. They all missed. As we sped on into the darkness the Huns lobbed a few long shots after us which fell around us, and then suddenly – we were hit. From the port wing, outboard of the engine, a little trail of vapour streamed back and slowly grew less and less until it died away. I checked over the instruments but could find nothing wrong and carried on, going fast. 'Is that the coast? Open up and go like Hell – or is it the coast? No. Just a bank of mist. False alarm – but it can't be far away now!

Then far in front we saw a flock of white seagulls and knew that the sea was ahead. As we weaved our way across the dunes a feeble spurt of tracer swung lazily up from the left and followed us until we were out of range. It was lighter out to sea. Very pleasant it was to see the sunset in front of us to the west. Throttling back a few miles outside the coast, I climbed a few hundred feet and took things easy. We passed over one of our convoys off Norfolk, were challenged by a destroyer and replied to everyone's satisfaction.

Far ahead we saw our own coastline and before long our own beacon gave us a friendly wink and our flarepath came into view.

The Germans had dropped a shell into one of our petrol tanks, but by some stroke of luck it had not exploded.

Late in the evening of 27 May the final large-scale daylight raid by the Mosquito IVs of 2 Group took place when fourteen Mosquitoes were given two targets deep in southern Germany. The briefing was very long and complicated. It meant flying at Low Level for well over three hours over enemy territory, of which a good two and a quarter would be in broad daylight. Led by Wing Commander 'Reggie' W. Reynolds DSO DFC and Flight Lieutenant Ted Sismore DFC, six aircraft of 139 Squadron set out to attack the Schott glassworks at Jena. A few miles further on eight Mosquitoes of 105 Squadron, led by Squadron Leader Bill Blessing DFC and Flying Officer G.K. Muirhead, were to bomb the

Flt Lt Ted Sismore DSO DFC lighting up prior to take-off for the raid on Jena.

Zeiss Optical factory, which at that time was almost entirely engaged in making periscopes for submarines. One of the 105 Squadron pilots taking part was Flight Lieutenant Charles Patterson, with the Film Unit cameraman Flight Sergeant Leigh Howard as his navigator. Patterson recalls:

> We saw the red ribbon running longer than we'd ever considered, right down into SE Germany near Leipzig and the target, the Zeiss optical lens works at Jena. It gave a great sense of anticipation and excitement that such a tremendously long trip was going to be undertaken but not undue alarm because it was so deep into Germany, an area that had never seen daylight flying aircraft before. We rather assumed that by going deep down not only could we achieve a great deal of surprise but there night be much light AA fire round this factory and what there was the gunners would be inexperienced.
>
> At 7 o'clock all around the perimeter the engines started up and everybody taxied out. Forming up on these trips with a full muster of Mosquitoes was quite a lengthy business, the leader circling slowly round and round the airfield for everybody to get airborne and catch up. 'The two formations swept across the hangars and the airfield at Low Level, an impressive sight and quite

Wing Commander Reggie W. Reynolds DSO DFC (at right) assumes command of 139 Squadron in May 1943 from acting OC Squadron Leader Vernon R.G. Harcourt DFC RCAF (KIA 21 May 1943). Note the unit's 'Jamaica Squadron' crest above the doorway at RAF Marham. (RAF Marham)

an exhilarating experience for the crews themselves. We settled down for the long flight right across to Jena in clear daylight as it was certainly a good 2½ hours before dusk. The Dutch coast was crossed with no difficulty but at the Zuider Zee we suddenly found ourselves flying slap into a vast fleet of little brown-sailed fishing vessels. In front of me the whole formation broke up and weaved in and around them, before we settled down again. On behind the Ruhr and down near Kassel we went, then on into the Thuringian Mountains where the Möhne and Eder dams are. Even then we were only two thirds of the way. You felt you were in a separate world, which

B Mk.IV Series II DZ467 GB-P of 105 Squadron was on its nineteenth operational sortie when it failed to return from the raid on the Zeiss Optical Factory at Jena on 27 May 1943. Pilot Officer R. Massie and Sergeant G.P. Lister were killed. Only three of the eight Mosquitoes dispatched by 105 Squadron bombed the target, while three of the six 139 Squadron aircraft attacked the Schott Glass Works. (RAF Marham)

has no end and will go on forever. On and on over the trees and the fields and the rising ground we went, mile after mile. Then suddenly, my navigator drew my attention to something. I looked across the starboard wingtip and I had a clear view of Münster cathedral quite a few miles away, the interesting thing being that I was looking up at the towers, not down on them!

We carried on past Kassel then suddenly we came across all the floods of the Möhne dam raid which had taken place only ten days before. For twenty minutes there was nothing but floods. It was fascinating and confirmed in our minds what an enormous success the raid must have been. We flew between the Möhne and Eder dams and suddenly came over a mountain ridge and there was a dam [Helminghausen] beneath us. On the far side the front formation was just topping the far ridge when flak opened up. It didn't look very serious. An enormous ball of flame rolled down the mountainside, obviously an aircraft but it wasn't long after that I learnt that it was two Mosquitoes, which had collided. Whether one was hit by flak or whether it caused one of the pilots to take his eye off what he was doing and fly into the Mosquito next to him, nobody will ever know. But two had gone.[94]

We flew on over this mountainous country, over ridges and down long valleys with houses on both sides. On my starboard wingtip we saw a man open his front door and look out to see these Mosquitoes flashing past. We saw the door slam in a flash of whipping past. Suddenly, the weather began to deteriorate and this had not been forecast. I think everybody was assuming that we'd soon fly out of it but it got worse and we were over mountains. We now began to fly right into clouds. Flying in formation in cloud and knowing you're right in the centre of Germany gives you a rather lonely feeling. Blessing put on his navigation

Flying Officer A.B. 'Smokey Joe' Stovel RCAF of 139 Squadron gets a light from his navigator, Sergeant W.A. Nutter, before setting off in Mosquito B.IV DZ593/K on 27 May 1943 to bomb the Schott Glass Works at Jena, along with five other Mosquitoes. A few miles further on, eight Mosquitoes of 105 Squadron bombed the Zeiss Optical factory. Stovel made it back and landed at 23.40 hrs. (Via Peter Pereira)

lights to try and enable us to keep formation. Everybody put on navigation lights. I was very nervous flying on instruments in cloud and although I did my best to keep the next aircraft in view, I lost him.[95]

H.C. 'Gary' Herbert in the 105 Squadron formation adds:[96]

A bit further on another 139 kite [B-Beer flown by Reynolds and Flying Officer Ted Sismore] feathered his port airscrew [after it took a hit and part of the aircrew entered the cockpit, injuring Reynolds in the left hand and knee] and turned back. He got home OK. Just before we turned to make the last run up the valley to the target the clouds came right down to the deck and the formation had to break up. When the clouds broke I found the formation OK but three other kites were gone.[97] So six kites out of the formation went on to attack.

Visibility was extremely bad and as we approached the target at nought feet we suddenly saw balloons over it. Then the fiercest cross fire of light flak I have ever seen opened up. I was last in the formation by this time. Free to go in how I liked I broke away and climbed up the mountain at the side of the town hoping to fox the gunners and dodge the balloons, which I expected would be spread across the valley. I didn't do either. As we went up the mountain they poured light flak down at us and we dived down the other side. The only thing to do was to weave straight in dodging the flak and praying not to hit a cable. We did that and as we screamed down the flak poured past us and splattered all over the town. They put a light flak barrage over the target hoping we would rim into it but somehow we dodged it and put our bombs fairly in the glass grinding section – a sixteen-storey building. We were hit in several places on the way out.

The heavy cross fire they put up over the glass grinding building (my target) was not directed at us but obviously to deter us from going through it. They don't know how close they were to succeeding! I was absolutely terrified and did not think anybody could get through that and survive and 'was' sorely tempted to turn away and bomb and alternative target. The only thing that made me go through was the thought that I couldn't face men like Hughie Edwards, Roy Ralston, Reg Reynolds and say, 'I lost my guts and turned away'. I now know that heroes are really cowards whose conscience would not let them hold their heads high in the presence of real brave men. Subsequent reports confirmed that I was not the only one who was tempted to turn away.[98] However, we managed to get away OK and only ran into one lot of flak on the homeward journey. We dodged it OK. When we got back we found that our hydraulics were out of action and had to put our wheels and flaps dawn by hand. The throttles wouldn't close and I had to cut the switches to get in. Made it OK. Two other kites crashed when they got back and both crews were killed.[99] Another kite was missing, making five crews lost – our heaviest loss. It was certainly my stickiest operation and everybody else reckoned it was the stickiest too. There were so many aircraft pranged on the flarepath when we got back that we were ordered to go to an alternative aerodrome – Swanton Morley I think. We came back by car, which took many hours in the blackout. By that time all the Bigwigs from Headquarters who were there to decide whether we should continue as a Low Level squadron or be switched to PFF work had left.

On 4 June the Mosquito crews learned of a change in their role. They would do no more daylight ops. Instead the two squadrons joined Fighter Command and they were the first Mosquito units to join the specialist Pathfinder Force (later No.8 (PFF) Group). This had been formed from 3 Group using volunteer crews on August 1942, under the direction of Group Captain D.C.T. 'Don' Bennett, and was headquartered at Wyton. On 13 January 1943 the PFF became 8 (PFF) Group and 'Don' Bennett was promoted to Air Commodore (later Air Vice-Marshal) to command it. The tough-talking Australian ex-Imperial Airways and Atlantic Ferry pilot wanted Mosquitoes for PFF and target-marking duties. In 8 Group 105 Squadron became the second *Oboe* squadron. On 4 July 139 Squadron left Marham for Wyton to begin a new career in 8 Group as high-level 'nuisance' raiders, flying B.IX Mosquitoes. They would also be required to go in with the early markers and carry out diversionary attacks, acting as bait for the enemy fighters to keep them at bay during the main *Oboe* raids. At Wyton 139 Squadron swapped places with 109 Squadron,[100] commanded by Wing Commander 'Hal' E. Bufton DFC AFC, who transferred their 18 Mosquito IVs and six IXs to Marham, which now became home to the PFF *Oboe*-equipped Mosquito marking force.

4

'MUSICAL MOSQUITOES'

Oboe was the code name for a high-level blind bombing aid, which took its name from a radar-type pulse, and sounded rather like the musical instrument. (All non-*Oboe*-equipped squadrons in 8 Group were termed 'non-musical'!) Mainly because of this device, Bennett's force was able to conduct 'eine kleine nacht musik' almost every night over Germany. Pulses were transmitted by Type 9000 ground stations at Hawkshill Down (Walmer), Kent, Trimingham near Cromer and Winterton (both in Norfolk), Sennen and Treenin (Cornwall), Worthy Matravers and Tilly Whim (Swanage), Beachy Head and Cleadon (Newcastle). A high-flying *Oboe*-equipped aircraft up to 280 miles distant could receive them. The 'cat' station sent the pilot and navigator a steady sequence of signals describing an arc passing through the target, with dots to port and dashes to starboard. If inside the correct line, dots were heard; if outside the line, dashes. A steady note indicated that the aircraft was on track. The 'mouse' station indicated distance from target, and was monitored by the navigator only. Flying the beam made considerable demands on the *Oboe* pilot, who for fifteen to twenty minutes had to maintain constant airspeed, altitude and rate of change of heading. The navigator monitored the aircraft's position along the arc, and only he received the release signal, from the 'mouse' station, when the aircraft reached the computed bomb-release point. Ten minutes away he received in Morse, four 'A's; four 'B's at eight minutes; four 'C's at six minutes and four 'D's at approximately four minutes. The bomb doors were then opened. Next was heard the release signal, which consisted of five dots and a two-and-a-half second dash, at the end of which the navigator released the markers or bombs. The jettison bars were operated and the bomb doors closed. As the pilot could not hear the 'mouse' signals, the navigator indicated to him the stage reached by tracing with his finger on the windscreen in front of him, the 'A's, 'B's and 'C's etc. When the release signal came through, the navigator held his hand in front of the pilot's face. Permitted limits were strict – up to 200 yards off aiming point and crews were expected to be at the target within a four-minute time span, from two minutes early to two minutes late. Sixty seconds off-time on release point were acceptable. Failure to meet these criteria and the crew were off the squadron! *Oboe* was to

DZ379/H was shot down by a night fighter on 17 August 1943, while flying with 139 Squadron on a diversionary sortie to Berlin for the Peenemünde raid. Flying Officer A.S. Cook (an American pilot from Wichita Falls, Texas) and his navigator, Sergeant D.A.H. Dixon, were killed. (Shuttleworth Collection)

become the most accurate form of blind bombing used in the Second World War and, in practice, an average error of only 30 seconds was achieved.[101]

Six Mosquitoes of 109 Squadron flew the squadron's first operation from Marham on the night of 8–9 July 1943, when the Main Force attacked Cologne for the third time in a week. Flight Lieutenant Stevens and Squadron Leader J.F.C. Gallacher DFC acted as primary marker. The *Oboe* sky-marking was accurate and over 280 Lancasters of 1 and 5 Groups devastated the north-western and south-western sections of the city. Over 500 people were killed and 48,000 more were bombed out, bringing the total number of displaced inhabitants that week to 350,000. On the night of 9–10 July 105 Squadron flew their first *Oboe* operation when Squadron Leader Bill Blessing and his observer, Flying Officer G.K. Muirhead, and Flying Officer William E.G. 'Bill' Humphrey and his observer, Flight Sergeant E. Moore, went to Gelsenkirchen. Both crews had spent a month of training at Wyton. Twelve other 'Musical Mosquitoes' were flown on the Gelsenkirchen operation by 109 Squadron crews. The raid by over 400 Lancasters and Halifaxes was not successful. The *Oboe* equipment failed to operate in five of the Mosquitoes and a sixth Mosquito dropped sky-markers in error 10 miles to the north of the target. On the night of 13–14 July 105 Squadron operated Mosquito IXs for the first time, when two *Oboe* Mosquitoes carried out a diversion for the main attack on Aachen by dropping Green TIs and a 500-pounder apiece over Cologne. Eleven other *Oboe* Mosquitoes went to Cologne ahead of the Main Force. Eight of the 'Musical Mosquitoes', marked with Red TIs, and three others dropped their mixed bomb loads of three 500-pounders and one 250lb bomb. Mosquito IXs could carry six 500lb bombs, including one under each wing, although for long-range operations these were frequently used to carry additional wing tanks.

Meanwhile, the training of *Oboe* marker crews continued at Marham, where 1655 Mosquito Training Unit was tasked with instructing the specialist Pathfinder Force. All pilots had to complete a laid-down syllabus of thirty hours' flying – ten in the Dual Flight and twenty in the Bomber Flight, the latter complete with navigator. No pilot was allowed to touch the controls of a Mosquito until he had 1,000 hours as First Pilot under his belt and had been selected to fly Mosquitoes. Flight Lieutenant Jack Richard 'Benny' Goodman,[102] who converted to the Mosquito at 1655 MTU at Marham after flying a first tour on heavy bombers, recalls:

The best *Oboe* crews could place a bomb within a few yards of the aiming point from 28,000ft. However, since they had to fly straight and level for several minutes in the final run to the target they were vulnerable to flak and fighters. Moreover, they could only approach a given target from two directions – in the ease of Ruhr targets, almost due north or south – the Germans quickly realized this and set up searchlight cones over the aiming point which they plastered with heavy flak. Another little trick was to position Ju 88s near the searchlight cones, at a higher level than the Mosquitoes. Thus, when coned, a Mosquito might first he blasted with heavy flak and then the barrage could suddenly cease. If the pilot wasn't in a position to react instantly, the next happening would he a highly unpleasant squirt of cannon fire from the night-fighter. The average time for a trip to the Ruhr was 2½ hours, while a run to Berlin took about 4½ hours. To carry out such sorties in a Wellington had taken something like 5½ hours and 8 hours respectively. For this reason alone, Mosquitoes were greatly to he preferred to Wellingtons – it is better to be shot at for a short time than for a long time!

Flight Sergeant Edwin R. Perry, who had been posted to 1655 MTU in April and who teamed up with Flight Sergeant V.J.C. 'Ginger' Myles, his observer, recalls:

Another 17 joined us to make up ten crews who were to be taught to fly the Mark IV Mosquito. When we joined 1655 initially it was to continue Low Level flying over the East Anglian countryside, initially using the Oxford. We were then formed into crews, (Ginger and I stayed together for the rest of our 8 Group experiences) and commenced a programme of Low Level cross country exercises in the Mosquito flying at around 250 knots. Low level practice bombing also featured on the Whittlesey range near Peterborough. After the change in emphasis in training we concentrated on night flying which, with so many airfields in the country each with its own red two letter identification beacon within a few miles, was in many cases easier for the navigator to monitor his position than with day – navigation. There were also white aerial lighthouses of fixed position enabling accurate bearings to be made of these with a hand bearing astro compass. The aircraft was also being equipped with Gee, a piece of radar equipment which measured the distances from a master and two slave stations to give a very accurate position, but then limited in range up to 4° east longitude. Gee took up less room than the 1154/5 and was easier for the observer to use but had the disadvantage that the positions on the Gee grid map had to be transferred to the Mercators projection used for navigation. It was also known that VHF voice radio could be heard for long distances, up to 200 or more miles, and there was therefore no loss in establishing position on approach home when high altitude flying without MFDF or HFDF Morse code facilities.

After three weeks 1655 was detached to Finmere where we were the only unit. However we later flew back to Marham to complete the course, my pilot for that flight being Flying

Officer Ivor Broom DFC (later Air Marshal Sir Ivor) who had made quite a name for himself in Malta. Normally his observer was an amiable Warrant Officer named Tommy Broom and it was claimed when they went on operations they went on a 'sweep'. Tommy really enjoyed his beer and raw onions, which was the normal supper in the Marham Sergeants Mess. He 'strained' the beer through a magnificent moustache but after one splendid drinking session. Tom went to bed and on awaking found some rogue (never identified) had removed one side while Tommy blissfully slumbered on. A side effect was that nobody recognised him when he turned up at the 'Flights' next morning! 1655 was a happy unit. When at Marham our free time was spent in Kings Lynn, where the Duke of York was a favoured hostelry or we might go up the coast to Hunstanton or Sandringham. And so, at the end of 22.5 months service and 315.5 hours flying (50.45 at night), I was considered to be suitably trained for operational duties as an observer in Bomber Command Mosquitoes of PFF's Light Night Striking Force. Victor Miles and I were posted to 139 (Jamaica) Squadron on 17 July 1943 and we stayed there until 16 December 1943 at the very comfortable pre-war Sir Edwin Lutyens-designed station, Wyton.

Mosquito training and operational flying at Marham was interspersed with several accidents. On the afternoon of 15 July four Mosquitoes flew on ASR duty over the North Sea, searching in vain for a missing aircraft for three hours. On 18 July a Norwegian crew of Captain Stene and Lieutenant Lochen were killed when their Mosquito crashed near Cranfield during a cross-country navigation exercise. On 24 July another Mosquito was written-off in a night-landing accident. The next day Pilot Officer C. Prentice RNZAF and observer Pilot Officer J.L. Warner were injured when their Mosquito crashed on approach to Marham. The following day a 105 Squadron Mosquito suffered an undercarriage retraction on the ground at Foulsham. On the 26th, during a night-flying test, Flying Officer Bill Humphrey and Flight Sergeant E. Moore of 105 Squadron experienced an engine failure on take-off and the Mosquito crashed at Fincham.

On the night of 24–25 July the Battle of Hamburg began, and was to last until 3 August 1943. The city was beyond *Oboe* range so the Mosquitoes flew diversionary and nuisance raids to Bremen, Kiel, Lübeck and Duisburg. 'Window', which was dropped for the first time, helped keep bomber losses to a minimum. Just twelve aircraft – 1.5 per cent of the force – failed to return. Essen, which was the target for over 700 aircraft on the night of 25–26 July, was not beyond the range of *Oboe*, and so seven *Oboe* Mosquitoes of 109 Squadron and four of 105 Squadron successfully marked the target for the Main Force. Twenty-six aircraft were lost but the raid was a success, with much damage to Essen's industrial areas in the eastern half of the city. Hamburg was bombed again on 27–28 July by over 780 aircraft, and the PFF marking was carried out by H2S. This was the night of the firestorm, which killed approximately 40,000 people. Following the raid about 1,200,000 people – two thirds of Hamburg's population – fled the city in fear of further raids. By 6 August, the battle ended and 75 per cent of the city had been laid to waste. On the night of 30–31 July three of 105 Squadron's Mosquito IXs and six of 109 Squadron, each carrying four red TIs, departed Marham to mark Remscheid on the southern edge of the Ruhr, which was the target for over 270 aircraft. Flying Officer Kenneth Wolstenholme with Squadron Leader J.F.C. Gallacher DFC flew one of the 105 Squadron Mosquitoes.[103] The *Oboe* ground-marking and the bombing by the comparatively small Main Force were exceptionally accurate, and 83 per cent of the town was destroyed. This brought the Battle of the Ruhr to an end after 18,506 sorties, in which 58,000 tons of bombs had been dropped for a loss of 872 aircraft. By the end of the month Marham Mosquito crews had flown thirty-two Mk IX sorties.

August 1943 proved a relatively quiet month for the Marham Mosquitoes, which operated a mix of target-marking and bombing operations on just four nights, while Bomber Command concentrated its main efforts on Italian targets at Milan, Genoa and Turin. On 22–23 August, when the I.G. Farben factory at Leverkusen was the target for the Main Force, Marham dispatched thirteen Mosquitoes. One of the six 105 Squadron Mosquitoes had a 'technical failure' and was unable to bomb, so Flying Officer Ken Wolstenholme took over and marked. Each Mosquito dropped two Long Burn Red TIs and two red TIs, but *Oboe* was not operating as well as it should, and the Main Force bombing was directed against at least twelve other towns in and near the Ruhr instead. The I.G. Farben factory received only minor damage from the few bombs that did hit Leverkusen. At Brauweiler, the other 'Musical Mosquitoes' of 105 Squadron also had problems marking with *Oboe* and two Mosquitoes returned early with engine trouble. The four other Mosquitoes unleashed their 2,000lb bomb loads visually.

For the following night, 23–24 August, when over 720 aircraft visited Berlin, Marham again provided the *Oboe* markers so necessary for the Main Force to do their work. Three of 105 Squadron's Mosquitoes and five from 109 Squadron were to mark the bombers' route by dropping Red LB TIs between the Dutch towns of Westerbork and Zweeloo, and Green TIs just over the German border at Georgsdorf, 270 miles west of Berlin, to keep the heavies. Despite reservations in some quarters, who feared it might alert enemy night fighters, the object was to keep the bombers away from known flak areas and to achieve a heavy concentration of bombs at the target. Ken Wolstenholme and his observer, Squadron Leader Gallacher, were forced to abort after take-off when a flock of birds smashed into their Mosquito, but the other Mosquitoes carried out their marking duties. The Main Force attack was partially successful but fifty-seven bombers were shot down by a combination of night fighters and flak. A few nights later, on the 29–30th, four *Oboe* Mosquitoes visited Cologne. Meanwhile, Lieutenant 'Bud' Fisher DFC USAAF and Flight Lieutenant Robert W. 'Bob' Bray DFC, in *J-Jig*, and three other 105 Squadron Mosquitoes marked Duisburg. On 30–31 August 600 aircraft of the Main Force attacked Mönchengladbach and the neighbouring town of Rheydt. With marking by twelve *Oboe* Mosquitoes, four of 105 Squadron, led by new CO Wing Commander Henry John 'Butch' Cundall AFC[104] with Squadron Leader A.C. Douglas DFC, and eight of 109 Squadron were described as 'excellent'. In particular Cundall and Douglas had only a 40-yard error.

On the night of 31 August–1 September over 620 bombers visited the Big City again. Three Mosquitoes of 105 Squadron and six of 109 Squadron route-marked for the heavies by dropping red TIs near Damvillers, in north-east France, and Green TIs near Luxembourg. Bombing was carried out using H2S equipment and TIs but the latter were

Flying Officer F.M. 'Bud' Fisher DFC, an American pilot from Pennsylvania, in front of his Mosquito, DK337 GB-N *Uncle Sam*. On 22–23 September 1943 Fisher and his navigator, Flight Sergeant Les Hogan DFM, were one of twelve *Oboe* Mosquitoes that visited Emden as a diversion for the Main Force attacking Hanover. They crashed while flying Mk.IX LR506/E 1 mile north-west of RAF West Raynham and both men were killed. (RAF)

dropped to the south of Berlin while the main bombing was up to 30 miles away and was unsuccessful. The enemy used 'fighter flares' to decoy the bombers away from the target and about two-thirds of the forty-seven aircraft lost were shot down over Berlin by night fighters. In a separate operation thirty OTU Wellingtons, six *Oboe* Mosquitoes and five Halifaxes of the Pathfinders bombed an ammunition dump in the Forêt de Hesdin in northern France. All of Marham's Mosquitoes returned safely from the night's operations. During early September the *Oboe* Mosquitoes marked more 'special targets'. On the night of 2–3 September thirty OTU Wellingtons, six *Oboe* Mosquitoes and five Lancasters of the Pathfinders were dispatched to ammunition dumps in the Forêt de Mormal, near Englefontaine in France, about 40km south-east of Valenciennes. Flying Officer Don C. Dixon, an Australian from Brisbane, and Flight Lieutenant Tommy W. Horton DFC of 105 Squadron, carrying two red LB TIs and two red TIs, and four 109 Squadron Mosquitoes marked successfully. Crews dropped their TIs from 26,000ft, for the heavies' bombs fell squarely on the dumps. The following evening six *Oboe* Mosquitoes carried out a similar operation in the Forêt de Raismes, 10km north-west of Valenciennes, for thirty OTU Wellingtons and six Halifaxes. Flight Lieutenant Tommy W. Horton DFC and Lieutenant 'Bud' Fisher of 105 Squadron and the four Mosquitoes of 109 Squadron again marked with two red LB TIs and two red TIs. On 8–9 September when 257 bombers, including five American B-17 Flying Fortresses, attacked the German long-range gun batteries near Boulogne, the *Oboe* Mosquitoes marked the target with green LB TIs and red TIs. The marking and bombing was poor and the gun batteries were largely untouched. Knowing that the Mk.I version of *Oboe* would soon be jammed, trials began with *Oboe* Mk.II (codenamed 'Penwiper') on 11 September by Wing Commander H.J. 'Butch' Cundall AFC with Flight Lieutenant C.F. Westerman in attacks on Aachen. (Aachen was the target for *Oboe* II trials again on 3 and 7 October).

On 22–23 September twelve *Oboe* Mosquitoes visited Emden as a diversion for the Main Force attacking Hanover. Most of the Mosquitoes bombed on DR after the *Oboe* system failed. On 23–24 September the *Oboe* Mosquitoes were dispatched to Aachen as the Main Force went to Mannheim. Two of 105 Squadron's Mosquitoes route-marked at a point near Simmerath, near the Belgian-German border, for six more Mosquitoes that successfully bombed the town. On 29–30 September four *Oboe* crews dropped 500lb and 250lb bombs on Gelsenkirchen and nine *Oboe* Mosquitoes set out to mark Bochum with red TIs for 352 heavies. Many bombs fell accurately in the old part of the town. The Mosquito flown by Lieutenant 'Bud' Fisher DFC and Flight Sergeant Leslie Hogan DFM crashed 1 mile north-west of RAF West Raynham, killing both crew members. Bad weather while returning from Gelsenkirchen forced Squadron Leader Peter Channer DFC and Warrant Officer Kenneth Gordon to land at RAF Coltishall.

In October the *Oboe* Mosquitoes flew operationally on twelve nights during the month, 109 Squadron flying 101 sorties and 105 Squadron flying seventy-six. On 1–2 October a steelworks at Witten, north-west of Hagen, was ground-marked with red TIs by twelve *Oboe* Mosquitoes for training purposes. Eight of the Mosquitoes bombed at Witten and two, whose *Oboe* system failed, dropped their bombs on the fires at Hagen created earlier by 240 Lancasters and eight Mosquitoes of 1, 5 and 8 Groups. On 3–4 October twelve *Oboe* Mosquitoes attacked the Goldenbergwerke power station and Knapsack power station near Cologne, and four others carried out Mk.II *Oboe* trials to Aachen. Knapsack was attacked again on 4–5 and 20–21 October, and again on the 22nd when twelve Mosquitoes of 105 and 109 Squadrons set out in the early evening. Flight Lieutenant Gordon Sweeney DFC and Flight Lieutenant William George Wood of 105 Squadron failed to return. On 24–25 October raids were made on Rheinhausen and Büderich, and on 31 October Oberhausen was bombed.

On the night of 3–4 November twelve *Oboe* Mosquitoes ground-marked Düsseldorf for 589 heavies, and thirteen other *Oboe* Mosquitoes (each carrying three 500lb MC and a 250lb GP bombs) set out to attack the Krupps factory at Rheinhausen. Twelve Mosquitoes bombed successfully while the unlucky 13th aircraft returned with two 500-pounders hung up in the bomb bay. On nights when the Main Force was not operating the *Oboe* Mosquitoes were dispatched to keep the enemy defences alert. On 4–5 November twenty-four Mosquitoes attacked a chemical works at Leverkusen and four Mosquitoes visited Aachen again, all returning without loss. On 5–6 November twenty-six Mosquitoes carried out small-scale raids on Bochum, Dortmund, Düsseldorf, Hamburg and Hanover. Flight Lieutenant John 'Flash' Gordon DFC and Flying Officer Ralph Gamble Hayes DFM were returning over Norfolk in a 105 Squadron Mosquito. They tried to land at Hardwick, an American Liberator base, when at 21.10 hours, they crashed into a field at Road Green Farm, Hempnall, about 10 miles south of Norwich. Both men were killed.

With no major raids planned for the Main Force the *Oboe* Mosquitoes spent most of November dropping their bomb loads of six 500lb MC bombs on Dortmund, Bochum,

Flying Officer Ralph Gamble Hayes DFM (left), navigator, and (right) his pilot, Flight Lieutenant John 'Flash' Gordon DFC, of 105 Squadron, who were killed on the night of 5–6 November 1943 over Norfolk. They tried to land at Hardwick, an American Liberator base, when at 21.10 hours they crashed into a field at Road Green Farm, Hempnall, about 10 miles south of Norwich. (RAF Marham)

Essen, Duisburg, Krefeld and Düsseldorf, and using DR when *Oboe* failed. The operation to Essen on the night of 7–8 November was typical of the non-Main Force nights, apart from thirty-five aircraft mine-laying off the French coast and a handful of OTU sorties; the only Bomber Command aircraft that were airborne were six *Oboe* Mosquitoes from Marham. The *Oboe* equipment failed because one of the ground stations was not in operation and the Mosquitoes were sent a recall signal. Two of the *Oboe* aircraft received the signal and returned but the other four continued to the target and dropped their 24,500lb MC bombs from 32,000–35,000ft on a DR run from the last Gee fix. Two of these Mosquitoes returned home on one engine and one of them put down at RAF Coltishall.

On the night of 9–10 November eighteen *Oboe* Mosquitoes attacked blast furnaces at Bochum and a steelworks at Duisburg. The Mosquito flown by Pilot Officer R.E. Leigh and Pilot Officer J. Henderson of 109 Squadron was hit by flak at the target and they crash-landed at Wyton on return. As the Mosquito touched down the tail assembly broke away from the fuselage but both men escaped uninjured. On 11–12 November Cannes was the target of the Main Force while twenty-nine Mosquitoes raided Berlin, Hanover and the Ruhr. Marham dispatched twelve *Oboe* Mosquitoes to Düsseldorf. One of the four Mosquitoes of 105 Squadron, each carrying four 500lb MC bombs, was flown by Pilot Officer Angus Caesar-Gordon DFM and his second tour navigator, Flying Officer R.A. 'Dick' Strachan, who were on their first Mosquito operation. Strachan recalled:[105]

The flak started about four or five minutes before the target and immediately it was apparent that it was intense and extremely accurate. *Oboe* entailed the pilot flying dead straight and level for ten minutes on the attack run. Suddenly a tremendous flash lit up the sky about 50 yards ahead of our nose and exactly at our altitude. Within a tenth of a second we were through the cloud of dirty yellowish-brown smoke and into the blackness beyond. I shall never forget the spontaneous reaction of both my pilot and myself. We turned our heads slowly and looked long and deep into one another's eyes – no word was spoken – no words were needed. Despite continued heavy flak, we completed our attack run and dropped our bomb-load on the release signal, within a quarter of a mile of the aiming point and, with luck, some damage to a German factory. Turning for home and mighty glad to be out of the flak, I glanced out of the window at the starboard engine and immediately noticed a shower of sparks coming from the starboard engine cowling. A quick glance at the oil temperature gauge showed that it was going off the clock. Only one thing for it and the pilot pressed the extinguisher button and then feathered the engine. The sparking ceased but we now had 300 miles to go and only one engine to do it on. I remember thinking this wasn't much of a do for our first operation. But at least we had a good deal of altitude and still had a fair amount of speed, even with just one engine. The danger was interception by a German night fighter and I spent a lot of time craning my neck around to check the skies about our tail. The other thing I remember was a terrible consciousness of our own weight, sitting as I was on the starboard side. However this feeling wore off and the remainder of the flight home to base was uneventful. Then came the strain of a night landing on one engine…again that awful awareness of how heavy I was…but after one anti-clockwise circuit, a superb approach and magnificent landing. I recall the great feeling of relief as the wheels touched the runway. I also remember the urgent desire to get my hands round a jug of beer to relieve the dryness in my throat and to celebrate a safe return from what was to prove my worst experience on Mosquitoes. Needless to say, the beer was not long in forthcoming.

On 12–13 November seven Mosquitoes attacked Düsseldorf, Essen and Krefeld, and the following night eight *Oboe* Mosquitoes attacked the blast furnaces at Bochum again. Both raids were flown without loss. On the night of 15–16 November ten *Oboe* Mosquitoes attacked the Rheinmetall Borsig AG ironworks at Düsseldorf, while two others bombed Bonn. The Mosquito flown by Flight Lieutenant J.R. Hampson and Pilot Officer H.W.E. Hammond DFC RCAF was shot down. Both men survived and they were later sent to Stalag Luft III. A flak shell exploded a few feet under Flight Lieutenant Humphrey's Mosquito and turned the aircraft upside down, and Humphrey was hit in the foot and leg. The Mosquito went into a spin but the crew managed to make it home and Humphrey landed at Hardwick whereupon one of his engines stopped.

On 17–18 November eighty-three heavies attacked Ludwigshafen. Twenty-one Mosquitoes visited Berlin, Bonn and the August Thyssen AG foundry in Duisburg and the semi-finished products of the Bochumer Verein in Bochum. None of the Mosquitoes was lost. On the night of 18–19 November the Main Battle of Berlin began with a raid on the Big City by 440 Lancasters, while another bomber force visited Mannheim and Ludwigshafen. Ten Mosquitoes went to Essen and six each went to Aachen and Frankfurt. While returning from Aachen Flight Lieutenant R.B. Castle and Pilot Officer J. Griffiths, in a 105 Squadron Mosquito, overshot the landing area at Marham and crashed at 23.31 hours. They were not seriously injured but the Mosquito was a write-off. On the next raid on the IG Farbenindustrie AG chemical works at Leverkusen, on 19–20 November, failure of equipment prevented most of the *Oboe* marking being carried out and the bad weather prevented other PFF aircraft from marking the target properly. As a result bombing was widely scattered and twenty-seven towns were bombed, mostly well to the north. On 22–23 November, when the Main Force raided Berlin, twelve *Oboe* Mosquitoes set out for Leverkusen again. Berlin was once more the target for the Main Force attack on 23–24 November, when six *Oboe* Mosquitoes again braved the flak and searchlight defences protecting the Goldenbergwerke power station at Knapsack, near Cologne. Pilot Officer Eric Wade BEM and his observer, Pilot Officer Alfred Gerald Fleet, died when their Mosquito crashed at 19.50 hours, 5 miles north-west of Swaffham at Contract Farm, Narborough. Throughout the rest of November the *Oboe* squadrons bombed familiar targets such as the Krupps foundry at Essen, the Rheinmetall Borsig AG ironworks at Düsseldorf and the steel producers Vereinigte Stahlwerke AG at Bochum.

On 3 December the Marshal of the Royal Air Force, Lord Trenchard, made a lunchtime visit to Marham and he congratulated the squadron on the excellent work they had done leading the Main Force in the Battle of the Ruhr. He also praised their current role of precision attacks on special targets. The *Oboe* Mosquitoes were operational on fifteen nights during December, with return visits to targets such as Hamborn, Leverkusen, Krefeld, Düsseldorf Liege, Aachen and Bochum. Usually the operations were flown without loss but there were early losses. On the night of 2–3 December Flying Officer L.F. Bickley and Flying Officer J.H. Jackson of 109 Squadron failed to return from a raid by six *Oboe* Mosquitoes on Bochum. Both men evaded. Then, on the night of the 12–13th, Pilot Officer Benjamin Frank Reynolds and Pilot Officer John Douglas Phillips of 105 Squadron were killed when they crashed at Herwijnen in Holland on the north bank of the Waal River. They had probably been hit by flak towards the end of the attack on the Krupps works at Essen. On the night of the 16–17th, when Berlin was the main target for the heavies, thirty-five Stirlings and Lancasters and twelve *Oboe* Mosquitoes were dispatched to bomb two V-1 flying bomb sites at Tilley-le-Haut, near Abbeville in Northern France, and in a wood at Flixecourt.[106] Neither raid was successful. The attack on Tilley-le-Haut by twenty-six Stirlings failed because the six *Oboe* Mosquito markers of 105 and 109 Squadrons could not get their green and yellow TIs closer than 450 yards from the tiny target. At Flixecourt the nine Lancasters of 617 Dam Busters Squadron dropped their 12,000lb Tallboy bombs accurately on the Green TIs and LB TIs placed by Squadron Leader Bill Blessing and Wing Commander F.A. Green DFC. However the markers were 350 yards from the V-1 site and none of the Lancasters' bombs were more than 100 yards from the markers.[107] Five more raids on V-bomb construction sites were flown during the rest of the month, two each on 22–23 and 30–31 and one on the night of 29–30 December, yet only one site was bombed accurately.

Crew discipline and navigational accuracy were put to the test on the night of 23–24 December, when twelve *Oboe* Mosquitoes were sent to raid Aachen and then to carry on to a second site to route-mark Berlin for 379 heavies heading for the Big City. Sixteen Lancasters were lost and the losses would have been higher had it not been for the cloud covering the Berlin area, which grounded many German night fighters, and the diversion raid at

Leipzig by seven Mosquitoes. There were no bombing raids on Christmas Eve, and only a few Mosquitoes were airborne on 28–29 December when operations resumed again after a period of bad weather. A raid by over 700 aircraft on Berlin took place on the night of 29–30 December, with small numbers of Mosquitoes being sent to a number of targets in Germany and France without loss. This was followed on 30–31 December by the last raid of the year, when twenty-one *Oboe* Mosquitoes were dispatched to targets in Cologne, Duisburg and the Vereinigte Stahlwerke AG steelworks at Bochum again. A further attempt was also made to mark a V-1 flying bomb site at Cherbourg that had been missed on an earlier raid. Unfortunately, the markers were placed 200 yards from the target. All the bombs dropped by the ten Lancasters of 617 Squadron, though well grouped, missed the site completely, as did four 500-pounders dropped through 3/10th low cloud by Flying Officer Bill Humphrey and his observer Pilot Officer L.C. Poll of 105 Squadron.

In January 1944 the *Oboe* Mosquitoes were operational on nineteen nights, with 105 and 109 Squadrons flying sorties on eleven nights during the period up to the 14–15th. It was much the same routine as in 1943, with area marking and attacks on industrial targets such as the Ruhrstahl AG steel works at Witten, J.A. Henckels Zwillingwerke AG at Solingen, the Krupp AG works at Essen, the Verstahlwerke at Duisburg and the Deutsche Edalstahlwerke AG at Krefeld. The Krupp Stahl AG works at Rheinhausen, the Rheinmetall Borsig AG ironworks at Düsseldorf and the Mannesmannröhrenwerke AG iron and steel tube plant at Untererthal were also bombed, as were the Gutehoffnungshütte AG foundry at Obershausen and the Chemische Werke industrial chemicals plant at Hüls. No less than twenty-one V-1 rocket-sites were also visited by the *Oboe* Mosquitoes during January. Losses at night remained at a thankfully relatively low rate. Returning from a raid on Duisburg by five Mosquitoes on the night of 7–8 January, a 109 Squadron Mosquito flown by Flying officer C.R.G. Grant RAAF and Flying Officer K.F. Hynes hit a tree returning to Marham and crash-landed at Narborough. Grant scrambled to safety but a crane was needed to move wreckage to allow Hynes to be freed. On the night of the 13–14th Flying Officer P.Y. Stead DFC and Warrant Officer A.H. Flett DFM of 109 Squadron were shot down at 26,000ft by Oberleutnant Dietrich Schmidt of III./NJG1, flying a Bf 110. Flett was killed but Stead survived and was taken prisoner.[108] Squadron Leader J. Comer and his observer, Pilot Officer P. Jenkins DFM, of 105 Squadron were just setting out for Düsseldorf on the night of 20–21 January, when at 20.43 hours their Mosquito became uncontrollable and they baled out over Norfolk. The aircraft crashed 3 miles east of Kings Lynn at Waveland Farm, Grimston. Returning home from their target on the night of 23 January Flight Lieutenant Kenneth Wolstenholme and Pilot Officer V.P. Piper crash-landed at RAF Manston after their Mosquito lost elevator control.

By way of a change, on the night of 25–26 January fourteen Mosquitoes of 105 Squadron were dispatched to bomb the Nazi HQ at Aachen, while 109 Squadron attacked four V-1 sites in northern France. Eleven of the *Oboe* Mosquitoes of 105 Squadron identified the target at Aachen and, amid light and accurate flak, forty 500lb bombs were released through cloud. A number of hits were scored. Two days later the *Oboe* Mosquitoes returned to Aachen and dropped 'spoof' green TI route markers just north of the town without loss, although Flight Lieutenant J.W. Jordan landed at RAF Manston with an overheating starboard engine. On the night of 28–29 January, while 677 aircraft headed for Berlin, twenty-three *Oboe* Mosquitoes took off from Marham to bomb German night fighter airfields in Holland. Six Mosquitoes of 109 Squadron were sent to attack Leeuwarden and four more to raid Deelen, while 105 Squadron dispatched five to Gilze-Rijen. Six more went to Venlo and two visited Deelen.

On the night of 30–31 January twenty-two *Oboe* Mosquitoes attacked the G&I Jager GmbH ball-bearing factory at Elberfeld, while over 530 aircraft visited Berlin again. Warrant Officer I.B. McPherson's Mosquito received several flak hits in the port engine and Flight Lieutenant A.W. Raybould had the nose of his Mosquito shattered, but all aircraft returned safely. In February the ball-bearing factory at Elberfeld was attacked on no less than eight more nights. Just before the third attack on 4–5 February by eight *Oboe* Mosquitoes, Flight Lieutenant John Fosbroke Slatter and his observer Pilot Officer Peter Oscar Hedges of 105 Squadron were killed on their NFT (Night Flying Test). During the late afternoon they were involved in a collision with a Boeing B-17G 42-97480 of the 337th Bomb Squadron, 96th Bombardment Group, from Snetterton, Norfolk. The Mosquito came down at Colne Field Farm near St Ives, Huntingdonshire. Slatter and Hedges were killed, while the Fortress landed safely with minor damage.[109]

On 9–10 February Flying Officer R.G. Leigh RNZAF and Flight Lieutenant M.R. Breed RNZAF of 109 Squadron were shot down over Holland. In the early hours of the 26th Flying Officer Taylor and Pilot Officer Mander of 1655 MTU crashed at Fincham, killing both crew. Much of February was spent bombing airfields at Gilze Rijen, Deelen, Volkel, St Trond, Twente, Venlo and Leeuwarden, all without loss, and V-1 sites in northern France. On the night of 23–24 February, when seventeen *Oboe* Mosquitoes raided Düsseldorf, the Mosquito flown by Pilot Officer L. Holiday DFM was hit in the fuselage and his observer, Flying Officer C.L. French, was wounded in the thigh. They continued to Düsseldorf nonetheless and bombed the target.

During the first five days of March, two of 109 Squadron's *Oboe* Mosquitoes acted as 'formation leaders' for bomber units of the 2nd Tactical Air Force (2nd TAF) attacking flying bomb sites in Northern France. The formation bombed as soon as it saw the bombs of the *Oboe* Mosquitoes being released. Altogether eight of these daylight operations were flown, the first being to Conches on 1 March. That same night an operation to Stuttgart by over 550 aircraft of the Main Force was supported by eighteen *Oboe* Mosquitoes, which bombed German night fighter airfields at Deelen, Volkel, Florennes, St Trond and Venlo. The operations were flown without cloud cover over Holland and only broken cloud to the west. It was on this night that 109 Squadron dispatched its first Mosquito XVI sortie, to Deelen. Deliveries of the pressurised Mosquito B.XVI, an adaptation of the Mk.IX, and powered by the more powerful two-stage, 1,680hp Merlin 77/73 engines, had began on 19 December when two of the aircraft were received by 109 Squadron. The XVI also had bulged bomb boors to permit a 4,000lb 'Cookie' bomb to be carried.[110] All the airfields were bombed except Florennes, where *Oboe* failed, and all the Mosquitoes returned safely, although a heavy snowstorm over Norfolk made landings very difficult.

Flying Officer Grenville Eaton, a 105 Squadron pilot, flew his first Mosquito operation on 1–2 March in *A-Apple*, an *Oboe*-equipped B.IV. His observer was Warrant Officer J.E. 'Jack' Fox, who had flown his first tour on bombers. Eaton recalls:

Venlo, the target, was a German fighter aerodrome on the Dutch border near Aachen. (The first few trips were usually to 'less difficult' targets but they were certainly no less important in countering the threat of fighters.) With a full load of bombs, four 500 pounders, and of petrol, it took, perhaps, one hour following carefully planned and timed legs' all over East Anglia until setting course from Orfordness to the Dutch coast. Then, at the operational height of 28,000ft, we flew towards the waiting point [where the track to the target extended backwards for a further 5 minutes] and there, at the precise appointed time [to hear the call-in signal in Morse], we switched on *Oboe*.

The navigator worked out the flight plan and calculated the time to set course in order to reach the target at the correct time. On marking sorties it was important that TIs were dropped at the correct time in order not to compromise the Main Force. Having worked out the time to set course, navigators actually did this with six minutes in hand to allow for any errors to the forecast wind and so on. Having settled into the flight and arrived at the ETA for the waiting point, crews usually had to make some sort of correction. If the full six minutes had to be lost, the pilot did a 360° orbit, and most pilots became expert in achieving this in the six minutes. Lesser times to be lost were accomplished by making a dogleg. Grenville Eaton now had to find the beam and keep on it for perhaps ten to fifteen minutes to the target:

> Thanks to Gee, Jack Fox's navigation was spot on and we had a good run to target. His signals gave him our distance to target and finally, the bomb release signal, like the BBC time signal, five pips then the sixth, a dash, to press to release the bombs. We had a clear run. Holding steady for some seconds after bomb release to photograph the bomb explosions, we turned smartly onto the planned course home, keeping our eyes skinned for fighters, flak and searchlights, around 360° above and below. A gentle, slow dive at top speed and we arrived at the Dutch coast around 20,000ft and the English coast at 12,000ft. We landed at 03.30 hours. So, Jack's 31st, and my first 'op', took 3 hours 25 minutes. A simmering feeling of incipient fear throughout had been kept in check by being fully occupied. Now, home, we felt a tremendous feeling of relief and achievement, especially when we were told at debriefing that we had achieved a 'Nil' target error on this, out first *Oboe* trip. Finally, a heavenly operational aircrew breakfast of bacon, eggs, toast, rum and coffee. Smashing!

Weather conditions improved and the next night, 2–3 March, 105 Squadron flew its first Mosquito XVI sortie when six *Oboe* Mosquitoes formed part of the raid by 117 Halifaxes of 4 and 6 Groups on the aircraft assembly factory at SNCA du Nord, at Meulan-Les Mureaux. The factory, about 15 miles north-west of Paris, originally turned out Potez aircraft for the French Air Force, and was now producing about fifteen Messerschmitt Me 108s each month, as well as components for Bf 109s and Dornier Do 24s. Wing Commander H.J. 'Butch' Cundall AFC and his navigator, Squadron Leader I.E. Tamango, flew the XVI (ML938), and they led four other Mosquito IXs of 105 and two of 109 Squadron. As usual the *Oboe* markers were to go in first and ground-mark the target with Red and Green LB TIs for the Halifaxes. Unfortunately, *Oboe* failed and Cundall relinquished primary marker duties to Flight Lieutenant E.M. Hunter with Flight Lieutenant Crabb, and Flight Lieutenant Jacobs and Flight Lieutenant Tipton of 109 Squadron, who each dropped four Red LB TIs. Two 105 Squadron Mosquitoes flown by Squadron Leader L.F. Austin DFC with Squadron Leader C.F. Westerman DFC, and Flying Officer Don C. Dixon and his navigator Flying Officer W.A. Christensen, a fellow Australian from New South Wales, failed to drop their four Green

LB TIs. The reserve aircraft flown by Flight Lieutenant Ken Wolstenholme with his observer, Flight Lieutenant V.E.R. Piper, dropped four Red LB TIs. The raid was successful and the Halifaxes caused considerable damage to the main assembly shops, the factory testing hangars and the seaplane base, while other parts of the plant were 'extremely severely damaged'.

On 5–6 March four *Oboe* Mosquitoes set out to mark Duisburg for three Mosquitoes carrying 4,000lb 'Cookies'. Squadron Leader Peter J. Channer DFC was forced to abort before the target when his *Oboe* equipment blew up, although he managed to return safely to Marham. The other Mosquitoes encountered slight but accurate flak on the run-in to the target. Flight Lieutenant C.P. Gibbons' Mosquito of 109 Squadron was hit at 30,000ft, but he was able to carry on. Flight Lieutenant G.W. Harding of 105 Squadron reported a cloud of smoke and a red flare hanging over the target. Meanwhile, plans unveiled on 4 March in preparation for the Overlord invasion, planned for that summer, had put in motion precision bombing attacks on railway networks and marshalling yards, ammunition dumps and airfields in France. Seven rail targets at Trappes, Aulnoye, Le Mans, Amiens, Courtrai, Laon and Vaires-sur-Marne were selected for all-out attacks, which began on the night of 6–7 March when Trappes was marked by *Oboe* Mosquitoes to enable 261 Halifaxes of 4 and 6 Groups to bomb. Photo reconnaissance later revealed that the engine shed had been destroyed and six wrecked locomotives were seen lying in the almost demolished building. The water tower was completely destroyed, and throughout the yards there was a heavy concentration of craters affecting tracks and all the internal lines were blocked. There was also considerable destruction and derailment of tenders and rolling stock. Seventeen direct hits on the main Paris–Chartres lines had put all but one line out of action. Attacks on Le Mans and also the road and rail junction at Aachen followed on 7–8 March. The Aachen operation was the second for Flying Officer Grenville Eaton and Warrant Officer Jack Fox, as Eaton recalls:

The target was Aachen, an important road and rail junction just inside Germany. I was feeling more confident. Crossing Holland at 28,000ft, with a clear sky, we could see the distant Zuider Zee. We switched on *Oboe*, found we were early, so guided by the navigator, I wasted a precise number of minutes and seconds until finding and settling into the beam towards the target, about 15 minutes' flying time away. We noticed we were leaving long white contrails behind us – frozen water vapour crystals in the exhaust of each engine. Suddenly streams of cannon-shells and tracers enveloped us from the rear, hitting us in numerous places, but luckily missing Jack and me and the engines. I immediately dived to port, then up to starboard several times, then resumed height and regained the beam. The only protection was a sheet of steel behind my seat. Most instruments seemed to work, so we continued. Half a minute later, a second and noisier attack from the rear, so again I took evasive action, more violent and longer, and again regained height and beam. Now there was considerable damage to dashboard, hydraulics and fuselage. Shells had missed us, truly by inches. However, engines and *Oboe* still worked, so being so near we had to continue to target, deliver the load, and turn for home, changing course and height frequently, and assessing the damage as far as we could. Certainly, hydraulics, flaps, brakes, ASI and various other instruments were smashed – but we were okay.

At Marham, landing in pitch darkness was a problem, hut for safety I landed on the grass, by feel I suppose, at about 150 knots with no brakes. We hurtled across the aerodrome, just missing two

Flying Officer W.A. Christensen (left), a navigator from New South Wales, and (right) his pilot, Flying Officer Don C. Dixon, an Australian from Brisbane. (RAF Marham)

Wing Commander Roy Ralston DSO DFM and Flight Lieutenant Syd Clayton DFC DFM. (IWM)

Wing Commander John de L. Wooldridge DFC★ DFM. (IWM)

huge armament dumps, straight on through hedges and violently into a ditch. Jack was out of the emergency exit like a flash. I could not move, could not undo the safety belt. Jack leapt back, released me and we scampered away to a safe distance in case of exploding petrol tanks, and emergency services were quickly there. Debriefing was interesting, as not only was our run 'seen' on the CRT, but our bombing error was precisely calculated and we wondered whether all operations were to be like this one! Incidentally, we never saw the attacking fighter. Our aircraft was a write-off.[111]

On 11 March HRH the Duke of Gloucester, accompanied by Air Vice-Marshal D.C.T. Bennett CB CBE DSO, AOC 8 Group, visited the station and HRH inspected the aircrew, who were presented to him by Wing Commander H.J. 'Butch' Cundall DFC AFC. On 10–11 March three Mosquitoes of 105 Squadron attacked Duisburg again. Flight Lieutenant Ken Wolstenholme's Mosquito suffered flak damage to the starboard undercarriage door and starboard flap, but he returned safely to Marham.

Much of March 1944 then was spent bombing French marshalling yards and Trappes, Le Mans and Amiens. Diversionary attacks on Dutch airfields at St Trond, Venlo and Deelen were flown in support of Main Force operations to Stuttgart on the night of 15–16 March. Many of the heavies' bombs fell in open country south-west of the city due to poor marking. Amiens marshalling yards were the main target for the *Oboe* Mosquitoes that night. Two aircraft were detailed to mark with four Red LB TIs and two 500lb MC bombs, but Flight Lieutenant Almond returned early with generator problems. Technical failures prevented both Flight Lieutenant Ken Wolstenholme and Flying Officer Holland from attacking, but Flight Lieutenant Bill Humphrey was able to make two runs, dropping two TIs each time with excellent results. There was some cloud and very thick haze over the target and, as only four sets of TIs went down at very irregular intervals, it is doubtful whether much success was achieved. Some 132 Halifaxes and Stirlings were dispatched and 105 heavies claimed to have dropped 605 tons of bombs. Little concentration of bombing was reported by the Mosquito crews which, in view of the poor marking, was not surprising, but some of the Main Force were bombing to the north-east of the target before zero hour. Numerous searchlights were in operation and many fighter flares were seen. A subsequent Bomb Command report claimed that several parts of the north-east and southern areas of the yards were badly damaged while railway workshops, storage buildings, tracks, sidings, rolling stock, a road bridge, roundhouse, engine sheds, and lines under construction were all hit severely. Two Halifaxes and a Stirling failed to return, and in Amiens eighteen French civilians were killed.

Further support operations were flown for raids on 18–19 March when Frankfurt was raided and St Trond, Volkel and Venlo were again attacked. On the 22–23rd it was the turn of Leeuwarden, Venlo, Deelen and Juliandorp, and Marham dispatched ten *Oboe* Mosquitoes. Nine of the aircraft carried six 500lb MC bombs while Squadron Leader F.R. Bird and Flight Lieutenant Norman Clayes DFC carried three 500lb MC bombs and one White TI.[112] There was 10/10ths cloud at Leeuwarden but four aircraft successfully attacked the airfield with good results. Bombs were seen to burst and the TIs were seen to cascade as markers for Fighter Command Intruders. Three Mosquitoes attacked Venlo with excellent results through small amounts of cloud, but Flight Lieutenant J.H. Ford and his observer, Flight Lieutenant L.W. Millett, had a wing-bomb hang up. They returned safely to Marham.

Squadron Leader Wills and Flight Lieutenant Castle attacked Deelen through 5/10ths cloud with excellent results. However the Mosquito flown by Flight Lieutenant Charles Frank Boxall and Flight Lieutenant T.W. 'Robby' Robinson DFC also suffered a wing-mounted bomb hung up, when the grease from the bomb release froze and the 500lb MC bomb refused to drop. Boxall was forced to return with it to Marham, where at 22.50 hours on landing back the bomb freed itself and exploded. The wing disintegrated and Boxall died in the flaming aircraft. Robinson was injured but he survived and was taken to the RAF Hospital at Ely, suffering from shock and severe burns to his left foot and minor burns on the right foot. He also had a fractured left clavicle and facial abrasions.

The *Oboe* Mosquitoes were now carrying 'Cookie' bombs on a regular basis, and the bomb was known to be notoriously unstable. Also, the bomb bay doors were prone to creep and if not fully open before the release point the bomb would take the doors with it. Not surprisingly, crews preferred Graveley's hard runway to Marham's grass airfield for 'Cookie'-carrying operations. A decision had been taken to close Marham and begin the construction of three concrete runways and bring the airfield up to the standard for heavy bombers. It was a massive undertaking that would involve eighteen months' work and a cost of £1,740,000. On 7 March, 1655 MTU departed for Warboys and two weeks later 105 Squadron began the move to Bourn in Cambridgeshire, while in early April 109 Squadron began moving to Little Staughton. While the *Oboe* squadrons famously carried on their good work, Marham was placed under the custody of the Clerk of Works, from which it would finally emerge in early 1946, long after the Second World War had finished.

5

VALIANTS AND VICTORS

In February 1946 the Development Wing of the Central Bomber Establishment arrived at Marham from RAF Feltwell. The CBE's role was to develop bomber tactics for use in the Cold War and many trials took place involving improved H2S radar, SHORAN (Short Range Navigation) system and the Lancaster Automatic Gun Laying Turret (AGLT), a radar-directed gun. Most of the flight trials for the AGLT involved Lancasters and Lincolns with cine gun film to permit detailed interpretation of the operation of the turret. The project led to the remote-controlled barbette. One of the most interesting post-war trials involved devising ways of destroying massive concrete structures. These had been begun by a detachment of three USAAF B-17G Flying Fortresses at Mildenhall in December 1945, for high-level bombing trials beginning in January 1946. The Fortresses had their armament removed and they were modified to carry 4,500lb rocket bombs or a 2,000lb bomb with a special penetration head beneath each wing. On 28 February 1946 the three B-17Gs moved to Marham to join three Boeing B-29s to take part in Project *Ruby* which, together with modified Lancasters of XV Squadron, were involved in the bombing of former U-boat pens at Farge on the River Weser, north of Bremen. The huge structure had a concrete roof 23ft thick. It had almost been ready for use when on 27 March 1945 twenty Lancasters of 617 Squadron had attacked it and penetrated the roof with two 22,000lb 'Grand Slam' bombs, which brought down thousands of tons of concrete rubble and rendered the shelter unusable. It was thought that a target like this could probably withstand a 22,000lb bomb, but whether it could withstand repeated hits could only be determined by experiments and these had to wait until after the war. Project *Ruby* ended in July 1947.

In 1947 the CBE consisted of four main Wings. Development and Tactics were operational elements responsible for trials work, while Technical and Executive were support organisations. The RAF and the United States Air Force co-operated fully on many projects at Marham, and in July 1947 B-29s of the 340th Bomb Squadron in Strategic Air Command (SAC) arrived at the station on detachment. This was the start of a regular series of visits by USAF heavy-bomber units to Marham.[113] The Cold War heated up, and

Senior RAF Officers salute the arrival of the first four Boeing Washington B.Is (B-29) at Marham on 22 March 1950. (RAF Marham)

on 26 June 1948 the Berlin airlift began in response to the Soviet blockade of land travel into the city. In July SAC terminated B-29 deployments to Germany and moved two B-29 groups to the United Kingdom. B-29s of the 370th and 371st Squadrons, 307th Bomb Group, flew to Marham from MacDill Air Force Base.[114] Meanwhile, the 28th Bomb Group went to Scampton while the other two squadrons in the 307th Bomb Group were stationed at Waddington. On 16 July the 3rd Air Division (Provisional) was established at Marham to serve as headquarters for USAF B-29 rotational units in Britain. This was the first time that US combat forces were stationed in a major, friendly foreign country during peacetime.[115] That November, units of the 97th Bomb Group replaced the 28th and 307th Bomb Groups.

Meanwhile, the introduction of the RAF's all-jet bomber force was still several years in the future and Bomber Command was heavily reliant on the aging Avro Lincoln. Therefore, a decision was taken to acquire Boeing B-29 Superfortresses to fill the bomber gap until the arrival of the Canberra (in 1951) and the first of the V-bombers (1955) into service. Production of the B-29 had ended in 1946, but a large number of B-29s and B-29As were still in operation in SAC and many airframes were in storage. The RAF originally wanted seventy B-29s, or Washington B.Is as they were termed, and this was later increased to eighty-eight examples, which equipped eight squadrons. The US, under the MDAP (Mutual Defence Assistance Program), subsequently provided all of the B-29s. They were massive aircraft for their time, with 141ft wingspans and an all-up weight of 82,000lb, and so only Class A airfields such as Marham could accommodate them. Even so Marham lacked certain requirements. An urgent rebuilding programme was begun to add twelve concentric hardstands and an extension to the apron in front of the hangars, as well as many new barracks to house the large influx of personnel. The station was to be the home of the Washington Conversion Unit (WCU) responsible for the training of all air and ground crews of the B-29 squadrons. The CBE left Marham for Lindholme to make way for the Boeing Washington B.Is (B-29), the first four of which arrived on 22 March 1950.[116] By late summer 1951 most of the initial conversion work had been completed and crews were busy converting to the new bomber at Marham and Coningsby (15 Squadron) and were trying to achieve their monthly flying goal of 315 hours. Nos 35, 44 (Rhodesia), 57 and 207 Squadrons were the other four B-29 Squadrons. In 1951 the Washingtons took part in Operation Pinnacle, a major air defence exercise. In 1952 Washingtons of 90 Squadron won the Lawrence Minot Trophy for bombing efficiency. In 1953 115 Squadron repeated this success. With the large scale introduction of the English Electric Canberra B.2 to the RAF the Washingtons were gradually replaced and by the end of 1954 most had been returned to the desert storage area at Davis Monthan, Arizona. By January 1954 only seventeen B-29s were left at Marham, and that same month the first of the Canberra B.2s arrived. Departure of the Washingtons was marred by a fatal accident on 24 January, when Flight Lieutenant Williams and crew and WF495 were lost en route from Prestwick and no trace of the seven-man crew was ever found. The last Washington was flown out of Marham on 30 March.

For three years, from January 1954–June 1957, Marham operated Canberra B.2s and T.4s in the night medium-bomber role. The Norfolk station was the last of Bomber Command's six four-squadron Canberra wings, and that type also equipped 90, 115 and 207 Squadrons initially (each receiving ten to twelve aircraft) and, finally, 35 Squadron in April 1954. A new era was heralded at Marham on 21 January 1956 when 214 Squadron was reformed at the station and it took delivery of its first Vickers Valiant B(PR)I to become the third V-bomber unit. At 232 OCU at RAF Gaydon, Chief Instructors fondly told new intakes that the Valiant was 'a gentleman's aircraft'. Alan Gardener, who had been a Canberra navigator before flying in Valiants and who later served on Victor tankers at Marham, recalls:[117]

> We formed No.57 Valiant Course, so we were certainly no pioneers, the first aircraft having
> been delivered to 138 Squadron five years before. In those days the requirements in terms of
> flying hours, experience and 'assessments' ensured that the 'V-Force' really did represent the
> 'cream' of Bomber Command, if not the Royal Air Force. Although I had flown 900 hours
> on Canberras, my only experience of radar bombing – my new 'trade' – was gained at the

Boeing Washington B.Is of 115 Squadron in formation. (RAF Marham)

Bomber Command Bombing School at Lindholme. We trundled around the sky in a fleet of Lincolns whose wartime H2S sets functioned (usually) thanks to what must have been superhuman efforts by the radar mechanics. Powered by four 10,000lb thrust Rolls-Royce Avons, the Valiants were able to carry a 10,000lb nuclear bomb on a 3,500-mile sortie, cruising at 0.76 mach at 35-40,000ft. The Valiant was a nice big, comfortable aircraft to fly in. The crew compartment shared its general layout with the other 'V' bombers. The first pilot (Captain) and co-pilot sat side by side in ejection seats, with fully duplicated controls and instruments. Behind them and facing aft, the Nav (Radar), Nav (Plotter) and Air Electronics Officer shared a table that spanned the full width of the cockpit, while facing them were the controls and instruments appropriate to their trade. Heart of the weapon delivery system and good enough to remain in service for over 25 years, was the Navigation and Bombing System (NBS), which allied a greatly updated H2S Mk.9 radar with NBC, an electromechanical computer of startling ability. With this equipment, the Nav, could, by placing the electronic markers on his radar screen over suitable responses, put a 'fix' into his Ground Position Indicator, 'home' the aircraft to a selected point or, if that point were to be a target, 'fly' the aircraft on its bombing run. Bomb door opening and bomb release was achieved automatically.

Meanwhile, on 1 April 1956 207 Squadron, which had disbanded at Marham on 27 March, was reformed as the RAF's fourth Valiant squadron. In April 214 Squadron re-equipped with the B(PR)K.Mk.I multi-purpose version of the Valiant, which was capable of operating as a bomber, reconnaissance craft or as a flight refuelling tanker.[118] On 23 April three Valiants took part in a fly-past at Marham, in the presence of Premier Nikita Krushchev and other distinguished visitors from the Soviet Union that included Marshal Bulganin and A.N. Tupolev, the great Russian bomber design bureau chief. The visitors also watched displays by a Hunter and a Canberra. On 1 May, 90 Squadron disbanded at Marham and in mid-July 35 Squadron moved to Upwood. In June a Valiant from each of 214 and 543 Squadrons were flown to Idris, 15 miles south of Tripoli in Libya, to take part in Operation Thunderhead to test NATO defences in the Mediterranean theatre and southern Europe. On 1 July 214 and 207 Squadrons were joined at Marham by 148 Squadron flying Valiants. During July HM Queen Elizabeth was treated to a fly-by at Marham, consisting of seventy-two Canberras and twenty Valiants. That same month, on 26 July, international tensions were heightened again when President Gamal Abdel Nasser of Egypt announced that his government intended to nationalise the Suez Canal. Britain and France were determined to reverse the decision by military means and Operation Musketeer, a joint Anglo-French undertaking, was put into action to destroy the Egyptian Air Force.

Marham and all other front-line stations were immediately brought to operational readiness, as aircraft were prepared for the preliminary deployment to Malta and Cyprus. On 24 September four Valiants (three from 214 Squadron and one from 207 Squadron) left Marham for Luqa airfield in Malta as part of Operation Albert. Group Captain L. Hodges, the Marham Station Commander, acted as Force Commander. The main force of what was to be known as the Valiant Wing arrived on the island on 26 October. It comprised twenty-four Valiants, made up of four from 214 Squadron, commanded by Wing Commander Leonard Trent VC DFC,[119] six of 207 Squadron, commanded by Wing Commander D. Haig, and six of 148 Squadron, commanded by Wing Commander W. Burnett, while another eight were from 138 Squadron at Wittering. Though designed to drop thermonuclear bombs the Valiants were fitted with multi-carriers and six light-series bomb racks to carry conventional free-fall bombs, the biggest being the 1,000-pounder. Twenty-one of these weapons could be carried.[120] Chances of accurate delivery were poor, however, as many of the Valiants were bereft of their full complement of navigational and radar-operated bombing equipment. Instead they were forced to rely on the Second World War system of target-marking, while ex-Lincoln bomber sighting heads were fixed in temporary fittings. (As it turned out, those Valiants that carried navigation and bombing systems (NBS) mostly went unserviceable in the air). Bomber Command was ill-prepared to undertake a Musketeer-type operation; the command was geared to a 'radar' war in Western Europe and was not constituted nor organised for major overseas operations. The majority of the Valiant force had neither Navigation Bombing Systems nor visual bombsights and was not cleared for HE stores. The Canberra aircraft, forming the bulk of the force deployed, were equipped only with Gee-H as a blind bombing device, and it was not possible to position ground-based beacons to give coverage for this equipment over Egypt. It was considered that it would be prudent for the Valiants and Hal Far- and Cyprus-based Canberras to carry out night bombing attacks on Abu Sueir, Kabrit, Almaza, Fayid and Cairo West, the main Il-28 base, and this necessitated a reversion to the marking technique successfully used in the Second World War. The plan was to crater the runways, followed up at dawn by ground-attack strikes to destroy the aircraft. It was considered that the destruction of the EAF would be achieved in two days. Little opposition was expected. Flying Officer R.A.C. Ellicott of 214 Squadron recalls:

Sir Hugh Pugh Lloyd, C-in-C Bomber Command 1950–53, with armourers preparing to load bombs aboard a Washington of 115 Squadron at Marham, during an air exercise early in 1951. (RAF)

The looks and expressions of surprise can only be imagined when, within two hours of landing at Luqa, all crews gathered in the Bom ber Wing Operations briefing room for the first operational briefing and the curtains were drawn aside to reveal Egyptian airfields as the targets. Targets in Phase I were the Egyptian airfields operating Russian-built Il-28 bombers and MiG-15 fighters. The aiming points were the runway intersections and crews were briefed to avoid the camp areas. Further instructions were given that bombs were not to be jettisoned 'live' in case Egyptian casualties were caused. At dusk on 30 October operations commenced.

On the night of 30 October–1 November the Valiants and Canberras set off to bomb eight of the nine airfields in the Canal Zone and four more in the Nile Delta with 500lb

Crews of 207 Squadron brief for a bombing sortie during Operation *Musketeer*. (RAF Marham)

A Valiant crew debrief after a raid during Operation *Musketeer*. (RAF Marham)

Wing Commander Leonard Trent VC
DFC, who at the time of the Suez Crisis
in 1956 commanded 214 Squadron, whose
Valiants took part in Operation Musketeer.
(Via EDP)

and 1,000lb bombs. Five Valiants of 148 Squadron and one from 214 Squadron, plus four Canberras of 109 Squadron and three of 12 Squadron, attacked Almaza airfield near Cairo at 19.00Z hours. Intelligence reports stated that there were ten Vampires, ten MiG-15s, ten Il-28 bombers, nine Meteors and thirty-one twin-engined transports on the airfield. Canberras of 139 Squadron operating from Cyprus did the visual marking. The first Red TI markers from a PFF Canberra went down over Heliopolis, and the flares were dropped on the western hardstands 1,000 yards from the nominated aiming point. A second marker dropped TIs closer to the aiming point and called the bombers to drop on the most eastern set of TIs. Bombing was scattered, with the Valiants attacking from 42,000ft with free-fall bombs. XD814 of 148 Squadron was the first V-bomber in action. Because of the poor marking, the 50 per cent error circle was 1,550 yards and only one runway was hit, suffering superficial damage. It was a similar story at Kabrit and Abu Sueir where, although accuracy was better, damage was light. Little opposition was encountered and there was light AA fire in the target area but it was sporadic and well below the attacking aircraft. The Valiant piloted by Squadron Leader Trevor Ware was intercepted by an Egyptian Meteor NF.13 but its pilot could not hold on to the jet bomber, which climbed out of his range, and the Meteor flew away below the bomber.

The following night attacks were made on the airfields at Cairo West, Fayid and Kasfareet. Damage was again light, and at Cairo West the Ilyushins had already flew to Luxor. On the night of 2–3 November seven Valiants attacked Huckstep Barracks, which was bombed again two nights later together with the coastal batteries on El Agami

In 1959 214 Squadron operated the B(PR)I multi-purpose version of the Valiant for flight-refuelling trials. Pictured are B.K.Mk.I's WZ376 and WZ390. (Vickers)

Island. During the attacks on Huckstep the markers were well-placed and bombing was reasonably concentrated, but at El Agami most of the bombers failed to drop because the TIs were extinguished, probably having fallen into the sea. Although AAA defended many of the targets, this was usually light and almost always well below the aircraft. By 3 November the EAF had virtually ceased to exist. About 260 of its aircraft had been destroyed, including most of the 120 MiGs and fifty Il-28s that were in service when the conflict began. The Anglo-French airborne assault began on 5 November and the seaborne assault went ahead on the morning of the 6th when all immediate objectives had been taken. But mounting pressure at the UN, instigated by USA, led to a ceasefire on 8 November, and the RAF and French crews stood down. The total Bomber Command effort during the Suez campaign amounted to forty-nine Valiant and 278 Canberra sorties. Post-conflict analysis determined that the destruction of the EAF was largely due to attacks by the fighter-bombers. On 17 November all the Valiants returned to the United Kingdom.

Production of the Valiant ceased at the end of August 1957 when the last of 104 aircraft was delivered. By the end of 1957 Valiants equipped nine squadrons, Marham, Honington and Wittering being the main bases. In October 1958 the Valiants were invited to take part in the annual SAC Bombing Competition, which involved making three simulated atomic bomb attacks on a single night on San Jose in California and Boise and Batte in Montana, followed by an 800-mile cross-country route using astro navigation. In 1959 Valiant crews of 214 Squadron established four unofficial long distance records, from Marham to Nairobi, Salisbury, Rhodesia, Johannesburg, and from Heathrow to Cape Town. On 20–21 June 1961 a Vulcan B.IA flew non-stop from England to RAAF Richmond near Sydney, refuelled all the way by 214 Squadron's Valiants stationed along the route at Cyprus, Karachi and Singapore. Two years later Valiant tankers refuelled three Vulcan B.IAs of the Waddington Wing over Libya, Aden and the Maldives for the flight to Perth, Australia, and back.

On 26 June 1961, 49 Squadron transferred to Marham from Wittering and brought station strength up to thirty-five Valiants. Marham became occupied with nuclear quick reaction alerts (QRAs) and these became a regular feature of day-to-day operations. Alan Gardener recalls:

Squadrons each held one aircraft and crew on alert at all times, the aircraft armed with a 'Blue Danube' weapon and 'cocked' or 'Combat Ready' in correct parlance. In normal use, from climbing in to taking off would take 45 minutes. But if a crew checked each item of equipment in similar fashion to a pre-take-off check and left all switches in specified positions, it was possible to reduce this to about 5 minutes on a good day. The alert crew was required to stay together throughout its tour of duty. Flying clothing was worn, meals were taken in the aircrew buffet and the day spent in activities that could be immediately abandoned if a call to 'cockpit readiness' was tannoyed. It was an appropriate time to spend the passing hour or two studying the allocated war targets and planning routes. The crew's 'go-bag' was drawn from the Wing Weapon's Leader and the crew locked in the 'Vault' with suitable intelligence and briefing material. Outside the confines of the 'Vault', one member of the QRA crew would have the 'go-bag' with its contents, locked to his wrist at all times. At night, although originally allocated dedicated adjacent rooms in the Mess, it was obviously decided that too much comfort was a bad thing, for we were later provided with a 'QRA caravan' for sleeping purposes. This was a little like a miniature railway carriage (suburban!) with five individual compartments each complete with bunk, washbasin and heater, but not much else. Three of these devices were parked adjacent to the Ops Block. QRA could be an irritation; but at a weekend, when the rest of the station was away and gone, and the only people to be seen were those other poor souls on duty of one sort or another, it was a real pain. One of the techniques planned for our survival as a reprisal force in the event of a Soviet Nuclear strike was for all available V-bombers to disperse, in groups of four, to two dozen airfields around the British Isles. These were equipped with suitable accommodation, hardstandings, communications, Motor Transport and in most eases end-of-runway Operational Readiness Platforms, to function as emergency strike bases should the need arise.

The Valiant had been designed for high-level, long-range operations, but in 1960–61 Nos 49, 148 and 207 Squadrons had been assigned to NATO in a low-level tactical bomber role. Stresses on the airframe became too much and serious metal fatigue in the rear wing spars led to the Valiant fleet being grounded on 11 December 1964. At Marham on 1 March 1965, 207 Squadron disbanded and the three others followed on 1 May. Meanwhile, the decision had been taken for another former V-bomber to take over the role of aerial tankers.

Vickers Valiant B.Mk.I XD823 with nose probe for in-flight refuelling. (Vickers)

Valiant B(K)I XD812 of 214 Squadron at Khormaksar, Aden, in 1964. (Ray Deacon)

In January 1965 the Handley Page Company had begun working around the clock to convert six Victor B.1As to B(K)1A two-point tankers. That same month 92 Squadron's Lightnings were forced to 'puddle-jump' their way from the UK to their detachment in Cyprus via West Germany, southern France, Sardinia, Malta and Libya. Meanwhile, the conversion of Victors to in-flight refuellers was speeded up. The first to fly was XH620 on 28 April. On 24 May 55 Squadron, which had become non-operational as a Medium Bomber Force Squadron at Honington since 1 March, moved to Marham to operate in the in-flight refuelling role. Ironically, Second Lieutenant (later Sir) Alan Cobham, the great air-refuelling pioneer, had been one of the flying instructors at Narborough during the last two months of the First World War.[121] By 1932 Sir Alan Cobham was making preparations for a non-stop flight to Australia in an Airspeed Courier using flight refuelling. He sought Air Ministry help in providing tankers and Air Vice-Marshal Sir Hugh Dowding, Air Member for Supply and Research, suggested that India might be a more reasonable destination in view of the cost and organisation involved.[122] In 1934 Cobham started Flight Refuelling Ltd, and in the space of five years he had developed a successful transatlantic service that was refuelled in flight. In 1944 Cobham was awarded the contract to supply 600 sets of 'looped hose' flight refuelling equipment for the bombers of 'Tiger Force' in the Pacific. In April 1945 the Air Staff decided to abandon air refuelling for the Tiger Force, as the Americans were advancing in the Pacific and were offered bases nearer Tokyo, and the potential for overloading made the technique unnecessary.[123] Cobham bought back, at scrap value, all of the equipment already supplied to the Air Ministry. In December 1948 Cobham's equipment enabled the USAF Boeing B-50 *Lucky Lady II* to remain airborne for nearly four days.[124] Britain considered that the air refuelling technique then in use was unsuitable for high-speed and high-altitude operation.[125] but the advent of the probe and drogue changed this situation. Backed by Flight Refuelling's submission of numerous reports showing how range and bomb load of the new aircraft could be increased by employing air refuelling, in 1952 the Air Staff decided to adopt the in-flight refuelling system for the V-bomber force. Some Valiants would be equipped as tankers with removable refuelling equipment and all Valiant, Vulcan and Victor aircraft would be capable of receiving fuel.[126] During 1961–62 proposals were made for two- and three-point Valiant tankers, but these were turned down in favour of a three-point installation in the Victor. A number of Mk.I and IA Victor bombers became available as squadrons re-equipped with the Victor B.Mk.2. Three squadrons of Victor tankers were required to supplement the Valiant force and eventually replace it in the late 1960s; Treasury approval for the conversion was obtained in 1963. Following the discovery of fatigue defects, however, the Valiant force had to be withdrawn from service in January 1965, and the Victor conversion programme was then accelerated to make good this sudden loss of tankers. The prototype conversion (XA918) flew in September 1964 and was used to test the compatibility of all current receiver types.

55 Squadron's first two Victor tankers (XH602 and XH648) arrived at Marham on 26 May 1965, and in July a Tanker Training Flight was formed at the station. The two-point tanker was an interim measure only and was to be withdrawn and replaced with the more versatile three-point tankers when available. Two-point tankers did not permit Victor-to-Victor refuelling operations, but in August they provided the air-to-air refuelling element for 74 'Tiger' Squadron's Lightning F.3's deployment to Akrotiri, Cyprus. Meanwhile, six Lightning pilots from 19 Squadron at Leconfield converted to high-level, in-flight refuelling and then carried out low-level, in-flight refuelling trials from five of the K.1A tankers in preparation for 74 Squadron's return to the UK. Low-level tanking was possible but extremely difficult, and was best carried out over the sea where conditions are relatively smooth. The Victor's wing was prone to flexing in turbulence, and the whip effect of the basket end of the drogue could be quite frightening if a Lightning was not on the end to 'tone it down'.

Valiant B(K)I XD870 of 214 Squadron at Khormaksar, Aden, in 1964. (Ray Deacon)

Valiant B(K)I WZ390 of 214 Squadron at Khormaksar, Aden, in 1964. (Ray Deacon)

Valiant B(K)I WP223 of 214 Squadron at Khormaksar, Aden, in 1964. (Ray Deacon)

55 Squadron's full complement of six Victor tankers was finally reached in October. That month four Lightning F.3s of 74 Squadron were able to use all six Victor tankers at Akrotiri in Operation Donovan, when they were refuelled all the way to Tehran and back. On 1 December 1965, 57 Squadron moved to Marham from Honington but the first of their six Victor K.I/IA three-point tankers did not arrive until 14 February 1966. That same month 55 Squadron began receiving then first of 14 Victor K.IA tankers in place of their two-point tankers. On 1 July, 214 Squadron reformed at Marham as a Victor tanker squadron and, by the end of the year, was equipped with seven K.I/IA three-point tankers. In February 1967, Exercise Forthright 59/60 saw Lightning F.3s flying non-stop to Akrotiri and F.6s returning to the UK, refuelled throughout by the Victor tankers. In April, 56 Squadron's Lightnings flew to Cyprus carrying out six in-flight refuellings for the fighter versions and ten for the two-seat T-birds. In-flight refuelling from Victors also became a feature often used on QRAs in the UK. At night floodlights aboard the Victors had to be turned off to prevent blinding the Lightning pilots as they tanked over the North Sea. In June 1967 seventeen Victor tankers refuelled 74 Squadron's thirteen Lightnings which flew to Tengah, Singapore, in Operation Hydraulic, the longest and largest in-flight refuelling operation hitherto flown. All the Lightnings reached Tengah safely, staging through Akrotiri, Masirah and Gan. The Lightnings remained at Tengah for four years and during this time three 2,000-mile deployments were made to Australia non-stop using Victor tankers, the major one being Exercise Town House, 16–26 June 1969. Meanwhile, on 29 November 1967 an 11 Squadron Lightning established the record of eight-and-a-half hours' flying, refuelled five times, flying 5,000 miles.

By now a further twenty-four Victor K.I/IA three-point tanker conversions were in RAF service. Operating from hot and short airfields, the Victor K.I tankers were limited in the amount of fuel they could carry, and it was sometimes necessary to refuel the primary tanker from another tanker before proceeding to the rendezvous. A new tanker having greater capacity and more power was required. Plans were made for the conversion of twenty-nine (later reduced to twenty-four in 1975) Victor B.Mk.2 and SR.2 versions, the type having been phased out of service in the bomber role when the task of maintaining the nuclear deterrent passed to the Royal Navy's Polaris submarine fleet in 1969. Preliminary design for the conversion was initiated by Handley Page but, after the collapse of this company, Hawker Siddeley Aviation revised the design and completed the conversions at Manchester, the first flying on 1 March 1972. 55 Squadron re-equipped early in 1976, followed by 57 Squadron in June, but 214 Squadron, the last to operate the Mk 1 tankers, was disbanded in January 1977 as a result of Defence cuts. Designed for a fourteen-year life, the Victors were due for replacement by the early 1990s. The RAF planned to bring nine converted VC 10s into service to supplement the fleet.

The withdrawal of British forces from the Far East involved a rapid reinforcement commitment. In May 1968 four F.6 Lightnings of 5 Squadron at Leconfield flew non-stop from Binbrook to Bahrain in eight hours, refuelled along the 4,000-mile route by the Victor tankers. Deliveries of the Victor K.Mk.2 began in May 1974 for 232 OCU at Marham. This unit now took over from the squadrons' full-role conversion training, in addition to ground training in a simulator and the Air-to-Air Refuelling School. Night and day sorties were flown when weather permitted. Despite thunderstorms and sheets of rain over Norfolk late in the evening of Monday 19 August 1968, Victor B(K).1A XH646, flown by thirty-six-year-old Flight Lieutenant W.A. Gallienne with four crew, took off fully loaded with fuel on a training sortie. Just before 10.00 p.m. the Victor reached 1,400ft above Holt. Suddenly, a massive explosion shattered the peaceful tranquillity and many locals thought that Armageddon had arrived. Police Constable Ian Jarvis, who had only just moved into the police house next to the Police Station, had returned home as his wife was getting their child ready for bed. He went to the back door and at that instant heard the explosion. Incredulously he watched as a wing and a section of aircraft undercarriage spiralled down out of the flaming sky. A large part of fuselage with a wheel came down in Mrs Barnes' garden at 4 Gravel Pit Lane, flattening her shed only 9ft from her back door. Her neighbour at No.6, Mrs Brown, had a large part of a wing embedded in her garden a few feet from the house. In a bungalow at High Kelling, Rolley Nurse thought that the explosion was a thunderbolt hitting something close by. He rushed out into his garden and, seeing the fireball overhead, thought that a hydrogen bomb must have exploded. He ordered his wife and two children to keep down as tiny bits of debris fell everywhere, 'clattering around the garden' and sounding like 'heavy hail hitting his roof'. Thousands of small fragments fell on a 10-mile sq. area in fields east of Holt. PC Ian Jarvis left the scene of devastation and headed towards a field of potatoes where more wreckage was burning fiercely. As he stood looking at the flames a helicopter suddenly appeared overhead and shone a powerful searchlight across the field. The beam found the wreckage and the helicopter descended, and as it landed an airman appeared at the open door and jumped down beside him. He studied the twisted metal for a while and then turned to Jarvis and said, 'Where's the other one?' It was only at that moment that Jarvis realised that it had not been one aircraft that had exploded, but two.

The severe electrical storm had negated radar coverage throughout the area, and the Victor and a Canberra bomber flying in from Brüggen in West Germany had collided nose-to-nose and disintegrated in the conflagration. The air was thick with the stench of kerosene as ambulance crews, firemen, police and RAF personnel thronged around the scenes of devastation. In the darkness PC Ian Jarvis could hear grown men being sick. As the flames in the cockpit of the Victor were extinguished, fireman Jack Gillett noticed that the arm of one of one of the four bodies was sticking out. He took it and gently tried to put it back in. As each body was laid on a stretcher it was covered with a clear polythene wrap. The next day someone walking their dog on the edge of Holt Country Park found the body of one of the crew of the Canberra at the base of a young pine tree. Over the next few days the RAF systematically collected aircraft debris from all around Holt, and at Gresham's School recreation fields collected an airmen's helmet and a wad of scorched papers. A glove with the hand still in it came from Sheringham 10 miles away, and the other two bodies from the Canberra were also recovered. Incredibly, no one on the ground had been harmed in any way. The following Sunday St Andrew's church in Holt was packed to overflowing as a service of thanksgiving was conducted for the townsfolk's narrow escape, and prayers were offered for the souls of the seven dead airmen.[127]

The wreckage of the Canberra, which was involved in a mid-air collision over Norfolk on 19 August 1960 with Victor B(K).1A XH646, flown by Flight Lieutenant W.A. Gallienne. (EDP)

The rapid reinforcement commitment continued. On 6 January 1969 Exercise Piscator, the biggest in-flight refuelling exercise so far mounted by the RAF, took place when ten Lightning F.6s of 11 Squadron refuelled by the Victor tankers were deployed to Tengah, staging through Muharraq and Gan and back, a distance of 18,500 miles. Victors of 55, 57 and 214 Squadrons refuelled each Lightning thirteen times. Throughout the two-way journey 228 individual refuelling contacts were made, during which 166,000 imperial gallons (754,630 litres) of fuel were transferred. In-flight refuelling was used for a less belligerent role in the 1969 *Daily Mail* transatlantic air race, when Harriers of Air Support Command and Phantoms of 892 Squadron, Royal Navy, were refuelled numerous times by Victor tankers based on both sides of the Atlantic. During Christmas 1969 Exercise Ultimacy, involving ten F.6s of 5 Squadron, flew to Tengah for joint air-defence exercises in Singapore. Only one stop, at Masirah, was made en route, the first Lightnings leaving Binbrook before dawn on a foggy 8 December morning. At 03.45 hours they made their first rendezvous with their Victor tankers over East Anglia in the dark. Then it was on, across France and the Mediterranean and a rendezvous with more Victors from Cyprus. They continued eastwards, finally crossing Muscat and Oman and on to Masirah, the overnight stop. The next day a pre-dawn take-off saw the Lightnings away on the last leg of their trip, across 4,000 miles of ocean south-east to Gan, where Victors rendezvoused on schedule to refuel them, and then due east to Sumatra.

Wreckage from the mid-air collision on 19 August 1968, in fields near Holt, Norfolk. (EDP)

Victor K.IA XH621 of 57 Squadron refuelling a Lightning F.2A of 19 Squadron from RAF Gutersloh at 30,000ft in November 1973.

Some of 74 Squadron's Lightnings were in need of major overhaul, and pairs of Lightnings left for the UK refuelled by the Victors on the homeward trip, after stopovers at Masirah and Akrotiri.

In May 1970 three Phantom FGR.Mk.2s of 54 Squadron, participating in Exercise Bersatu Padu, flew to Singapore non-stop in a little over fourteen hours with the aid of nine in-flight refuellings. The run-down of the aircraft-carrier fleet meant that land-based strike aircraft had to operate further out to sea. In exercises in the mid-1970s tanker support enabled RAF Phantoms to mount a defensive patrol over a naval task force 900 miles from their base in Scotland, and Buccaneers from Honington were able to carry out attacks against simulated enemy shipping operating more than 1,100 miles from the coast. In February 1971, 23 Squadron tanked from Victors to Cyprus. On 25 August, 74 Squadron disbanded at Tengah and 56 Squadron acquired all of the Tigers' remaining F.6s, which, starting on 2 September, were flown over the 6,000-mile route to Akrotiri, a thirteen-hour trip, staging through Gan and Muharraq and completing seven air-to-air refuellings with Victor tankers.

Demonstrating the rapid deployment made possible by in-flight refuelling, in 1974 six Lightning F.6s were sent to Cyprus when a Greek-led coup by the Cyprus National Guard overthrew President Makarios. In July twelve armed Phantoms were dispatched from RAF Coningsby at short notice during the Turkish invasion of the northern part of the Mediterranean island. Flying through the night and refuelled by Victor tankers from Marham (which then landed at Malta), the fighters were available to the United Nations commander by first light the following morning. On 24 March 1975 a 57 Squadron Victor K.2 (XH618) flown by Flight Lieutenant Keith Hanscomb was involved in an in-flight refuelling accident with a Honington-based Buccaneer S.2 over the North Sea. The Buccaneer pilot approached too fast and his probe clipped the edge of the trailing drogue, sending it snaking towards the Victor's fuselage. The Buccaneer pilot tried a second approach, above and a little behind the Victor's starboard wing, and dropping down to tuck in behind. He flew into the Victor's jetwash, rolled and his starboard wing smashed the tanker's port elevator on the high T-tail and caused Handscomb to lose control. The Victor's tail broke off and the starboard side of the tailplane also sheered away. Hanscomb ordered his crew to bale out, but without ejection seats the three backseaters stood no chance.[128] As Hanscomb ejected the tanker exploded and his four crew were killed. The Buccaneer pilot, meanwhile, managed to land safely. Hanscomb was found floating in his dinghy by the crew of the German freighter SS *Hoheburgh*, and he was rescued by a RAF Whirlwind SAR helicopter. Hanscomb recovered from his injuries to return to flying.

In November 1975, and again in July 1977, Harriers were flown to Belize with the aid of in-flight refuelling to counter invasion threats from Guatemala. In January 1976 Marham saw the return to Canberra operations when 100 Squadron arrived from West Raynham to operate as the target facilities unit with eleven Canberras. On 18 February 231 OCU and its six Canberras arrived from Cottesmore, which was needed by the PANAVIA Tornado Training Unit. On 15 August 1977 Canberra E.15 WH948 of 100 Squadron was abandoned on a training sortie after getting into difficulties and Squadron Leader Tony Gordon and Flight Lieutenant Roy Smith ejected safely. The Canberra crashed at Oulton. On 19 June

1978 another 100 Squadron Canberra (WJ753) crashed on the threshold at Marham, injuring three of the crew. The pilot suffered two broken legs and one of the other occupants broke both ankles. On a happier note, that same month four Boeing B-52 Stratofortresses landed at Marham to take part in the annual bombing competition. The runway at Marham was resurfaced and all aircraft moved to Sculthorpe nearby. A third Canberra crashed on 11 November 1980 when WH667, which was taking part in an APC, suffered an engine failure during take-off. Squadron Leader G. Thompson and Flying Officer M. Wray were killed. In December 1981, 7 Squadron disbanded at St Mawgan; that unit's TT.18s were transferred to Marham and were absorbed by 100 Squadron. In January 1982, 100 Squadron moved to Wyton and in July they were followed by 231 OCU. The moves were all part of the reorganisation to allow Marham to become the new home for the strike/attack variant of the Tornado the following year.

In the meantime the Victor tankers continued to operate from Marham although, on 28 January 1977, 214 Squadron disbanded for the last time, leaving just twenty-four K.2 tankers of 55 and 57 Squadrons as the only aircraft capable of in-flight refuelling the RAF's Lightning, Phantom, Buccaneer and Jaguar strike aircraft.[129] The in-flight refuelling crews were a closely-knit family who took great pride in their exclusive role and unashamedly referred to themselves as the 'Tanker Trash'. In keeping with the traditional rivalries found on every RAF station, reputations counted for nought. Once, the Victors had been a part of the V-bomber elite, and it must have come hard when on 25 April 1982 the first eight Tornado GR.1s of 617 'Dam Busters' Squadron arrived, commanded by Wing Commander Tony Harrison, and upstaged them. Not to be outdone, the old guard was soon referring to the shiny new upstarts as 'The Dim Bastards'. According to the Victor fraternity, MRCA stood for 'Much Refurbished Canberra Aircraft'.[130]

While the new arrivals found their feet, it was the 'Tanker Trash' that were suddenly and unexpectedly thrust into the ascendancy again. On 1 April South Georgia and the Falklands were invaded on the orders of the Argentine Junta in Buenos Aires, and the veteran Victors' and Vulcans' presence in the South Atlantic was urgently required as part of the British determination to regain the islands, code-named Operation Corporate. On 18 April the advance party and five Victor K.2 tankers left Marham for Wideawake airfield on the British-owned island of Ascension, 3,375 miles from the Falklands. The next day four more Victors flew the 4,100 miles from Marham to Ascension, and by the end of the month fourteen Victors were stationed at Wideawake. Squadron Leader A.I.B. 'Al' Beedie of 55 Squadron, who with Squadron Leader Tony Cowling formed the radar team aboard Squadron Leader John Elliott's Victor, recalls:

Beginning on 20 April, Victors, supported by five more operating in the air refuelling mode, flew three maritime reconnaissance operations, each more than fourteen hours duration, to waters in the region of South Georgia.[131] On 30 April/1 May two Vulcan B.Mk.2s of 101 Squadron, supported by ten Victors, set out on a demanding 7,860-mile round trip to bomb Port Stanley in an incident-filled, complex operation.[132] At the start the primary Vulcan [XM598] aborted after its cabin could not be pressurized and the Victor fleet, too, suffered malfunctions. Victors refuelled Victors until only two remained with the reserve Vulcan

[XM607], flown by Flight Lieutenant Martin Withers and Flight Lieutenant Dick Russell.[133] Just before the fifth refuelling of the Vulcan one of the Victors [Squadron Leader Bob Tuxford flying XL189] attempted to refuel the other Victor in very turbulent conditions and the receiving Victor [XH669 flown by Flight Lieutenant Steve Biglands] had its probe broken during the transfer. The two Victors exchanged roles and the provider took back the fuel. Although dangerously low on fuel itself the Victor then transferred enough fuel to the Vulcan to allow it to make its attack, before heading back towards Ascension and calling for another tanker to meet it. Withers' successfully dropped his 21 1,000lb bombs on Port Stanley airfield. The Vulcan was then refuelled a sixth time and returned to Ascension after being airborne for 15 hours 45 minutes. At the time it was the longest-range operational bombing operation ever flown.[134]

Squadron Leader Bob Tuxford of 55 Squadron recalls:

We did a number of work-up sorties before leaving for Ascension. We had an inclination of what was ahead, but I think it's fair to say no one expected to be launching eighteen-ship sorties and assisting a Vulcan to drop the hardware. It was a massive operation. We were taken aback with the logistical aspects. Air-to-air refuelling was our business, but normally escorting fighters around the world in much reduced numbers. The tanking support for this mission took eighteen individual Victor sorties – a very complicated operation, but one we thought absolutely achievable. We had a fuel planning cell at 1 Group that looked after the tanker force. Mostly ex-navigators, their business was to produce fuel plans – BLACK BUCK was just a variation on a theme. We saw the plan for the very first time on the evening of 30 April, but it was our experience using formation procedures that allowed us to run with it quickly. Martin Withers has acknowledged that the plan was mind-boggling to him. He had Dick Russell with him in the cockpit to bring some air-to-air refuelling expertise into the Vulcan crews. [The Vulcan crews had just twelve days in which to hone their refuelling skills.] I flew over fourteen hours that night. I went through every emotion from excitement in the launch phase to worry in the early stages.

Much of the 'excitement' for me came in the sixth and seventh hours when I was refuelling one of the other tankers, Victor K.2 XH669 piloted by Steve Biglands, which broke its probe in my basket. That necessitated changing places and receiving back the fuel we'd just passed in pretty shocking weather. The degree of difficulty at that stage was as hard as anything I'd had to deal with before. Despite a shortage of fuel in the whole formation, I was able to give the final offload to the Vulcan, which then went onto the Falklands, albeit with less fuel reserves than hoped. As I 'turned the corner', it was seven hours back to Ascension and we had five hours worth of fuel. I didn't have any options to divert; there was no option but the South Atlantic. We were very focussed at that point, not sure if the Vulcan could finish the job. But once we'd intercepted the code word that indicated the job was done we went from a subdued state to an elated one and then concentrated efforts on recovery, which would require another tanker. The original plan hadn't allowed for such a contingency so I was relying on their knowledge at Ascension on how the plan had gone and the fact the formation was short of fuel, so they would launch additional recovery aircraft, which indeed they did.

The Vulcan crews were not very familiar with air-to-air refuelling operations – the managers at the Vulcan bases did not have the best available information to them on the fuel consumption rates the aircraft would endure, especially fully laden, and undertaking multiple formation changes. So, the figures were not as accurate, in retrospect, as we would have liked. A number of things also went significantly wrong, Steve Biglands' unfortunate breaking of the probe being the biggest. We were flying in towering cumulous clouds at night. Your visual references for formating on the aircraft in front are reduced. Therefore with the turbulence, the distracting lightning, St. Elmo's Fire all around the cockpit windows, the whole process of achieving a stable contact and maintaining it for long enough to get the fuel on becomes much more difficult. On approaching the Falklands, the whole formation had burnt a lot more fuel than had been planned. Unfortunately, that ended up with me, the final tanker, 20,000lbs' short.

There is a weak link on the front end of the probe that is designed to shear if too much lateral force is put upon it. One of two things can happen; the probe tip can lodge inside the coupling of the basket, which would render it useless, or the tip breaks off and falls into the sea, if it doesn't enter the engine intakes. At this point, I wasn't aware whether I would be able to use the centre HDU [Hose Drum Unit] again. But everything premised on my ability to change places with Steve Biglands and take back the fuel we had just given him. If I couldn't do that, then it didn't matter my hose may be damaged. So, I took back the fuel, so I had enough to go on with the mission. Then we had to decide if the hose would be satisfactory. We brought Withers's Vulcan behind, they visibly inspected it but that wasn't quite confirmatory enough, so we made a small additional transfer of about 5,000lbs. That demonstrated how flexible this whole refuelling plan was. We were effectively making it up as we went along. Once I knew he could take on fuel, we could then continue with the mission.

If we hadn't been able to transfer to Withers, the mission would have been aborted. I had grounds for aborting the mission somewhat earlier, as I was prejudicing my own recovery, as I wasn't sure we could get another tanker on the way home. I hasten to add that I discussed the options available with my crew and each of the other four members came back and said. ''Let's press on and get the job done'. That was in the full knowledge that we would be two hours short of fuel in getting back to Ascension, about 600 miles south.

We gave the Vulcan sufficient time to effect the mission and my AO, [Airborne Electronic Officer] Flight Lieutenant Mick Beer, intercepted the code word 'Polo' designed to communicate the mission had been a success. I was then able to make arrangements for my own recovery. Two Victors were scrambled from Ascension. They were from the recovery wave of six tankers for the mission to bring the Vulcan back post-strike. The six aircraft were required to provide two Victors at the RV in case of problems. Fortunately, Group Captain Gerry Price, the Station Commander from RAF Marham who was running the air bridge at Ascension made the decision to divert two of the Victors to assist us. Another of our tanker crews, Flight Lieutenant Alan Skelton, had developed a fuel leak and also required assistance. They met us three hours south of Ascension when we had about an hour's fuel left.

I'm very proud, both for my crew and the whole of the tanker force. Any one of those eighteen tankers failing would mean the mission failing. Pretty much the whole of 1 Group's tanker force was on the island and it was thanks to some pretty skilful flying from every pilot

Victor K.IA XH650 of 55 Squadron refuelling Lightning F.3 XF700/K of 29 Squadron.

that enabled the whole plan to be accomplished. It was very much more than a simple bombing mission. The Argentines then knew we could attack them on the mainland.'[135]

BLACK BUCK 2 went ahead on 3 May and was flown by the same Vulcan with a different crew, who took off from Wideawake with a small group of Victor tankers. A larger formation of Victors left later and flew at a higher speed than on BLACK BUCK I to catch up with the Vulcan well along the route to Port Stanley. This operational change worked well enough but the runway was not hit, although several Argentinean aircraft and buildings were very badly damaged. BLACK BUCK 3, scheduled for 16 May, was cancelled because of bad weather. BLACK BUCK 4, flown on 28 May, was the first anti-radar mission, but five hours out from Ascension the HDU, the mechanism that winds and unwinds the refuelling hose, failed in the key Victor tanker and the mission was aborted. Two nights later, on 30–31 May on a mission to the Port Stanley area, BLACK BUCK 5, supported by eighteen Victor sorties, was successful and the Vulcan launched four AGM-45A Strike missiles, which damaged the antenna of the Argentinean Westinghouse AN/TPS-43 surveillance radar installation. BLACK BUCK 6 went ahead on 2–3 June but the Argentineans repeatedly switched off their radars. Vulcan XM607 was forced to divert to Rio de Janeiro in Brazil, after an in-flight refuelling accident involving the loss of its probe on the return leg of the anti-radar strike. BLACK BUCK 7 was flown to bomb Port Stanley airfield on 11–12, and was the last bombing operation involving a Vulcan. Fourteen Victor tankers carried out eighteen refuelling sorties. The mission was a success, with the Vulcan dropping a full load of 1,000lb high-explosive and anti-personnel bombs on the airfield without hitting the runway, which was spared because the RAF would need it.

The occupation of the Falklands ended on 15 June with the surrender by Argentinean forces. The Victors' participation in the war had been crucial. Not only did the Victors tank for the Vulcans on the BLACK BUCK series of missions, but they air-refuelled Harriers from Britain to Ascension, and after the surrender the tankers were kept fully occupied supporting Nimrod and C-130 Hercules operations. In total the twenty-three Victors logged 1,980 hours and thirty minutes (including 1,105 hours by thirteen Victors of 55 Squadron) throughout the entire conflict.[136]

A few months later, on 16 October, the Victor force was reduced by one aircraft when Victor K.2 XL232 crashed during take-off at Marham, as Wing Commander Al Beedie recalls:

> I was scrambled early that morning with my Victor crew to go and support a fighter. We'd just started the take-off roll when there was a muffled thump. There were no adverse engine indications. My captain said: 'Did anybody hear that?' as if to say, 'Has your knap bag fallen over?' I said I'd heard it. He then made the best decision of his life. He decided to abort. He closed down the throttles and started slowing down. I got out the periscope to view the undersurface of the aircraft and discovered that we were massively on fire because one of the engines had blown up and the debris had cut through the fuel tanks. The whole of the back of the aircraft was literally boiling oil fire into the sky ... I told the chaps it'd be a good idea to stop as quickly as possible and then we'd all get out and run as fast as we can. Have you ever tried running in an immersion suit, flying boots and a Mae West over a thick grass airfield? It's jolly difficult.

At Marham the 'Tanker Trash' soldiered on in front-line service, fulfilling day-to-day air refuelling operations for Strike Command's Jaguars and Phantoms, while all around them the station moved vigorously into the Tornado age. The Tornado GR.I strike-wing became reality on 1 May 1983 when 27 Squadron, the third and final UK-based Tornado interdictor-strike squadron, arrived at Marham under the command of Wing Commander John Grogan, and its Tornado GR Is began occupying the HAS 'farm' on the south side of the airfield. Officially, the date of the squadron's formation was 12 August, by which time a full complement of thirteen Tornadoes had been delivered. Each aircraft was soon displaying the squadron markings, consisting of a green elephant motif (recalling its Martynside Elephant aircraft from the First World War) in a yellow disc on a red bar painted along the fin RWR fairing. Meanwhile, on 16 May 617 Squadron commemorated the fortieth anniversary of the famous Dams Raid by entertaining the survivors of that epic operation. In a further tribute of the great raid, the Tornadoes' individual aircraft identity letters painted on the fins were those carried by twelve of the aircraft flown by Wing Commander Guy Gibson VC DSO DFC's crews in May 1943. In September three 617 Squadron Tornadoes visited Canada, flying the 3,500-mile journey to the Toronto International Airport with the aid of Victor and Vulcan tankers. On 28 October Tornado ZA558/F of 617 Squadron was lost when it crashed into the sea 10 miles north-west of Cromer, Norfolk. The navigator ejected and was uninjured but the pilot was killed. That same month 617 and 27 Squadrons began moving into the north-eastern hardened aircraft shelter (HAS) site at Marham.

A Victor K.2 of 232 Operational Conversion Unit refuels two F.6 Lightnings of 11 Squadron during an exercise in September 1974.

Routine training continued throughout 1983 and 1984. Between 28 January–8 February 1984 four of 27 Squadron's Tornadoes were flown to Thumrait airfield in the Gulf Sultanate of Oman for a goodwill visit. The 'Flying Elephants' participated in and won a bombing competition with the Sultan of Oman's Air Force Hunters, and Jaguars and the Tornadoes also visited Abu Dhabi and Saudi Arabia. During a 27 Squadron deployment to Goose Bay in July for western vortex, Tornado GR.I ZA494 crashed after a flap problem. The crew ejected safely.[137]

In October 1984 the RAF returned to the United States, after a gap of four years, to take part in the annual US Strategic Air Command Bombing Competition.[138] 617 Squadron's six Tornadoes needed tanker support, provided by 55 Squadron's Victors, to compete in Operation Prairie Vortex at Ellsworth Air Force Base, South Dakota, against B-52s of Strategic Air Command and F-111s of the Tactical Air Command. F-111Cs of the Royal Australian Air Force also took part. In total forty-two crews were competing for three trophies. The competition involved two phases of bombing sorties over the low-level ranges in Montana, Nevada, South Dakota and Wyoming, and extended over eight weeks. The first six weeks of the detachment was spent as a work-up period to allow everyone to acclimatise, settle in and sort out the aircraft before the competition proper began. The first phase comprised a single five and a quarter hour daylight hi-lo-hi bombing mission, in which terrain following and ECM were employed to avoid detection and attacks by interceptors and simulated SAMs; live practice bombs were dropped on invisible targets using offset blind bombing techniques. A low-level dash and high-level cruise return completed the mission. Phase 2 involved a six-hour mission and was flown over two separate courses, one in daylight and the other at night. Multiple targets were attacked at high and low-level using tone bombs while evading multiple threats from interceptors and missiles. Throughout the missions timing was recorded to within one-second accuracy, as was navigation and bombing. It must be remembered that the Tornado was the only aircraft in the competition that demanded in-flight refuelling, by Victor K 2 tankers of 55 Squadron, requiring split-second timing to avoid acquiring penalty points. The Tornadoes required at least two AAR

Victor K.1 XA918 refuels F.2A Lightnings XN730 and XN784 of 19 Squadron RAF Germany.

Canberra PR.9 XH169/AC of 39 (I PRU) Squadron overhead Marham in May 1994. (Author)

brackets per sortie and in total 111 day and night join-ups were successfully made. The Le May and Meyer trophies had never been out of the USA before, but 617 Squadron won both of these trophies and the Mathis was missed only because the radar failed in one of the Tornadoes at a crucial point in the competition.[139] It was certainly one in the eye for Richard DeLauer, Under Secretary of Defense for Research and Engineering in the US DoD, who had said that the Tornado was 'vulnerable, heavy and expensive. I just don't think it's a good plane!'

In October 1985 six Tornadoes of 27 Squadron, together with Victor tankers of 57 Squadron, competed in that year's Bombing Competition at Ellsworth. Squadron Leader Terry Cook recalls:

The early sorties were designed to be mini replicas of the competition missions with both Victors and Tornadoes flying for about 2½ hours in preparation for the 6½ hour competition routes. The whole RAF detachment was supporting two teams in the competition with two Tornado crews and two Victor crews in each team. Each crew flew three competition sorties spread over three weeks with no allowance given for mistakes or if aircraft failed to take-off on time. The first two Tornado missions were 6½ hours long and covered 2,800 miles over four states of the mid west. On each sortie the crew dropped one bomb from medium level and four from Low Level whilst using the Skyshadow electronic countermeasures (ECM) pod to confuse simulated surface to air missiles (SAMs). The bombs were electronic 'tone' bombs where the aircraft generates a tone for weapon release while the aircraft is being tracked by a ground based radar. The radar then calculates where the bomb would have fallen. For the final competition mission the Tornadoes flew a Low Level route through the deserts of Utah, Arizona and Nevada to avoid USAF fighters and SAMs before dropping 2 practice bombs on targets very close together. A complication for the crews was that all the targets were merely map references on the ground and had to be attacked using offset aiming techniques. Offset bombing allows the crew to mark a known point either visually or on radar while the aircraft's main computer makes the necessary calculations for the aircraft to bomb the target. Before flight, therefore, the range and bearing of the offset point from the target needed to be accurately calculated in order to give the best bomb scores.

Twice on each competition sortie the Tornadoes had to refuel from the Victors. Without the benefit of British Military Air Traffic or Fighter Controllers the airborne rendezvous had to be carried out by either aircraft type or, more usually, a combination of both. Once in company, the Victor crews assumed responsibility for navigation and timing in order to allow the Tornado crews a short period of relaxation. Without the benefit of modern, electronic navigation aids the Victors always took the Tornadoes to the end of the refuelling leg (approximately 200 nautical miles) within a few seconds of the required time! There is no doubt that had the Victors been allowed to enter the navigation parts of the competition they would have achieved very creditable results against the much better equipped USAF KC-135 tankers. On many sorties the Victors also acted in other roles, especially in negotiating extra refuelling airspace to meet and refuel Tornadoes that were short of fuel. One Victor crew even offered to fly along the Low Level route at medium level and to act as a relay between the Tornado, which had a poor radio, and the various range controllers.

With just three competition sorties per crew we all worked hard to have all the aircraft serviceable and to launch two Tornadoes and four Victors on each competition day. Generally all the aircraft were available to fly although the Tornado crews usually had a preference as some aircraft dropped better scoring bombs than others. For the final day of the competition, one Victor and two Tornadoes were not available due to a series of problems; indeed, one Tornado was at a base in Wyoming after suffering an engine failure. All six competition aircraft, however, launched on time for the two sorties.

The RAF was invited to the 1985 SAC Bombing and Navigation Competition to compete for the Best Tornado award and for 3 major competition trophies; the Le May individual crew trophy and the Meyer and Mathis team trophies. After 'TOM' had won the Meyer and Le May trophies in 1984 we expected the USAF to compete much harder. Indeed, one USAF team even sported 'Tornado Buster' badges on their flying suits. They were disappointed. The results could hardly have been better, with Tornado crews taking second place in all three trophies and First Place in the Meyer[140] and Le May[141] trophies – again!

Less than a year later, on 30 June 1986, 57 Squadron disbanded. Its K.2s were handed over to 55 Squadron, which would continue to operate the Victor tankers for seven more years after that. No one could possibly have foreseen that before then the Victors would still have one more war to fight.

6

'TANKER TRASH' AND THE TORNADOES

In August 1990 55 Squadron's Victors were supporting RAF Jaguars at the Reconnaissance Air Meet in Texas when the recall of all tankers to the UK was ordered. Within twenty-four hours the 'Tanker Trash' were back at Marham, and within forty-eight hours they were operating over France and Sicily to deploy fast jets to the Persian Gulf, where conflict had begun on 2 August when Iraqi President Saddam Hussein's armies invaded Kuwait. On 7 August President George Bush ordered Operation *Desert Shield* to liberate Kuwait. USAF Lieutenant General Charles A. Horner, the allied coalition's supreme air commander, began coordinating all air actions related to the build-up and, within days, established HQ Central Command Air Forces (Forward) in Saudi Arabia. Initial Air Force planning was largely concentrated on defending Saudi Arabia from invasion and the first priority, therefore, was the neutralization of advancing Iraqi tank and troop columns. The coalition air forces faced 750 Iraqi combat aircraft, 200 support aircraft, Scud surface-to-surface missiles, chemical and biological weapon capability, 'state-of-the-art' air defences, ten types of surface-to-air missiles, around 9,000 anti-aircraft artillery pieces and thousands of small arms. The Iraqi air force had twenty-four main operating bases and thirty dispersal fields, many equipped with the latest in hardened aircraft shelters. As many as forty-five of the most important targets were situated in and around Baghdad, a city covering 254sq. miles and one which was considered to be seven times more heavily defended than Hànôi had been in December 1972.

All the RAF's refuelling assets were needed to deliver the Tornado GR.1s, F.3s and Jaguars from Europe to Tabuk and Dhahran in Saudi Arabia and the former RAF Muharraq, now Bahrain International Airport. In London on 9 August, the MoD had announced the forthcoming dispatch of a dozen each of Tornado F.3 air-defence fighters and Jaguar GR.1A attack aircraft. Operation *Granby*, the British contribution to *Desert Shield/Desert Storm*, had begun. The Tornadoes were already halfway deployed in Cyprus for an APC. On 23 August plans for the dispatch of a Tornado GR.1 squadron were announced. On 27 August twelve Tornado GR.1s left Brüggen in Germany in hastily applied 'Desert Pink' camouflage, and were flown to Bahrain. A second squadron, of

II (AC) Squadron's Tornado GR.Is after arrival at Marham in December 1991. Nearest aircraft is ZA552/X followed by ZA373/H, ZA369/II and ZA404/W. (RAF Marham)

Laarbruch aircraft but mainly Marham crews, left for Bahrain in two elements on 19 and 26 September, but transferred to Tabuk in the far west of Saudi Arabia from 8 October onwards. Finally, it was decided to send to Dhahran twelve additional Brüggen GR.Is, the first of which arrived on 3 January. (Between 2–4 January 1991 a third Tornado squadron was deployed to Dhahran to complement the Tornado F.3s, and six more Tornado GR.1As were received at the base between 14–16 January.) All the Tornado GR.I/IAs deployed to the Gulf were from RAF Germany, including even those held in reserve at Marham, as these were powered with the more powerful Mk.103 version of the RB199 reheated turbofan. At Muharraq Group Captain David Henderson was in command, while XV Squadron commanded by Wing Commander John Broadbent was the leading unit, although 9, 17 and 31 Squadrons and Marham's 617 'Dambusters' and 27 Squadrons provided crews. Normal peacetime training now stood the Tornado crews in good stead, as Wing Commander John Broadbent later recalled:

The normal training routine on the Squadron was based upon the assumption that aircrew would achieve on average about 20 hours' flying a month. Within this quota, the emphasis was placed upon developing low flying skills for two major reasons. First and foremost, notwithstanding the experience of the Gulf War, in most circumstances Low Level still remains the most effective and survivable option for Tornado at least at the outset of hostilities. This would be especially true of operations in Europe, our primary theatre. Here, weather considerations alone could easily preclude the use at medium level of the present generation of precision guided munitions. 'Dumb' bombs would be the sole remaining option and, although they are suitable for area targets, even Tornado's excellent weapon system lacks the accuracy to make them a truly cost effective alternative. Secondly, Low Level operations are the most demanding and, as they require the greatest crew skills, they therefore need the most rigorous training. This policy paid off handsomely in the Gulf conflict. Once the operational conditions were judged to be favourable, the RAF was able to move to medium level and be effective immediately only because this was an easier environment for the crews to operate in than the Low Level one for which they were trained. Consider for a moment the opposite scenario. Imagine that we had trained and had intended to operate at medium level but that the tactical situation suddenly demanded a change to Low Level operations. Frankly, such a course of action would be quite impossible to execute at short notice because our crews simply would not have the required skills to be effective.

The training programme was based around three main detachment/exercise cycles, which ran concurrently. Although their periodicity was broadly 12, 18 and 24 months respectively, this was by no means rigid and squadrons could bid to modify the agenda if they so wished. Typically, in the annual cycle we would be scheduled to attend an Armament Practice Camp at Decimomannu in Sardinia where we would concentrate solely on improving our basic weaponry skills. Next, once a year we would expect to take part in the NATO Squadron Exchange Programme which, as the name suggests, would give us an opportunity to compare tactics and doctrine with one of our sister squadrons. As an example of the value of such programmes, in July 1990 XV Squadron exchanged with the 81st Tactical Fighter Squadron, a USAFE unit based at Spangdahlem in Germany. Six months later, in the Gulf conflict, the 81st was supporting XV on operational missions using procedures that we had practiced together the previous summer. Finally on the annual cycle, we would deploy to Goose Bay in Labrador where we would practice those events such as bad weather operations using the terrain following radar, or very low flying, which for reasons of crowded airspace or environmental pressures were not easily possible in Europe.

Turning now to the 18-month cycle, we would expect to deploy to Decimomannu again, but this time to take advantage of the Air Combat and Manoeuvering Installation where we would aim to improve our air combat skills. Once every 18 months the trappers' who would come from the Tornado Weapons Conversion Unit would visit us. Their function as standardisers was to check our aircraft systems knowledge and ensure that we were operating in accordance with standard operating procedures. Lastly in this cycle, another external team of evaluators would rigorously check our nuclear procedures. Every two years, in this the final round of major events, each squadron would have the opportunity to take part in a 'FLAG' exercise in North America. FLAGEX's offer training as close to real operational missions as it is possible to get in peacetime. For example, the experience XV Squadron gained on its red flag in March 1990 flying as part of large multi-national packages was to prove invaluable a year later in the Gulf. As part of the preparation for such exercises, squadrons would also conduct specific work-up training either in the UK or Goose Bay. Completing the training programme would be the two most rigorous external evaluations of all: MAXEVAL, which was a national check of war-fighting capability and TACEVAL, its NATO equivalent. Both of these exercises would last about four days and would put the airbase through a demanding series of evolutions designed to test every aspect of operational proficiency. Interspersed with these major cycles would be a plethora of national and NATO exercises, as well as various station training programmes, all designed to keep our personnel and equipment at the very peak of efficiency. Within this busy and demanding framework, we at squadron level would seek to ensure that our own individual needs were not forgotten and that we maintained continuity and expertise in the diverse skills required by the modern fighting unit.

The Tornado GR1 units formed in the Gulf were considerably bigger in manpower terms than their peacetime counterparts for a number of reasons. Firstly, although in the Gulf the Squadrons were established for 12 aircraft, the same as in peace, some engineering practices were different. Aircraft earmarked for the Gulf were prepared in such a way that deep maintenance would not be required for some time. Aircraft approaching a scheduled maintenance period were rotated out of theatre and replaced with newly prepared ones thus keeping the total available at squadron level at 12. The net result was that we had the potential to generate more flying than was the case under normal conditions. Secondly, it has long been recognised in RAF circles that, for true 24-hour operations, an aircrew to aircraft ratio of 2:1 would be more appropriate than our peacetime figure of 1½:1. The latter figure was as much related to how much flying we could reasonably generate from our peacetime resources in an 18 hour flying day as it was to the operational requirement. Since no such airframe or environmental restrictions applied in the Gulf, in order to take advantage of the Tornado's 24-hour capability, we boosted our manning to 24 aircrews and 200 groundcrew. The inevitable consequence of this was that no single squadron could meet the manning requirements from within its own resources. In my own case, although from November XV was the lead squadron for the Muharraq Tornado detachment and as such provided half of the total manpower, the other half was formed from elements of three other squadrons. By the end of hostilities there were no less than five squadrons from three different airbases and two Commands represented in my detachment. This situation was less than ideal but, since the whole Tornado force works to the same basic operating procedures and is regularly standardised, in the event there were no real difficulties.

When the Gulf crisis erupted in August of 1990, the high quality of our routine training had ensured that our personnel were well prepared for the prospect of imminent hostilities. The Tornado F.3 crews proved this by mounting combat air patrols within hours of arriving in theatre. By the same token, the Tornado GR.1 crews could have flown operational missions immediately had the situation demanded. Nevertheless, clearly it would have been irresponsible not to have taken advantage of the months preceding the UN's January deadline to conduct training aimed specifically at preparing crews for the Gulf. Therefore, except for those first aircrews deployed in August, all subsequent crews underwent a 20-sortie syllabus in the UK before being sent into theatre. In the main, the extra missions were aimed at improving performance in those areas, which were least practised in peacetime for safety, cost or environmental reasons. The syllabus concentrated on air-to-air refuelling, very low flying by day and night, and heavy weight operations. Once in the Gulf, crews maintained their proficiency by flying profiles designed to mirror the potential war missions as closely as possible. A short, two-hour profile to Saudi Arabia mirrored those missions we might fly to northern Kuwait whereas the longer, four hour profile to Oman mirrored the possible missions to the Baghdad area. All included air-to-air refuelling, many were conducted at night and some were conducted in packages of allied aircraft. Every crew experienced handling the aircraft at its maximum all-up weight in the full war fit of JP233 or eight 1,000lb bombs.[142] The terrain varied enormously from the steep-sided, rocky gorges and 1000-foot sand dunes of Oman to the classic featureless desert of Saudi Arabia.

Wing Commander John Broadbent in front of Tornado GR.I ZA491/N *Nikki* at Muharraq in 1991. (John Broadbent)

The training routine continued unabated through November and across Christmas into the New Year. On 9 January, in order to ensure that everyone's body clocks had had a chance to readjust, I took the precaution of initiating the wartime shift pattern. The schedule was based upon the anticipated tasking which called for mostly night missions in the first days of any conflict. The mood of the Detachment took on a serious, reflective note and, even as the last few days ebbed away and the UN deadline approached, most crews still hoped for a political settlement. But it was not to be. On the afternoon of 16 January, I was called by my Detachment Commander and ordered to gather my crews so that they could receive final briefings to prepare them for hostilities. The training was over and Operation *Desert Storm* was about to break. We were about to find out the hard way whether we were as well prepared as we thought we were.

By the time the Gulf War began at 23.40Z on Wednesday 16 January, the coalition had built an air force of 2,790 aircraft, over half of which were combat aircraft. Included in this total was the RAF contribution of 135 aircraft, which included forty-six Tornado GR.1/IA attack and reconnaissance aircraft. The RAF had dispatched almost its entire tanker fleet to the Gulf region. A maximum of nine VC 10 K.Mk.2/3s of 101 Squadron and two TriStar K.Mk.Is of 216 Squadron were at King Khalid Airport just outside Riyadh. On completion of their fighter-bomber positioning assignments one Victor arrived at Muharraq on 14 December for a formal handover from 101 Squadron VC 10 detachment,

JP233 being loaded under the fuselage of a Gulf War Tornado. (RAF Marham)

which had been operating at the Saudi base for three months. The next day three more Victors arrived, followed shortly by two more crews, as Wing Commander David Williams, OC 55 Squadron, recalls:

The initial requirement from RAF Strike Command was that the Victor detachment should support the Tornado F.3 and Jaguar missions only and the VC 10 detachment would support all Tornado GR.I sorties. After all ground training was completed flying began on 16 December to air-refuelling 'towlines' scattered throughout the Saudi Arabian airspace. It became apparent that the rigid apportioning of receivers to tankers was impractical and the Victors supported all types of aircraft from the UK, Canada, France and the United States Navy and Air Force that were probe and drogue compatible. After two weeks of intensive flying, four crews returned to the UK so that the remaining four crews could be brought into the environment and be fully trained to a war footing by 12 January 1991. On this date additional Victor aircraft together with the two initial crews were positioned at Muharraq and by 16 January 55 Squadron was a total of six aircraft, eight crews and ninety-nine ground crew. Further training sorties were flown until 16 January when at 2250 Zulu, two Victors led the first Muharraq Tornado GR.I bombing mission into Iraq. The sortie was flown along olive low trail, which was a track south of the Iraq border but concluded with a northerly heading to cast off the receivers into the heart of Iraq. olive trail then became the bread and butter for the rest of the war. To meet all contingencies and to ensure that fuel was available for the Tornadoes on their return from the mission, all Victor aircraft were refuelled to the maximum 123,000lb for take-off. The early sorties were affected

Tornado dispensing its JP233 clusters of anti-personnel mines from the front and retarded runway-cratering bomblets from the rear section. (BAE SYSTEMS)

by very poor weather along the refuelling tracks and consequently, the aircraft consumed treble the normal fatigue. As experience grew, the take-off fuel was adjusted and the fatigue penalty was reduced.[143]

Wing Commander John Broadbent recalls:

I knew that in the early stages of any conflict at least, the Tornadoes would primarily be used for night operations. This meant that most of my 24 crews were allocated to the night shift. As the UN deadline loomed I thought that it was prudent to initiate the night shift system so that our5 body clocks would adjust to the conditions. Then, in the afternoon of 16 January, whilst the night shift was sleeping, I got the 'phone call from Group Captain Dave Henderson the Bahrain Detachment Commander. He said, 'Bring everybody in'.

'In?' I queried.

'Yes. Brief everybody.'

In the first week of January I had lost the twelve Tornado crews who had the most theatre experience when 14 Squadron went home. (Aircrews changed over every six weeks in the Gulf). In their place I got six from 27 Squadron and six from 617 Squadron. 14 Squadron's ground crews, who were on a three-month detachment, stayed! XV Squadron, my squadron, plus attrition reserves from 9 Squadron, made up the rest of the Muharraq detachment. I was in charge of elements of five squadrons from three air bases in two commands: RAF Germany and Strike!

I told the crews to rest but how could they now? There were some really serious looking young men around. We had all hoped it wouldn't come to this, that instead Saddam would come to his senses and back down. This was not our back yard. We weren't fighting for the White Cliffs of Dover. It's very difficult in the cold light of day in a distant land to fight for a principle. None of our people would choose to die in the desert, given the option, but their attitude was: 'Let's get it done, as professionally as we can and lets get home as soon as possible'. Ours was arguably the most dangerous mission going in the Gulf. Nevertheless, while there was a military reason for what they were being tasked to do, my people were determined to execute it to the best of their ability. Equally, I was determined too and knowing what the overall picture was, I knew I had a good chance of arranging it. Following the initial brief for the Operation, crews were assigned to their specific missions so that they could put the final touches to the plans. My position as Tornado Squadron Commander had entitled me to be one of the very few people at Muharraq to be involved in pre-planning missions for *Desert Storm*. In peacetime training exercises we were used to picking up other people's plans and flying them at short notice. Of course, you would hardly expect to get shot at on a training flight on the North German plain and so the precise angle of cut on a runway was not life-threateningly critical. This was in marked contrast to the Gulf where we fully expected to be engaged by a well-equipped, battle-experienced enemy. Hence, our attitude to planning changed somewhat and we would pore for hours over maps deciding on best aiming points, approach directions, weapon loads and fuse settings to ensure maximum weapon effect at minimum risk.[144]

One advantage of having been involved in the planning phase was that I had been able to set up the shift system in such a way as to ensure that I would be in a position to lead the first mission. I put XV Squadron crews into the first two waves. (27 and 617 Squadrons would cover the following night). Squadron Leader Nigel Risdale and I would lead the first eight Tornadoes. Our target was [Al] Tallil airfield in southwest Iraq, a huge airfield twice the size of Heathrow. We were to cut the two 11,000ft parallel runways and the access taxiways leading from the HAS's [hardened aircraft shelters] with our JP233 anti-airfield weapons. Other, US packages were planned to strike the airfield first. Their time over target was 04.00 hours; ours was eight minutes later at 04.08 hours.[145]

It was a funny feeling, emptying the contents of your pockets into little plastic bags to be collected by the pretty Squadron Intelligence Officer. It was an odd moment when she gave us our 'Goolie Chits', evasion maps and gold sovereigns before we trooped off. We gave ourselves plenty of time to prepare. Very few people in the detachment knew we were going to war at this stage. Not even the ground crews knew. We'd carried JP233 on night training missions before, so this appeared no different. We tried to make it look like a normal training mission. It worked.

It was very lonely taxiing out with radio and lights out. Group Captain David Henderson and his OC Ops, Ray Horwood, gave us a brief wave. Our all-up weight of 30 tonnes with drop tanks and two JP233s (alone weighing 10,000lb) meant we could not taxi to the into-wind runway. The net result was a very short taxi followed by a tailwind take-off. All eight of us got airborne, checked in with the Airborne Warning and Control System (AWACS) aircraft and 20 minutes after take-off, met up with our VC 10 tankers who would take us to our entry point into Iraq. Tanking conditions on this first night were quite good, which was in sharp contrast to what was to occur over the following few nights. All eight aircraft refuelled successfully at around 15,000ft and about one hour and 20 minutes after take-off we left the tankers and headed north. We descended to 500ft in the black night sky towards Iraq and the unknown. Then we went down to 200ft as we approached the target area. On the ingress frequency we heard the support packages of fighter sweep Wild Weasels and jammers and F-15s confirm that they too were on time. I could not of course see them in the darkness, but it was reassuring to hear them. The American package of about 30 aircraft was going to the same target and would bomb from medium altitude (around 20,000ft). We were to bash through one minute after them, at 04:08 local, so that our JP233 minefield would be undisturbed.

Up until this point, it had been just like a training sortie but now came the real test. Would our tactics work? What would it be like to be under fire? Would we all come back? We all experienced some apprehension as the Iraqi border slid down our moving maps and we entered enemy territory for the first time. We had selected the crossing point because Intelligence had indicated that it was well clear of enemy threats and I for one was considerably relieved that they were proved right on the night. The early part of the Low Level phase proceeded uneventfully with just a few distant lights to be seen. The silence was broken only by the comforting call of 'picture clean' from the AWACS indicating that no enemy aircraft were airborne. However, this quiet scene was not to last.

When we were about 70 miles from the target, Nigel could see through his NVGs [night vision goggles] the glow from a major battle, which was in progress in our 10 o'clock and as yet over the horizon from us. Nigel said, 'There's a bloody great punch-up going on,' or words to that effect. I wasn't wearing NVGs. I looked up and just saw darkness. Glancing at my watch, it was 11 o'clock – 4 o'clock local, the time the first American aircraft was due over Tallil. I had a quick look at my map to confirm that we would be shortly turning left to start our final run to the target. It seemed probable that the flak that Nigel could see was emanating from our target and was aimed at the American aircraft preceding us. This was confirmed minutes later as we turned towards the airfield and the flak moved into our 12 o'clock. It was obvious the firefight was coming from Tallil and that we'd have to fly through it. I asked, 'Just how fast can this Tornado go?' Nigel hit the burners, then took the burners out before we came over the visual horizon of the target. The firefight was right on our nose. Triple-A fire was hosing the sky. Occasionally, a friendly HARM high-speed anti-radiation missile was on its way down and distinctly unfriendly SAMs [surface-to-air missiles] would light the sky up. It was all just incredible. Many descriptions of what it looked like have been attempted but none do it justice. My own recollection is one of criss-crossing chains of multi-coloured, incandescent balls of tracer arcing up into the night sky. These were interspersed with masses of red speckles of what I assumed was small-arms fire. As far as we could tell, little if any of the fire was actually aimed at us, but it was difficult to convince your bowels of the truth or even relevance of that fact.

As we approached the airfield, it seemed highly improbable that you could penetrate that seemingly bloody great wall of fire and hope to emerge unscathed out of the other side. My wave of four were converging on the airfield on a heading of 343°; the rear four on a heading of 078°. There would be one Tornado over target every 20 seconds, so that after two minutes 20 seconds all eight would have delivered their JP233s at Low Level and cleared the target at 550 knots. We rushed over the target wings level for 5-6 seconds to get the JP233s away. Balls of tracer and cannon fire were coming towards us like a pretty firework display. It was like trying to run through a shower without getting wet. I recall saying 'good luck' or something equally inane to Nigel and then putting my head down to make sure that I had the target marked perfectly on the radar. I motored my seat down so nothing could not distract me. In peacetime our cockpit seats would have been high. Nigel pushed the speed up to as fast as we could go and got the height down to the absolute minimum compatible with the correct functioning of our JP233. Seconds later we were over the airfield and the cockpit was surrounded by tracer flashes. The JP233 started to dispense automatically with a thunderous roar; lighting up the undersurface of the aircraft with a dull red glow as it did so. Far more quickly than I had anticipated, since I had imagined that this part of the mission would appear interminable, the heavy thump of the now-empty weapon dispensers being automatically jettisoned signalled that the attack was over. The aircraft leaped forward freed of its huge weapon load and we were out the other side and safe. Feelings of relief and almost euphoria washed over us 'Holy Shit – I've survived!', I thought. Exhilaration! I felt ten foot tall – if not taller. Our attack was perfect.

But our euphoria was soon to be cut short. I waited a couple of minutes before checking the rest of the formation in. All responded until I got to No. 5 – nothing. '5 Check'. Still nothing. 'We've lost "Gordo" (Gordon Buckley), leader of the back four', I thought. 'We've lost him. I'm not surprised. Bloody good mate. Paddy Teakle too. Two really good hands. Never see them again.' My exhilaration was gone…In our Tornado clangers were going off WAH, WAH, WAH, red lights were flashing, and 'Kojaks' (warning sirens) were blaring away. We were not going as fast as we should. We suddenly realized we had lost an engine. In the heat of battle we had not realized it. We did not jettison our tanks and in any case the aircraft was much lighter without the JP233s. We retraced our steps across the desert and turned back to the tanker. We were pretty quiet because we thought we had lost 'Buckers'. I was convinced that we had lost him when, despite repeated efforts to raise him on the radio, 20 minutes later we had reached the tanker with still no sign of him. Then, climbing up to the tanker, we heard him! He had heard us calling him but he had a weak transmitter and we could not hear him! I now have sympathy with those that say you have to experience pain to understand pleasure because when he did eventually check in my joy was complete. The rest of the mission was relatively uneventful; even having to shut down an engine on the transit back to Muharraq seemed totally innocuous after what we had experienced over Iraq. We were first back at Muharraq at six in the dawn sky, four hours and five minutes after take-off, to an enthusiastic welcome. And we were just in time to encourage the guys waiting to go out in the next wave [to Ar Rumaylah airfield for daylight lofting or 'toss-bombing' of 1,000 pounders]. Squadron Leader Pablo Mason looked grey. The world's press was waiting. Rupert Clark, my own No.4, told the press, 'It went on rails!'[146] The guys couldn't have done better. I couldn't have asked them to do more. (Post-strike photos showed a very successful outcome and no more than a 20ft error). There was lots of 'Biggles banter' with the troops. We said the usual, that it was 'a piece of piss', 'nothing to worry about', etc! I rushed into squadron HQ still wearing my G-bags. Throwing open Dave Henderson's door I shouted: 'We're all back!'

My formation was lucky, we all returned. Others were not so fortunate and over the next three days the Muharraq detachment was to lose three crews in quick succession, including John Peters and John Nichol from the formation we had waved off with such enthusiasm shortly after dawn on 17 January.[147] The leadership challenge following the losses at this time was not as great as one might imagine since I noted a marked stiffening of attitudes amongst the aircrews and a grim determination to get the job done. Nevertheless, we all felt a great deal of satisfaction

Flight Lieutenant Rupert Clark and his navigator are interviewed on their return from their first Gulf War sortie on 18 January.

and relief when the Allied forces gained air supremacy so swiftly. The effectiveness of the RAF's JP233 attacks certainly played its part in this achievement. My own formation flew its third and final JP233 mission on the night of 20 January and we moved medium level the following day. The rest, as they say, is history.[148]

On the night of 17–18 January Marham crews formed a four-ship Tornado attack on Ubaydah bin al Jarrah airfield, and another four were given Al Tallil airfield at Shaibah close to the city of Basrah as their target. Each of the eight Tornadoes was loaded with two JP233s. Other Tornadoes would return to take-out the taxiways the following day. The al Jarrah formation took off at midnight local time, and the 'Norwich' formation took off for Shaibah two hours later, as their shorter journey required just one pre-attack refuelling from a VC 10. One of the pilots on the Shaibah strike was newly promoted twenty-four-year-old Flight Lieutenant David Waddington of 27 Squadron. Waddington had been part of the original team of Tornado crews that had deployed to the Gulf essentially for training and on alert should the Iraqis invade Saudi Arabia. After six weeks, when it was decided to put more Tornadoes in theatre, he and the rest of the 'Marham Group' had split from the 'Germany Group' and had moved to Tabuk. As part of the rotation of crews Waddington returned to England just before Christmas 1990. He was not scheduled to return to the

JP233 clusters exploding. (Hunting)

Gulf until April 1991. His proposal to his fiancée, Claire Holderness, a young nurse, was accepted and they made plans for a summer wedding. However, as the Gulf crisis escalated early in the New Year Waddington was called back and re-deployed to Bahrain in January. This time he and his fellow pilots sensed a definite increase in tension as the 15 January deadline approached.

After taking on fuel, the four Tornadoes heading for al Jarrah dropped to 300ft crossing the Iraqi border, and steadily descended to 200ft over the desert to the target, where the sky was lit up by AAA fire five minutes before they went in. Flying parallel to the runway in 'card four' formation (the leading pair 2 miles apart, the trailing pair thirty seconds' flying time behind them), they turned towards the airfield. The spacing was closed up to 1 mile and the interval to fifteen seconds, then ten. With one minute to go, Flying Officer Nigel Ingle and Flight Lieutenant Paul McKernan of 617 Squadron in ZD744 felt a bump and thought they had been hit, but the Tornado was still flyable – just. Flight Lieutenant Beet and Flight Lieutenant Osborne, and Flight Lieutenant Ruddock and Squadron Leader Crowley, each dropped their two JP233s at one-fifth and three-fifths along the runway's length. Flight Lieutenant Waddington and Flight Lieutenant Hammans, and Ingle and McKernan, released their pair at the two-fifths and four-fifths points. After turning for home Ingle could not maintain control above 350 knots and when he eventually found the VC 10 tanker he could

Tornado GR.Is 'EE' and 'Q' and ZA471/E Emma in the foreground. (Air Commodore Ian MacFadyen)

only maintain formation by adopting 45°-wing sweep. He managed to reach Muharraq safely where inspection revealed that the Tornado had suffered a bird strike that had removed a large section of the port wing's leading edge. The Tornado was immediately patched and flown back to Brüggen for repair. Three days later it was re-delivered to the Gulf and went on to complete thirty-five missions.

All went well as the 'Norwich' formation flew the ingress route over Iraq to Shaibah at 550 knots, relying only on the radar altimeter to keep them 200ft above the desert and a map to locate the electricity pylons to the north and east of the airfield. Firing started within 2 miles of the Iraqi border and continued remorselessly until the aircraft were back over the border into friendly territory. All the JP233s were successfully released but there was heavy triple-A fire from the ground and the Iraqis also sent up SAM missiles. Waddington recalls:

There were one or two missiles, which with the benefit of hindsight were probably unguided. I was just so focused on getting through that there was no real fear, more apprehension. We just wanted to get out the other side but we were busy doing our job in the cockpit. On leaving the target there was a huge explosion on the desert floor. Once the shooting stopped and we came out of Iraq and towards friendly territory we were over the sea climbing for our return to Bahrain and checked in with the AWACs. At that point they informed us that there were only three of us. There is a still a huge element of doubt over what happened and I do not think we will ever really know. [ZA392 flown by 27 Squadron's 39-year old CO, Wing Commander Nigel Elsdon and his 42-year old navigator, Flight Lieutenant Robert 'Max' Collier was hit three minutes after 'bombs away' and had crashed into the ground, killing both crew. The three other Tornadoes landed safely back at Muharraq after 1 hour 55 minutes in the air.] Even before then we knew that Peters and Nichol were missing because they had been flying from Bahrain in a different formation. So we knew this thing was dangerous and we knew that going against airfields was going to be dangerous by its very nature. I knew when I signed up that I could be called upon to do this sort of thing. It was under a UN mandate and it was war and although it was not the sort of thing we had envisaged I do not think there was any question as to why we were there. But this loss of Elsdon and Collier personally hit very, very hard together with the fact that the two Johns were missing. There was now an unspoken fear about who was going to be next.[149]

The Tornado crews were flying night combat sorties only, and at Muharraq on the 19–20th eight Tornadoes of 'Belfast' formation were made ready for a raid on Tallil air base in central Iraq. Four of the Tornadoes were armed with JP233s, and another four were loaded with eight 1,000-pounders fused for an airburst 15ft above the Iraqi gun emplacements. Fifty years earlier Marham's Mosquito low-levellers and shallow raiders had employed similar tactics. At 14.57Z seven Tornadoes (the eighth developed mechanical failure) headed for Tallil. The approach to the target was not as dangerous as before and the Tornadoes flew though the middle of Saudi Arabia, meeting no resistance whatsoever. Tornado GR.I ZA396 was crewed by Flight Lieutenant David Waddington and his forty-four-year-old navigator, Flight Lieutenant Robert Stewart who was also from 27 Squadron. Waddington recalls:[150]

We were only flying over Iraq for about 30 minutes until we hit the target. Absolutely pitch dark, nothing around us – just like doing a training sortie. I was the number two aircraft in the formation and consequently, with the tactics, among the first to arrive at the airfield. We were trying to do a surprise job dropping the 1,000 pounders to suppress the triple-A so that the last four aircraft, who were carrying JP233s, would have an easier time. It meant pulling the aircraft into a climb in a 'toss attack' and letting the bombs go at 30° climb about three miles from the target. We were just coming up to the pull-up point where we would release the bombs, three and a half miles from the target. I saw the bright yellow flame of a [Euromissile Roland SAM] launch at me, at 12 o'clock, which is the worst position. My exact words were 'Shit! Missile!' I broke left and shouted 'Chaff' at Robbie. All I could see was a flame like a very large firework coming towards me but once I banked the aircraft we lost sight of it. Then there was aan enormous wind – I think I was unconscious very quickly. My last thoughts were that I was going to die. [The blast shattered the canopy, caused the hydraulics and started a fire in the cockpit]. Fortunately for me Robbie in the back seat had been protected because of the equipment and he used the command ejection system to eject us out [at 540 knots and only 180ft above the ground]. My next memory after that was regaining consciousness on the ground. I have no recollection of the parachute landing but probably about half an hour later I came to. I realised that I had taken a lot of injuries, albeit superficial, to my face. Both arms were dislocated at right shoulder and left elbow. Asa result of that I could not recover my parachute and because it was still inflated I could not recover my survival equipment. The pockets of my G-suit were blown away but my life jacket still had the radio and other essentials for short-term survival. The collective feeling of the rest of the formation was that we had not got out and they expected that we were dead.

I realized that I could not stay where I was and had to put some distance between where I was then and where I wanted to be by daylight. At that stage I was still trying to make radio

CPU-123/B (British 1,000lb bomb fitted with Paveway II guidance system) and inscribed: 'WITH LOVE FROM THE FOX AND HOUNDS MARHAM XXX'. It was the only laser-guided bomb (LGB) employed by RAF aircraft in the Gulf War. (GEC-Marconi)

contact and although I suspected my radio was not working I kept trying to transmit. I was several hundred miles the wrong side of the border and had not been able to make contact with friendly forces. To be honest, the situation was still pretty poor. From where I was I tried to walk away. My legs were fine so I decided to try to escape and evade until daybreak. By then I had travelled four or five miles to a position where there were two pipelines. They were about 40ft apart so I tried to hide in the middle of them. But in the flat desert it was not too difficult for someone to follow a trail and some in the morning a couple of Iraqi soldiers spotted me. They started firing, pretty close to me. I don't think they were firing at me but they were sending me a clear warning. As thy got closer I could see that they were quite scared of me. They knew I was armed and they kept gesticulating to me to put my arms above my head and surrender. But I could not do that. Both my arms had been dislocated and I could not raise them. There was a bit of a stand-off as they wondered what was going to happen but eventually they disarmed me, took away my pistol and then led me away to their barracks little more than a shed in the desert.

Waddington was taken to Al Tallil airfield, his target the night before, and he was then moved to Baghdad where, blindfolded, he was interrogated by Ba'ath Party officials. His consistent refusal to answer questions, apart from the 'big four' of name, rank, serial number and date of birth, was met with severe beatings with fists and sticks, which left him unconscious or on the verge of consciousness. Eventually his blindfold was lifted and

Released Allied POWs on 10 March 1991. From top to bottom: John Nichol, Rupert Clark, Dave Waddington and Robbie Stewart. Waddington said that he wanted to come down the steps just to show his family that he was okay. There was still an element of doubt about who was alive and who was not. (EDP)

the Iraqis showed him his aircraft checklist, which had his name and aircraft type on it. The physical elements of the beatings then transferred to the psychological phase but soon they became less intensive and eventually stopped. Waddington was taken to hospital in Baghdad and an operation was carried out on his damaged elbow. In prison his weight eventually dropped from 10½ stones to just over 8 stones. His only contact with other prisoners was when he heard the guards speak to them. He was aware that the American F-16 pilot Captain Jeff Tice and the captured Kuwaiti A-4KU Skyhawk pilot, Mohammed Mubarak, were nearby.[151] He did not know what had happened to Robbie Stewart and considered that he had already made his escape on foot. What had actually happened to him was that when he landed he broke his leg in three places, and Iraqi civilians picked him up in the morning and handed him over to the military authorities in return for payment of $20,000. On or around 23 February the Americans bombed the prison holding the captured airmen but fortunately they hit the other half and not where the prisoners were, and several guards were killed. Later, Waddington supposed that while the worst moment of captivity was when he realised he had been shot down, the most frightening was the bombing of the prison, and psychologically the worst thing was being kept in a pitch black cell for three weeks or so. Just after the explosions the prisoners were able to do a quick roll call and Waddington shouted 'Does anyone know what happened to Robbie Stewart?' The reply came back, 'I'm here Dave'. Both men were repatriated after the end of the war.[152]

By 23 January five Tornadoes had been lost in action.[153] Although the Tornado force represented just 4 per cent of the coalition air strength it had suffered 26 per cent of the casualties. It was obvious to all that precision-guided weapons were the only salvation if the Tornadoes were to remain at medium level. Buccaneers fitted with the pavespike pod, which provided a manually controlled TV picture by day only, were deployed to act as laser designators for the Tornadoes.[154] What was needed urgently was a laser designator for use on the Tornado to direct Laser Guided Bombs (LGBs) on to the target at night. Ferranti had been involved in the development of such a system since 1973 and this culminated in the production of a Thermal Imaging Airborne Laser Designator (TIALD) pod, which had been under flight development on a Buccaneer at RAE Farnborough since early 1988. To permit day and night operation under varying weather conditions, TIALD was equipped with thermal imaging and a TV camera, which were mounted in a pod carried beneath the aircraft. The designator was integrated into the aircraft's navigation and attack (nav/attack) system to enable it to be directed and controlled, and the thermal or visual images were recorded by the infra-red recce recorder in the Tornado GR.1A. Before TIALD the RAF's ability to use LGBs depended on designation of the target by a manually controlled laser marker. This was operated either from a ground-based designator, as was used in the Falklands conflict, or from the air. In the latter case, the marker equipment was fitted to a Buccaneer and controlled by the navigator. Although it was employed successfully during the Gulf War, there were several limitations to this system. The main one was that the navigator needed to see the target visually, thus limiting its use to good weather by day. Additionally, it could not be integrated with a modern nav/attack system, and having located the target the navigator had to track it visually – not easy in turbulence or if the

Flight Lieutenant Dave Waddington (left) and Flight Lieutenant Robbie Stewart (with arm raised) on their return to Marham from captivity. Stewart's left hand is on the shoulder of Pilot Officer Simon Burgess, at twenty-three the youngest pilot in the conflict, while following behind is Squadron Leader Bob Ankerson. On 23 January Burgess and Ankerson had ejected, after the explosion of one of their bombs on release detonated the others aboard their Tornado. Both men were taken prisoner, although their families were unaware of this until they were released on 5 March. The bodies of Wing Commander Elsdon and Flight Lieutenant Collier of 27 Squadron arrived in the UK on 19 March 1991. (RAF Marham)

aircraft was taking evasive action. During the preparations for *Granby*, Ferranti were asked to accelerate development of TIALD and its integration into the Tornado system, the main problem being the extensive computer software changes required by this integration. This problem was overcome and it planned to complete the work within six weeks, starting from 30 November 1990. Within three weeks a modified pod was delivered to Boscombe Down and the RAF had allocated five Tornado GR1s for modification to carry the TIALD pod. 13 Squadron were selected to introduce TIALD into service and four experienced crews carried out development trials at the site.

On arrival at Tabuk the TIALD team was taken over by OC 617 Squadron. Wing Commander Bob Iveson is probably the only RAF officer to have flown on operations in both the Falklands and Gulf Wars. (During the Falklands War he was shot down flying a Harrier and had ejected.) The normal procedure was for two bomber aircraft to fly at

'Welcome Back 617 Gulf Crews' at Marham in 1991. (RAF Marham)

about 20,000ft in close proximity to the Tornado, which carried the TIALD pod but no bombs; this allowed two sticks of bombs to be dropped on two targets in a single pass by the TIALD aircraft. Each of the bombers carried a maximum of three LGBs. On the run up, the TIALD aircraft fired its laser designator for a period of about thirty seconds to illuminate the target. The laser energy was reflected back over a large area in the general direction of the designator. Within these reflections was a region in the form of an inverted cone known as the 'basket' (not to be confused with the AAR basket). It was necessary for the bomber aircraft to drop their bombs within this 'basket' if the laser seeker in the nose of the bomb was to receive signals of sufficient energy to acquire the target. It was also necessary for the canard control fins and tail wings to be able to deflect the bomb onto it from its normal trajectory. As soon as the bombs were observed to burst on the first target, the designator was aligned on the second target and fired to guide the bombs, which had already been released, from the second aircraft. Later, with experience, it became possible for the TIALD aircraft to designate four targets in a single pass.

Arrival of the TIALD-equipped Tornadoes allowed Tabuk to switch to precision missions on 30 February, and from then until the end of the Gulf War the Tornadoes at all three bases flew few free-fall bombing missions.[155] Flight Lieutenant Adrian Frost, a navigator on 617 Squadron who carried out the first operational TIALD sortie[156] recalls:

> The RAF's capability for the airborne designation of LGBs provided by the pavespike pod fitted
> to the Buccaneer was a 20-year-old design and was fitted with only a TV camera. Hence it could

Tornado GR.IA ZA398/S of II (AC) Squadron, Tornado GR.I 'JM' of 27 Squadron and Tornado GR.I 'X' of 617 Squadron with Victor K.2 XH672 *Maid Marian* of 55 Squadron in 1993. (RAF Marham)

provide only a daylight capability. The necessity for night operations meant that TIALD would be rushed into service as soon as possible. The only TIALD pods available at the time were two flight demonstrator pods with TI only, which had been flying on a Buccaneer test-bed aircraft. These had never been designed for carriage on the Tornado. Indeed, there were no Tornado aircraft capable of carrying the pods either. However, a rapid development programme, TAP (Tornado advanced programme) was undertaken at the Aeroplane & Armament Experimental Establishment (A&AEE), Boscombe Down. The two pods, affectionately called Sandra and Tracy [after the 'Fat Slags' cartoon characters in Viz magazine] entered operational service on 10 February, flying from Tabuk and destroying hardened aircraft shelters at the H3 south-west airfield complex in north-west Iraq. As testament to their outstanding success, the two pods flew 91 missions in 18 days, scoring 229 direct hits. Overall their success rate was bettered only by the F-117A Stealth Fighter.

The end of the war came suddenly and unexpectedly when a cease-fire was declared on 28 February 1991. Following the expiry of the United Nations ultimatum for Iraq to withdraw from Kuwait by 15 January, air operations had started on 17 January and had continued for a total of forty-two days, while the ground war – starting on 24 February – had lasted only for 100 hours. However, these operations resulted in the complete defeat of the Iraqi forces.

During *Granby* and *Desert Storm* ten of 55 Squadron's Victor K.2s, the oldest aircraft in the campaign, flew 299 sorties and by 18 March 1991 all had returned to Marham. On 15

Tornado GR.IT ZA411/Z of II (AC) Squadron in Desert Pink scheme for Operation *Jural*, with two BAe ALARM (Air-Launched Anti-Radar Missiles). Under the port wing is an ARI 23246/1 Sky Shadow ECM system, while on the right is a BOZ-107 chaff/flare dispenser. (RAF Marham)

October that same year 55 Squadron was disbanded and the last Victor flight was made six weeks later, on 30 November, when XH672 *Maid Marion* was flown to Shawbury to be dismantled for transportation to the RAF Museum at Cosford. During the Victors' thirty-seven years of flying from Norfolk aerial warfare had changed out of all recognition. During the 1991 Gulf conflict nine out of ten expended weapons were unguided 'dumb' bombs and about one in ten of the weapons were precision-guided. In the next war as far as the bombers – Tornadoes included – were concerned, weapons delivery would largely be laser or satellite-guided. Air superiority had been replaced by a desire for air dominance. In twenty-first-century wars this can only really be achieved by high technology aircraft and laser-guided weaponry. In Britain in early 1992 it had been decided that an interim capability be developed in which production TIALD pods were integrated onto the existing TAP (Tornado advanced programme) 2 software. The programme was called ITC (Interim TIALD capability), and work started at Boscombe Down in July of that year. No sooner had crews arrived to begin what should have been a twelve-week programme, than they were asked to begin flight trials six weeks earlier than planned. Flight Lieutenant Adrian Frost says:

> Obviously things were 'afoot' and speculations rose about the heightened requirement for designation pods and the possible deployment area. Over an tense four-week period, including long sorties and lengthy debriefs, new software for both pod and the aircraft were developed,

the net result being a capability far in excess of that originally required by SR(A) 1015. Speculation was soon quelled by the announcement of the decision to deploy TIALD pods to the Gulf on Operation *Jural*, this time not to designate bombs, but to provide surveillance of Iraqi military positions south of the 32nd parallel as the RAF's contribution to Operation southern watch.

On 27 August 1992, three crews from 617 Squadron and one crew from 13 Squadron joined crews from II(AC) Squadron to set up Operation *Jural*, the RAF's contribution to southern watch, which provided protection for Iraqi Sheihaits from Saddam Hussein's oppression, south of the 32nd parallel. The surveillance role was a new one for TIALD, although during *Desert Storm* imagery was taken of anything interesting on the way to targets and of targets after attacks, in order that battle damage assessment (BDA) could be carried out. As a result, enhanced features were built into the aircraft's main computer software for this new role, including the ability to provide a continual read-out of the position to which the pod is pointing. Operation *Jural* continued with Tornado GR1/GR1A squadrons rotating on a three-monthly basis. Typical TIALD surveillance missions took the form of large multi-national packages of American naval and Air Force aircraft and French fighters. The 'packages' of aircraft regularly numbered over 30, sometimes as many as 50. Sorties took place by day and night lasting up to four hours and, apart from the surveillance of ground targets/areas, included air-to-air refuelling (AAR) with RAF VC 10s.

Although TIALD was being used for surveillance, it must be remembered that it was designed as a designator pod. The ability to carry out the surveillance task is an indication of the flexibility of the pod and the aircraft software. During training sorties over Kuwait in September 1992 LGBs were released at targets on the Udairi Range with a 100% success rate, proving the capability of the new pods. Operationally, TIALD was again put to the test in January 1993 when Saddam Hussein ventured to put surface-to-air missiles south of the 32nd parallel. Two missions were carried out, one at night, the other during the day. Three of the four targets assigned were destroyed.

In day-to-day operations, TIALD is easy to use. The ITC TIALD system is fully integrated into the Tornado's NAS. The TIALD imagery is displayed on the existing rear cockpit displays. Control of the TIALD is by means of the navigator's hand controller (also used to control the radar target mark) and the keys associated with the TV display for minor functions. The TIALD sight-line can be automatically slaved to any target in the aircraft's computer or manually steered. Target tracking is automatic although the navigator can make final refinement of the aiming point. Apart from target designation, TIALD can be used to update the aircraft's NAS just as the GPS (global positioning system) and radar can. If the radar is used, the TIALD will follow the radar mark, helping the navigator to find the target and ensuring that he can immediately identify and refine the TIALD aiming point denoted by a bore-sight cross. Laser fire can be automatically selected or manually input. For post-flight analysis both TV and TI imagery is recorded.

As a result of its accelerated development and the experience of combat operations, TIALD is now a far more capable targeting system than that originally specified by the RAF in 1987. Further TIALD system enhancements were planned as part of SR(A) 1242 and the Tornado Mid-life Update Programme. SR(A) 1242 covered the procurement of an advanced LGB and extra TIALD pods for the Tornado. The contract for a planned 17 extra TIALD pods was awarded in

Tornado GR.I of 617 Squadron in Desert Pink scheme for Operation *Jural*. (RAF Marham)

A Tornado banking over HASs during Operation *Jural*. (RAF Marham)

Tornado of 27 Squadron taking on fuel from a Victor. (RAF Marham)

Victor K.Mk.2 XL190 of 55 Squadron. (RAF Marham)

On 18 April 1982 during the Falklands War the advance party and five Victor K.2 tankers left Marham for Wideawake airfield on Ascension, 3,375 miles from the Falklands. Next day four more Victors flew the 4,100 miles from Marham to Ascension. Squadron Leader A.I.B. 'Al' Beedie of 55 Squadron (pictured), who with Squadron Leader Tony Cowling formed the radar team aboard Squadron Leader John Elliott's Victor, beginning on 20 April, supported by five more Victors operating in the air refuelling mode, flew three maritime reconnaissance operations, each more than fourteen hours duration, to waters in the region of South Georgia. On 16 October 1982, Beedie, now a Wing Commander, scrambled clear of Victor K.2 XL232, which caught fire on take off at Marham. (Author)

Flt Lt Dick Russell, who flew as second pilot on Vulcan, XM607, flown by Flt Lt Martin Withers, which flew the first Black Buck mission on 30 April/1 May 1982 during the Falklands War. Russell, who had just turned fifty, was an experienced Victor AAR instructor at Marham and was added to the cockpit crew to bring some air-to-air refuelling expertise into the Vulcan crews. (Author)

Tornado GR.I ZA411 AJ-S of 617 Squadron taking off from a snow-covered Marham. (Author)

1993. Evaluations on a single-seat aircraft commenced during the summer of 1993 at the Defence Research Agency (DRA) Farnborough and the Central Trials and Tactics Organization (CTTO) Boscombe Down. The final phase of the trials was scheduled to cover night self-designation attacks and this phase took place early in 1994.[157]

With the disbandment in October 1993 and April 1994 of the two Buccaneer Squadrons at Lossiemouth, 12 (as 27 Squadron had been re-numbered in October 1993) and 617 Tornado Squadrons were moved up from Marham to take over the Maritime/Overland strike/Attack role by April 1994. Meanwhile, 39 (1 PRU) Squadron, whose PR.9 and PR.7s and T.4s gave Marham its third period with the Canberra, moved here from Wyton in December 1993. As part of the RAF's draw-down of strength in Germany the reconnaissance GR.IAs of II (AC) Squadron arrived from Laarbruch, to be followed by the second GR.IA unit, 13 Squadron, which arrived from Honington. For the final trip from Honington, the CO led a fly-past of nine Tornadoes in diamond formation over Honington, and then made a similar fly-past in front of the Queen at Marham before landing at their new base. Her Majesty was

Tornado GR.IA of 13 Squadron in a HAS at Marham in February 1997. (Author)

Honorary Air Commodore of Marham and the squadron crews were presented to her after they landed.

With the final closure of RAF bases in Germany on 17 July 2001 IX (B) and 31 Squadrons moved with their Tornado GR.4s from Brüggen to Marham.[158] This move, resulting from the UK's Strategic Defence Review, saw Marham become the RAF's largest and most potent operational, front-line base. On 21 August 2001 six Tornado GR.4 aircraft of 31 Squadron departed from Brüggen and flew over some of the former Royal Air Force bases, as well as bases of the German Air Force. The aim was to bid a final farewell on behalf of all RAF aircrew to those bases that played such a major role in the defence of Europe during the Cold War, both RAF and German. The aircraft took off from Brüggen and flew over Laarbruch, Kalkar, Buchel, Norvenich and Wildenrath, before flying one last time over Brüggen, and they landed at their new home of Marham at 13.31 hours. On Tuesday 4 September 2001 Group Captain Tim Anderson, Station Commander at RAF Brüggen, and Wing Commander John Scholtens, OC Operations Wing, RAF Brüggen, had the honour of flying over the last Tornado GR.4 of IX (B) Squadron to RAF Marham to complete the Marham

Tornado GR.Is 'AX' and 'AM' of IX (B) Squadron, with the BBMF Lancaster painted to represent W4964 *Still Going Strong!*, better known as *Johnny Walker*, of 9 Squadron. On 29 October 1944 forty-seven Lancasters (including eighteen from 9 Squadron and eighteen from 617 Squadron) attacked the *Tirpitz*, which was moored near the Norwegian port of Tromsø. Thirty-two Lancasters dropped Tallboy bombs on the estimated position of the capital ship but no direct hits were scored. On 12 November thirty Lancasters of 9 and 617 Squadrons attacked the *Tirpitz* again and at least two Tallboys hit the ship, which capsized and remained bottom upwards. It has always been a bone of contention between 617 and 9 Squadrons as to whose bombs actually capsized the *Tirpitz*, and over the years a piece of metal from the battleship has often been 'removed' from the respective mess of each unit! (RAF Marham)

Tornado Wing. They arrived at RAF Marham at 11.45 hours, where they were met by a Champagne reception before joining the rest of the squadron in the Officers' Mess for a Squadron Luncheon.

On 23 June 2006, 39 Squadron flew its last PR sorties when two of the unit's Canberra PR.9s returned to Marham, after flying reconnaissance over Afghanistan. Watching their arrival home was Squadron Leader Terry Cairns, who at sixty-one was the oldest operational pilot in the RAF, and had served for thirty-five years on Canberras. He retired from the RAF when 39 Squadron was disbanded on 28 July and its standard was laid up in St Clement Danes Church in London's Strand on 30 July.

On 14 June 2006 Marham's four Tornado GR.4 squadrons formed 138 Expeditionary Air Wing, one of nine main base wings in the RAF. The wing identities adopted by the Main Operating Bases of No.1 Group are drawn from those that participated in the North-West European campaign of 1944–45, as part of the Royal Air Force's Second Tactical Air Force (2TAF). As such, they represent a tangible link to the RAF's expeditionary

Tornado GR.4s of II (AC), IX (B), 13 and 31 Squadrons of 138 Wing. (RAF Marham)

heritage. The three Mosquito fighter-bomber squadrons of 138 Wing became legendary as the 'Gestapo Busters'; making pinpoint raids on headquarter buildings and barracks in the occupied countries of Europe.[159] 138 EAW continues at the forefront of strike and reconnaissance operations throughout the world and it will continue to do so for the foreseeable future, carrying on the fine traditions set by their forebears who flew Wellingtons, Mosquitoes and Stirlings from Marham in the Second World War.

APPENDIX

UNITS STATIONED AT MARHAM

Units	From/To	Aircraft
Units of 31 Squadron	September 1916	F.E.2b/Avro 504
51 Squadron	7 August 1917–14 May 1919	F.E.2b. B.E.2e
191 NTS	6 November 1917–July 1918	F.E.2b. B.E.2c
192 NTS	10 October 1917–14 November 1917	F.E.2b. F.E.2d
38 Squadron	5 May 1937–November 1938	Fairey Hendon
115 Squadron	June 1937–November 1938	HP Harrow
38 Squadron	December 1938–12 November 1940	Wellington I
115 Squadron	12 November 1940–24 September 1942	Wellington I
1 RNZAF Unit	1 June 1939–27 September 1939	Wellington I
218 Squadron	25 November 1940–February 1942	Wellington
218 Squadron	January 1942–7 July 1942	Stirling
3 Group TTF	14 February 1940–18 November 1941	
1418 Flight	6 January 1942–1 March 1942	Wellington
1483 (Bomber)	July 1942–29 June 1943	Wellington Ic & III/
Gunnery Training Flight	Defiant I & II	
ABTF	13 July 1942–15 March 1943	
1483 Flight	13 July 1942–29 June 1943	Lysander/Wellington
1427 Flight	15 September 1942–2 October 1942	Stirling/Halifax
105 Squadron	22 September 1942–23 March 1944	Mosquito IV/IX
139 Squadron	29 September 1942–4 July 1943	Mosquito IV
MCU	29 September 1942–18 October 1942	Mosquito
1655 MTU	28 September 1942–1 May 1943	Mosquito IV
109 Squadron	5 July 1943–2 April 1944	Mosquito IV/IX
1655 MTU	28 September 1942–1 May 1943	Mosquito IV
	July 1943–7 March 1944	
CBE	25 September 1945–14 April 1949	Various

Jet Conversion Flight/ Unit	Gloster Meteor/Oxford	
15 Squadron	29 November 1950–4 February 1951	Lincoln
BC WTS	23 February 1950–1 July 1950	Washington B.I
WCU	1 July 1950–1 September 1951	
	16 June 1952–27 March 1953	Washington B.I
BC JCF	16 November 1953–30 September 1954	
115 Squadron	13 June 1950–1 June 1957	Washington B.I/Canberra B.2
149 Squadron	9 August 1950–17 October 1950	Washington B.I
90 Squadron	4 October 1950–1 May 1956	Washington B.I/Canberra B.2
44 Squadron	7 February 1951–9 April 1951	Washington B.I
35 Squadron	1 September 1951–16 July 1956	Washington B.I/Canberra B.2
207 Squadron	4 June 1951–27 March 1956	Washington B.I/Canberra B.2
214 Squadron	January 1956–May 1965	Valiant B(PR).1
148 Squadron	1 July 1956–1 May 1965	Valiant B(PR).1
242 Squadron	1 October 1959–30 September 1964	BAC Bloodhound SAM
49 Squadron	26 June 1961–1 May 1965	Valiant B(PR).1
1 AEF	1 April 1963–?	DH Chipmunk
55 Squadron	24 May 1965–15 October 1993	HP Victor K.I/K.2
57 Squadron	1 December 1965–30 June 1986	HP Victor K.I/K.2
214 Squadron	21 January 1956–1 March 1965	Valiant B(PR).1
1 Group SU	February 1968–December 1968	Victor B(PR).I
232 OCU	6 February 1970–4 April 1986	HP Victor K.I/K.2
TTF	1965–May 1970	
231 OCU	12 February 1976–31 August 1982	EE Canberra
100 Squadron	5 January 1976–5 January 1982	EE Canberra
617 Squadron	1 January 1983–April 1994	Tornado GR.I
27 Squadron	1 May 1983–October 1993	Tornado GR.I★
★Re-numbered as 12 Squadron October 1993–December 1993	Tornado GR.I	
II (AC) Squadron	1 December 1991–?	Tornado GR.I/4
XIII Squadron	1 February 1994–?	Tornado GR.I/4
39 (I PRU) Squadron December 1993–23 June 2006	EE Canberra PR.7 &9/B.2/T.4	
611 VGS	April 1996–1 May 1996	
31 Squadron	August 2001–?	Tornado GR.4
IX Squadron	September 2001–?	Tornado GR.4

NOTES

CHAPTER ONE — BOMBER STATION

1 *RAF Marham: Transition To War* by E.C. 'Johnnie' Johnson. West Norfolk Aviation Journal, No.2 (summer 1994)

2 The Great Government Aerodrome, *RFC Narborough: The Story of a First World War Airfield*. Narborough Airfields Research Group, 2000.

3 'A few days after our arrival, however, two airmen – one aircraft hand and one airframe fitter, were arrested. It was said at the time that someone fed up with being unable to leave the camp to see his girlfriend had named them to the SIB. It was rumoured that they were going to fly the aircraft to the Civil War in Spain but how they expected to get there with no navigation aids and probably insufficient fuel no one really knows. Perhaps they realised it too, for one of them lost his nerve and pulled the throttles back just as they got airborne. They were both uninjured in the crash, jumped out of the cockpit and disappeared into the darkness of the airfield perimeter and walked back to camp. Their Courts Martial took place a few weeks later and I think they were sentenced to twelve months in the military prison at Colchester, known in those times as the "glass house".'

4 Marham's first Wellington (L4230) was delivered to 38 Squadron on 28 September 1938.

5 *RAF Marham: Transition To War* by E.C. 'Johnnie' Johnson. West Norfolk Aviation Journal, No.2 (summer 1994)

6 The Wellington had been conceived by the brilliant British scientist, Dr Barnes Wallis, using geodetic or lattice work structure. Like many of its genre, the Wellington was weakly armed. The Wellington and the Handley Page Hampden, the Armstrong Whitworth Whitley and Bristol Blenheim – all twin engined bombers – would form the mainstay of Bomber Command early in the coming war.

7 The Vickers Armstrong Wellington was affectionately known as the Wimpy after the Walt Disney cartoon character 'J. Wellington Wimpy' in *Popeye*. On 1 June 1939 1 RNZAF Unit began forming at Marham to fly Wellingtons. A decision had been taken early in 1937 that the New Zealanders would have a complement of thirty Wellingtons, six of which would be ready to leave for the Antipodes in August 1939. When war clouds gathered the New Zealanders were put at the disposal of the RAF and the unit moved to RAF Harwell, where it became 15 OTU.

8 *RAF Marham: Transition To War* by E.C. 'Johnnie' Johnson. West Norfolk Aviation Journal, No.2 (summer 1994)

9   On 29 September, a complete formation of five 144 Squadron Hampdens were destroyed over the German Bight between Heligoland and Wangerooge Island by Bf 109s of I./ZG26. The serious loss inflicted soon convinced the Air Staff that a profound change of its daylight policy was necessary.

10 Also known as Eastmoor landing ground, this site was established in 1939 as a satellite for Marham about 4 miles north-east. Several Hawker Hurricanes of 56 OTU at Sutton Bridge were occasionally dispersed at Barton Bendish in the early war years. From September 1939 twelve Wellingtons of 38, 115 and later 218 Squadron were dispersed here and were refuelled and rearmed at Marham. Ground crews were transported back and forth by road, although some were carried in the Wellingtons. To conceal them from the air, the tails of the Wellingtons were moved under bordering beech trees. (When the satellite was not required for flying, large pipes were laid across the landing ground and large fields in the area had trenches dug to prevent enemy aircraft from landing).

11 With rain showers and overcast at 400ft, the Wellington I was flown by thirty-year-old Sergeant E T. 'Slim' Summers AFM, one of the most experienced pilots on 38 Squadron, having accumulated 1,102 flying hours (of which 167 hours were on Wellingtons). 'Slim' was a very colourful and ebullient character and he had earned his Air Force Medal earlier that year, on 2 January 1939. On 15 May he had saved the life of his rear gunner during a low-level bombing exercise in a Wellington. The starboard engine had failed and 'Slim' was unable to turn the aircraft against the port engine. A fire broke out between the tail and centre section and the aircraft was landed in a field near RAF Marham, on the port engine. A normal landing would have blown the flames into the area of the rear turret. After touchdown the bomber ran into a hedge and the undercarriage collapsed. The crew quickly vacated the aircraft, which was still burning, but 'Slim', who was wearing an old-style aircraft harness, became caught up in the side window. He extricated himself by releasing the harness, and although the aircraft was burnt out the crew escaped serious injury. 'Slim's' fame spread and he was known locally, for when he was not on duty Summers lived at the Whitington 'Bell' near Stoke Ferry with his wife. On 8 August 1939 he was asked if he would fly a Wellington out of a field at Roudham Heath near Thetford, after it had crash-landed with the undercarriage retracted during a night exercise. The daredevil Summers successfully got the Wellington off and flew it back to Marham. On the fateful day of 5 November 'Slim' attempted a very dangerous manoeuvre near the ground (it is thought he was trying to fly wingtip low between two trees). It must be assumed that he did not allow for the keel action of a heavy aircraft in a steep turn; he also failed to judge the height of the trees. The aircraft crashed inverted at Boughton, killing all seven on board. See *Wellington: The Geodetic Giant* by Martin Bowman (Airlife, 1989 and 1998); Summers and L.A.C.D. George, one of the six fitters, are buried in Marham village churchyard, which contains two First World War and sixteen Second World War, including six German graves, in the main plot.

12 'The romance followed on from that funeral. John had been very friendly with one of the girls who worked in the NAAFI. She was a favourite with us all in that little band of friends. She was rather a shy girl but had a lovely smile. When the crash occurred, she had been at home for the weekend, so I had the unenviable job of breaking the sad news to her on her return and offering my sympathy. This same NAAFI girl and I married and we celebrated our Golden Wedding Anniversary in 1994. Well I did say she had a nice smile and she always did!' *RAF Marham: Transition To War* by E.C. 'Johnnie' Johnson. West Norfolk Aviation Journal, No.2 (summer 1994); (Early in 1940 four Wellingtons of the New Zealand Flight were stored at Barton Bendish. On 20 November 1940 a Wellington Ic of 38 Squadron, flown by Sergeant I.N. Robertson, made a belly-landing at Barton Bendish having failed to maintain height on take-off during a non-operational flight. The aircraft was repaired on site and returned to service. During this period the airfield was used as a decoy

site with a flarepath in operation at night. From June to September 1941 detachments of 26 and 268 (Army Co-Operation) Squadrons were stationed at Barton Bendish with Curtis Tomahawk IIa low-level reconnaissance aircraft and a number of Westland Lysanders. 218 Conversion Flight followed with Wellingtons, before moving to Oakington on 2 October 1942. In 1942 Downham Market opened as Marham's satellite in place of Barton Bendish, which was unsuitable for 218 CU's Stirlings.)

13 *RAF Marham: Transition To War* by E.C. 'Johnnie' Johnson. West Norfolk Aviation Journal, No.2 (summer 1994)

14 Kellett, the son of an Anglo-Irish Surgeon Rear-Admiral, joined the RAF rather than the Navy after being told that Cranwell cadets were given motorcycles to assist their training. In the late 1920s, while serving in Iraq, he force-landed in the desert and was saved by a fellow pilot from capture by hostile tribesmen, who were advancing on the rescuing aircraft as it took-off. In 1936 he had the unusual experience of being seconded to the Imperial Japanese Army to advise on engineering for the Japanese Air Force, his services being recognised by the Emperor with the Order of the Sacred Treasure of Japan. He returned home in 1937 and took command of 148 Squadron, equipped with Wellesleys. On 5–7 November 1938, as leader of the RAF's Long Range Development Unit, he flew one of two Wellesleys to establish a new long-distance, record-breaking non-stop flight of 7,158.95 miles in just over forty-eight hours from Ismailia, Egypt, to Darwin, Australia. Kellett was awarded the DFC in 1940, and in the autumn of 1942 he was shot down in a raid on Tobruk and taken prisoner, being sent to Stalag Luft III where he was SBO at the time of the celebrated Wooden Horse escape. He was awarded the CBE in 1943. Air Commodore Kellett CBE DFC AFC died aged eighty-four in January 1990.

15 Later, in May 1943, after a long convalescence and a post in fighter training schools, Specht became Gruppenkommandeur, II./JGII. He scored thirty-two confirmed victories, including fifteen Viermots (four-motor bombers), and was awarded the Ritterkreuz (Knight's Cross) before being reported MIA on 1 January 1945 during the disastrous Bodenplatte operation.

16 Pilot Officer D.W.W. Morris and R3152/J, and Flight Sergeant L.G. Moores and P9298/H, on the 20th; Flying Officer D.F. Laslett and P9297/F on the 21st, and Flying Officer V.A.W. Rosewarne and R3162 on the 30th.

17 In all, Marham had five decoy sites, at South Acre (Q), South Pickenham (Q/K), Swaffham (Q/K), Wormegay (Q) and Barton Bendish (Q/K).

18 *RAF Marham* by Ken Delve. PSL, 1995.

19 When Bomber Command took the decision in May 1940 to start the strategic bombing of Germany by night, there was little the Luftwaffe could do to counter these early raids. The subject of night fighting was raised at a conference of German service chiefs just before the war and, according to Kommodore Josef Kammhuber, it was dismissed out of hand with the words, 'Night fighting! It will never come to that!' Up until May 1940 the night air defence of the Reich was almost entirely within the remit of the Flak arm of the Luftwaffe. No specialised night fighting arm existed, although one fighter, Gruppe (IV./(N)JG2), was undertaking experimental Helle Nachtjagd (illuminated night fighting) sorties with the aid of searchlights in northern Germany and in the Rhineland. IV./(N)JG2 flew the Bf 109D with the cockpit hood removed as a precaution against the pilots being blinded by the glare of the searchlights. The Helle Nachtjagd technique used in 1940 and early 1941 was entirely dependent on weather conditions, and radar-guided searchlights simply could not penetrate thick layers of cloud or industrial haze over the Ruhr and other industrial centres in the Reich. Kammhuber realised that Helle Nachtjagd was only a short-term solution and

soon concentrated all his energies in developing an efficient radar-controlled air defence system. *Battles With the Nachtjagd: The Night Air War Over Europe 1939–1945* by Theo Boiten and Martin W. Bowman. (Schiffer Publishing, 2006)

20 *RAF Marham: Transition To War* by E.C. 'Johnnie' Johnson. West Norfolk Aviation Journal, No.2 (summer 1994)

21 Flying Officer Rodney Gibbes had a lucky escape on 1 June 1940 when he was pilot of Wellington R3154, which crashed at Lastingham Hills, Yorkshire. Two of his crew were killed and Gibbes and the other members of his crew suffered shock and minor injuries. On 2–3 September 1941 a Wellington of 218 Squadron flown by Squadron Leader Gibbes DFC was hit by flak and crashed in the sea off Belgium. The crew came ashore three days later at Westgate near Margate, Kent. Gibbes was lost flying in the Mediterranean in August 1943. Peggy, his second daughter, married Sergeant Philip Wilks a 218 Squadron Wellington rear gunner, who survived the war and after a career with BOAC became landlord of The Ship. With Peggy as landlady, he remained there from the 1960s to the early 1980s.

22 Narborough House, less than 4 miles from the airfield, was the ideal solution. Late in 1940 the Army moved out as the RAF moved in, and the Rowley family transferred to the vicarage. The RAF used the whole of the house as a Sergeant's Mess, completely refurbishing the property.

23 'Razzles' and 'Deckers', consisting of small phosphorous pellets in celluloid strips, were dropped through flare chutes to start fires among crops and in forest areas. The incendiary devices had to be kept in tins of alcohol and water until dropped so that they would ignite when they dried out.

24 'Johnnie' Johnson saw service (1939–1950) at Marham, Malta, North Africa, East Kirkby, Chaveley and Horsham St Faith, and obtained the rank of Flight Sergeant in 1942. From 1950–1962 he was chief instructor at the Gloster Aircraft Servicing School on Meteors and Javelins, and during 1962–1985 was with the Ministry of Defence (Air) Aeronautical Inspection Service on specialist non-destructive tests based at Quedgeley, RAF Akrotiri, RAF St Athan and finally at HQ RAF Support Command, RAF Brampton. He retired in 1985 and was chairman of the Lowestoft & District RAFA until his death.

25 Rogers later gained a DFM and he was commissioned. He was KIA on 8–9 April 1943, flying as second pilot of a Halifax II of 76 Squadron.

26 Between January and October 1941, I./NJG2 claimed 125 aircraft destroyed for the loss of fifty-five aircraft and seventy-four aircrew. Dozens more aircraft were damaged in the intruder attacks. As a direct result of the Fernnachtjäger (long-range intruder) operations over England, the RAF was forced to end night-flying training in East Anglia, Yorkshire and Lincolnshire. Moreover, I./NJG2's continuous presence over England had a huge psychological impact on RAF aircrews. In mid-1941 it was planned to use the Dornier Do 217J over Britain as this type had greater endurance than the Ju 88, but on 12 October 1941 Adolf Hitler ordered all night intruder operations over the UK and the North Sea. See *Nachtjagd: The Night Fighter versus Bomber War over the Third Reich 1939–45* by Theo Boiten. (Crowood Press, 1997)

27 Rasper had trained as a fighter pilot during 1939–40. He and his Bordfunker Feldwebel, Erich Schreiber (KIA in 1943), claimed a 'Wellington' (more probably a Whitley) off Egmond on 15 December 1940 as their first victory. After his seventh Abschuss (victory) on 12–13 June 1941 (Wellington T2996 of 103 Squadron flown by Flying Officer Chisholm, who was KIA along with his crew), Rasper was awarded the 'Bowl of Honour' for 'exceptional achievements in the Air War' by Reichsmarschall Göering. After his eighth victory on 21 January 1942 Rasper was posted to a night fighter training uint where he was an instructor for three years until he became

operational again in early 1945 in II./NJG101. On 16–17 March 1945 he claimed his ninth and last Abschuss – a Viermot over Nürnburg. Leutnant Rasper flew his last sortie, a ground attack mission on 26 April 1945, when his aircraft was caught in radar-directed American flak at Low Level. He baled out and was taken prisoner but his funker was found dead near the wreckage of their aircraft. See *Battles With the Nachtjagd: The Night Air War Over Europe* 1939–1945 by Theo Boiten and Martin W. Bowman. (Schiffer Publishing, 2006)

28 In May German night fighters claimed forty-one bombers destroyed.

29 Evans-Evans was killed on 21–22 February 1945 while flying a Lancaster of 83 Squadron.

30 In captivity Alex Kerr recovered from his wounds fairly rapidly and a year later, on 11 May 1942, was recaptured after an attempted escape. With Bill Legg it was far more serious. A fellow prisoner, Dr Chatenay, carried out several operations on him. Chatenay was a young French doctor who took a great interest in Bill's case. He carried out miraculous feats of surgery with limited medical supplies under primitive conditions. The open hole in Bill's back never healed. He was repatriated in October 1943 under an exchange of POWs with the Germans. In August 1944 he recommenced flying duties as an instructor. The other crew survivors were repatriated at the end of the war. Exactly fifty years after the original incident, on 10 May 1991, the three bomber crew members met Von Bonin at Hohn German Air Force base. It was a very emotional occasion. Von Bonin embraced them all. He said that in 1941 when he had attacked their bomber he had been very annoyed with himself because he had forgotten to arm his cannon. Meeting them now he was very pleased that he had not set the 20mm cannon button to 'Fire'. Eckart-Wilhelm von Bonin eventually reached the rank of Major and was decorated with the Ritterkreuz (Knight's Cross) on 5 February 1944 when he had gained thirty-one victories. At that time he was Kommandeur of II./NJG1. He ended the war working for the Luftwaffe Inspector of Jet Aircraft. Two of Von Bonin's brothers serving in the Luftwaffe were killed on the Eastern Front. The Russians captured their father, Oberst Bogislav von Bonin, a Luftwaffe officer, in March 1945 and since then he remains missing. Eckhart-Wilhelm von Bonin died in January 1992.

31 Major Walter Ehle, thirty-five night and four day victories in ZG1 and NJG1, Ritterkreuz, KIA 7–18 November 1943 in crash at Horpmoel near St Trond airfield.

32 It is quite possible that Leutnant Russmann of St III/NJG3, who claimed a Wellington south of Papenburg at 01.45 hours, flew the Bf 110.

33 Although the surviving crew members were all confined to POW camps, Alan McSweyn soon successfully made his escape, though his fellow escapee died from exposure while they were crossing the Pyrenees. Alan was back in England by Christmas 1942, nearly six months after he was shot down. Awarded the Military Cross, he then served with Transport Command until returning to his native Australia in January 1946.

34 Woltersdorf was KIA on 1–2 June 1942 in crash at Twente airfield, shot down by a 3 Squadron Hurricane. He had fifteen night and eight day victories in ZG76 and NJG1.

35 A navigational and blind-bombing device, which was introduced into RAF service during August 1941. It consisted of the reception by equipment in the aircraft of transmission from a 'master' ('A') and two 'slave' stations ('B and C') situated on a base line about 200 miles long. The difference in the time taken by the 'A' and 'B' and 'A' and 'C' signals to reach the aircraft were measured and displayed on a CRT (Cathode Ray Tube) on the navigator's table in the aircraft. From then on the aircraft could be located on two position lines known as Gee co-ordinates. Accuracy of a Gee fix varied from less than ½ mile to about 5 miles, depending on the skill of the navigator and the strength of the signal. Gee range varied with the conditions from 300–400 miles.

36 1418 Flight was formed at Marham with four Wellingtons in December 1941 to develop Gee before it went into widespread use. This Flight moved to Tempsford on 1 March 1942.

37 The starboard engine of a Wellington IC of 75 Squadron, flown by Sergeant F.T. Minikin, cut as the bomber crossed the coast at 6,000ft and crashed in the sea near Corton, 2 miles north of Lowestoft. Both pilots, who were injured, were picked up. The rest were killed in action.

38 R1502 had crashed at 00.28 on 14 July at Onderdijk, 5km south of Medemblik.

39 In total Major Egmont Prinz zur Lippe-Weissenfeld scored fifty-one victories in NJG1 and NJG5, and he was awarded the Ritterkreuz with Eichenlaub. He was KIA on 12 March 1944 in a flying accident near St Hubert in the Ardennes.

40 Oberleutnant Helmut Lent (4./NJG1), Leutnant Eckart-Wilhelm von Bonin (6./NJG1) and Unteroffizier Benning of 1./NJG3 each destroyed a Wellington. Lent's victim has been identified as W5513 of 104 Squadron and von Bonin's as R1613 of 214 Squadron. Unteroffizier Benning's victory was either T2737 of 149 Squadron or W5726 of 305 Squadron.

41 Oberst Werner Streib, sixty-seven Nachtjagd victories (including thirty Viermots) in 150 sorties with NJG1, plus 1 as Zerstörer in I./ZG1. Ritterkreuz with Eichenlaub and Schwerter. Died 15 June 1986 in Munich.

42 R1772 piloted by Sergeant R.B.D. Hill was shot down over Kiel Bay by a Bf 110. Hill was killed and was buried in Kiel War Cemetery. Five crew baled out safely and they were taken prisoner. R1798, flown by Sergeant I.P.McH. Gordon, was shot down on its return from Berlin by Oberleutnant Helmut Lent of 4./NJG1 as his twenty-third Abschuss (victory) at 04.58 hours, near Drachtstercompagnie in Friesland province, with the loss of all the crew.

43 Becker, born in Dortmund in August 1911, volunteered for the Luftwaffe in 1934 and became a Stuka pilot before joining the Bf 110 Zerstörer and becoming a night fighter pilot in July 1940. In 1941–42 Becker – 'The Night Fighting Professor' – became one of the leading 'Experten' in the Nachtjagd. Instrumental in introducing the Lichtenstein AI radar in 1941, though most night fighter aircrew liked to rely on the 'Mk I Eyeball', Becker had one of the (still experimental) sets installed in his Do 217Z night fighter at Leeuwarden. His and Nachtjagd's first AI victory was in the early hours of 9 August 1941 in a Do 215B-5 night fighter, when forty-four Wellingtons of Bomber Command attacked Hamburg. Becker shot down six RAF night bombers during 8–9 August and 29–30 September 1941. He shot down forty bombers in 1942. See *Battles With the Nachtjagd: The Night Air War Over Europe 1939–1945* by Theo Boiten and Martin W. Bowman. (Schiffer Publishing, 2006)

CHAPTER TWO – THE NIGHT OFFENSIVE

44 Warrant Officer Snowdon and crew in Wellington X9873 was the only a/c lost, while four Whitleys FTR from the raid on Hamburg. It was Gildner's twentieth victory and he added a twenty-first, a Whitley, later that same night.

45 Sergeant H. Taylor and Pilot Officer G.G. Soames. There were no survivors from either crew.

46 In March 1942 forty-one bombers were brought down by German night fighters, compared to forty-six bombers in April.

47 On 23–24 April the Stirling flown by Sergeant S.V. Davidge of 218 Squadron was lost when it crashed near King's Lynn. The raids on Rostock had many of the characteristics of the successful bombing raid a month earlier on Lübeck, an historic German town on the Baltic with thousands of half-timbered houses. Lübeck was an ideal target for a mass raid by RAF bombers carrying

incendiary bombs and that night, 28–29 March, 191 aircraft claimed to have hit the target. A photo-reconnaissance a few days later revealed that about half the city, 200 acres, had been obliterated.

48 599 were Wellingtons, including four of Flying Training Command, and no fewer than 367 of the aircraft came from OTUs. The rest included eighty-eight Stirlings, 131 Halifaxes and seventy-three Lancasters, the remainder being made up of Whitleys, Hampdens and Manchesters.

49 Eight claims were submitted by four crews of II./NJG1 at St Trond, including three by Oberleutnant Walter Barte and his Funker, Unteroffizier Pieper, of the 4th Staffel. Seven of these claims were later confirmed by the Reichsluftfahrtministerium (RLM or Reich Air Ministry). Barte's first claim of the night, for a Wellington shot down north of Maastricht, was later officially turned down.

50 Falconer died on active service on 8 May 1944.

51 At Leeuwarden on 26 February 1943, thirty-year-old Hauptmann Ludwig Becker, Staffelkapitan 12/NJG1, a great night fighting tactician with forty-four night victories, waited to fly his very first daylight sortie. Shortly before taking off from Leeuwarden at 11.35 hours in a formation of 12 Bf 110s of IV./JGI led by Hauptmann Hans-Joachim Jabs, in pursuit of the American daylight raiders, Becker was informed of the award of the Eichenlaub (Oak Leaves) to be added to his Ritterkreuz (Knight's Cross). They intercepted the B-17s and B-24s, returning with claims for two shot down, but Becker's Bf 110 was lost without a trace. The 'Night Fighting Professor' and his Funker, Feldwebel Josef Staub, fell victim to the gunners of B-17s or B-24s. *Battles With the Nachtjagd: The Night Air War Over Europe 1939–1945* by Theo Boiten and Martin W. Bowman. (Schiffer Publishing, 2006)

52 Twelve aircraft – eight Wellingtons, two Stirlings, one Halifax, one Lancaster FTR. Nachtjagd was credited with eight victories.

53 Throughout the war, 4,059 cases were considered – 746 officers and 3,313 NCOs. The 'charges' against most were dismissed and only 2,726 (389 officers, 2,337 NCOs) were actually classified as LMF; in total less than 0.4 per cent of all the aircrews of Bomber Command. The NCO total was higher, because there were more of them then officers.

54 The Air Ministry issued the new policy of area bombing in Directive No.22 on 14 February 1942. Instead of attacking individual targets in a German city, the city itself now became the target. This dramatic change was prompted after an independent inquiry had revealed that, despite the best endeavours of the crews, bombs had been strewn far and wide over western Germany during 1941. Bomber Command simply did not have the tools yet to find, bomb and destroy specific targets at night.

55 Altogether, 233 aircraft, including 124 Wellingtons, set out for Emden that night. Nine bombers failed to return. Crews reported good bombing results and this was confirmed by later photographic reconnaissance. Emden reported that approximately 300 houses were destroyed and that 200 were seriously damaged, with seventeen people killed and forty-nine injured.

56 In the period 7–8 June until 18–19 June the Stirlings flew twenty-three *Gardening* sorties over four nights.

57 Freegard had flown his first op on 17 June to St Nazaire, followed by a mine-laying operation on the 18th. Two days later he went to the port of Emden in north Germany.

58 Oberleutnant Walter Barte of 4./NJG1 claimed a Manchester, L7301 of 50 Squadron flown by Flying Officer Leslie Thomas Manser, which had been seriously damaged by flak on the approaches to Cologne and he finished it off for his fifth victory. Manser and his crew could have safely baled out after leaving the target area, but only when it was clear that there was no hope of reaching England did Manser order the crew to bale out. Manser went down with the aircraft and was killed.

He was awarded a posthumous Victoria Cross on 20 October 1942. Barte also claimed a Wellington 30km north of Hasselt and a Wellington north-north-east of Maastricht. Barte survived the war with nineteen night victories and four day kills in NJG1 and NJG3. Oberleutnant Heinrich Prinz zu Sayn-Wittgenstein of II./NJG2 claimed a Manchester and a Wellington. Oberleutnant Reinhold Knacke StI/NJG1 claimed a Halifax 3km east-south-east of Weert, a Wellington 10km east of Weert and a Wellington 3km south-west of Middelbeerer. Stabsfeldwebel Gerhard Herzog of I./NJG1 claimed two Wellingtons, as did Oberleutnant Helmut Woltersdorf of 7./NJG1. Nachtjagd claimed thirty heavies. See *Battles With the Nachtjagd: The Night Air War Over Europe* 1939–1945 by Theo Boiten and Martin W. Bowman. (Schiffer Publishing, 2006)

59 1483 (Bomber) Gunnery Training Flight arrived a week later with Wellington IC and III and Defiant I and II aircraft, to train bomb aimers and air gunners who came directly from training schools without going to OTUs. In particular the bomb aimers performed exercises using Gee before the Flight returned to Newmarket Heath on 29 June 1943. 1427 Training Flight moved to Marham with Stirlings on 4 August 1942. This flight, which moved to Stradishall on 2 October 1942, trained ATA (Air Transport Auxiliary) pilots on four-engined bombers.

60 Warrant Officer II George Vincent Booth RCAF (USA), observer, Flight Sergeant Warnford Francis Victor Pink, WOP RAFVR and Sergeant John Munro, rear gunner, were buried in Nijmegen (Jonkerbos) War Cemetery. Wellington III X3561 KO-X crashed 7km south-east of Roermond. Two other Wellingtons of 115 Squadron, flown by Pilot Officer K.J. Stanford DFM RNZAF (six POW) and Sergeant J.H. Fletcher (five KIA) were lost. Two Wellingtons were claimed by Oberleutnant Reinhold Knacke, St Kpt 1./NJG1: X3561 5km south-east of Roermond and X3750 8km east of Eindhoven for his twenty-second and twenty-third victories. Of 291 bombers despatched, twelve aircraft – ten Wellingtons, one Halifax and one Hampden FTR (Failed to Return).

61 Seventy-six prisoners escaped from the North Compound of Stalag Luft III on the night of 24–25 March 1944 before 'Harry' (the name of the tunnel) was discovered. ('Tom' had been discovered in the summer of 1943 and was blown up by the Germans. 'Dick' was used subsequently to store tools and equipment for Harry.) Fifty of the escapees who were captured, including Squadron Leader Roger Bushell SAAF, who as 'Big X' organised the successful escape, were taken to remote spots and shot in the back of the head by the Gestapo. Only Bram van der Stok, Royal Netherlands Navy; Flight Lieutenant Jens Einar Mueller, Royal Norwegian Air Force, and Flight Lieutenant Peter Rockland RAF made 'home runs'.

62 Eight men were from 'A' Flight, six from 'B' Flight.

63 He was to fly his first operation as an aircraft captain in Wellington X3412.

64 Listening stations in Britain would pick up the resulting continuous note. When the aerial touched the water the signal would stop. The listeners would have the DF loop fix of the position of the bomber when the signal vanished.

65 Clerides was a Greek Cypriot who had been educated at an English Public School. Recovering his senses and finding the aircraft plunging to earth, he immediately called up on the intercom. Not realising he was no longer connected to the system and receiving no reply, he assumed the others had baled out. Scrambling back to the emergency hatch in the rear of the fuselage he baled out. In the meantime Fereday had regained control and flattened out at 8,000ft. Without navigational instruments he was flying by the seat of his pants. The undercarriage and the open bomb bay were causing excessive drag. Clerides landed safely in the outskirts of a town. A crowd of civilians soon surrounded him. Mistaking his Greek features for those of a Jew the cry of 'Jude' went up from someone in the mob. In a trice they were rifling his pockets, punching and kicking him. Luckily a

detachment of the Luftwaffe arrived and rescued him. He was whisked off to hospital in Bremen where an immediate operation was carried out on his leg. After the war Clerides qualified as a barrister. He became President of the Greek Cypriots.

66 On Friday 21 August 1942 the body of Sergeant Kelvin Shoesmith RAAF was recovered from Ho Bay in Denmark. Frank Skelley's body was washed ashore on the Dutch coast.

67 W1153 of 102 Squadron.

68 Oberst Helmut Lent, 102 Nachtjagd victories (including sixty-one Viermots and one Mosquito) in 396 sorties with NJG1, 2 and 3, plus 8 as Zerstörer in 3./ZG76. Ritterkreuz with Eichenlaub, Schwerter and Brillanten. Died after landing accident at Paderborn, 7 October 1944.

69 7.2 per cent of the total force despatched – fifteen Wellingtons, eight Halifaxes, two Hampdens of 420 Squadron, two Lancasters and four Stirlings. Two other aircraft crashed on return.

70 On 28–29 July when 256 aircraft attacked Hamburg again, sixteen Wellingtons and nine Stirlings failed to return. Two of the Wellingtons were from 115 Squadron and they were piloted by Sergeant A.C. Williamson RNZAF and Pilot Officer L.M. Mason RNZAF.

CHAPTER THREE – LOW LEVELLERS AND THE SHALLOW RAIDERS

71 KIA, 13 November 1942.

72 Piffer, an Austrian, was killed on 17 June 1944 when USAAF P-47 Thunderbolts shot his Fw 190A-8 'White 3' near Argentan. He was posthumously awarded the Ritterkreuz (Knight's Cross) on 20 October 1944 for his twenty-six victories in the West. See *Defending The Reich: The History of JG1* by Eric Mombeek (JAC Publications, 1992).

73 Rowland, a post-war captain for BEA, learned this at a stopover in Hamburg in 1963. Klein had later lost a leg in a crash-landing after he was shot down by a P-51 Mustang. In July 1993 Parry met Fenten face-to-face also, when the German flew his light aircraft to Horsham St Faith (Norwich Airport) and they flew a memorable flight around the city!

74 Oberfeldwebel Timm was KIA on 28 May 1944 flying Bf 109G-6 'Yellow 3'.

75 By the end of November 1942 105 Squadron had flown 282 operational sorties and lost twenty-four aircraft.

76 107 houses and ninety-six shops were completely destroyed; 107 Dutch workers and civilians living around the factory were killed and 161 wounded.

77 See *The Mosquito Log* by Alexander McKee. (Souvenir Press, 1988)

78 *The Mossie*, Mosquito Aircrew Association, Vol. 18, January 1998.

79 Flying Officer C. Vernon Pereira, a Trinidadian, flew eighty ops on Mosquitoes on 139 and 105 Squadrons, and was awarded the DFC and Bar.

80 Flight Sergeant Frederick Alfred Budden and Sergeant Frank Morris in DZ420/F, which crashed north-west of Tours at Vengeons.

81 By the end of the year he had taken up an appointment in Air Command Far East Asia and held the rank of SASO (Senior Air Staff Officer) until the end of 1945. He remained in the post-war RAF and was awarded the OBE in 1947. In 1958 he was promoted to Air Commodore and finally retired from the service in 1963. He returned to Australia, was knighted and in 1974 became Governor of West Australia.

82 On 1 May 1943 Flying Officer Onslow W. Thompson DFM RNZAF and Flying Officer Wallace J. Horne DFC took off in DK338 for an operation to Eindhoven, when an engine failed just after take-off and the aircraft crashed near Marham, killing both crew.

83 Four Fw 190s intercepted the Mosquitoes on the homeward journey and Flying Officer A.N. Bulpitt and his navigator, Sergeant K.A. Amond, were last seen being pursued by two Fw 190s and crashed into the sea. The Mosquito flown by Flying Officer J.H. Brown and Flying Officer Pounder slowed down to signal to another Mosquito that his bomb doors were open. Brown made off for the coast down a winding valley, pursued by two Fw 190s in line astern that caught the Mosquito crossing the coast and the leader scored hits in the fuselage just forward of the tail plane. The Fw 190s continued to follow the Mosquito out to sea for about 20 miles while Brown took violent evasive action. When they ran out of ammunition the Fw 190s were immediately replaced by two more and the combat finally ended 50 miles out to sea. Pounder then set course for Leuchars and they made landfall about 3 miles south. Brown made four attempts at a landing without hydraulics to operate the undercarriage, and with no air speed indicator, rudder controls or elevator trim. He finally made a successful crash-landing. Six days later Brown and Pounder had a similar experience after being hit by flak over the Renault works at Le Mans and they returned with tail trim, rudder controls, hydraulics and wireless all out of action. They returned to Marham at 20.15 hours and circled before finally crash-landing on the second attempt 'with no trouble', as Brown put it.

84 9.8 tons of bombs were dropped on the John Cockerill works. Pace and Cook crashed into the Ooster Schelde off Woensdrecht.

85 Flight Sergeant Peter J.D. McGeehan DFM and Flying Officer Reginald C. Morris DFC were killed.

86 Mosquito DZ477, flown by Sergeant Massey DFM and Sergeant 'Lofty' Fletcher DFM, was hit by flak in the port wing close to the fuselage. Petrol began to pour out and they feathered the port engine in case of fire. After leaving the target the port engine would not unfeather, and they had to carry on with one engine. As they approached the enemy coast a cone of searchlights tried to pick them up but they were too low to be caught in the beams, although they must have been silhouetted as there was a considerable amount of light flak and they were hit again in the fuselage. The controls became very sloppy and 30 miles from the coast the remaining engine began to run rough. They then switched in to emergency and obtained assistance to land at Docking in Norfolk. They were unable to land on the flarepath due to a violent swing, which materialised as the starboard engine was throttled back, but they landed alongside it and finally crashed into a windsock. They were uninjured but the aircraft was written off.

87 Wooldridge spent three months in command of 105, and on 25 June he was posted to 3 Group at RAF Stradishall. On 1 September 1943 he was posted back to the PWD. His replacement at Marham was 109 Squadron's Wing Commander Henry John 'Butch' Cundall AFC (later Group Captain Cundall CBE DSO DFC AFC). Wooldridge wrote *Low Attack* and after the war he composed music, worked as a conductor, with the Philharmonia Orchestra especially, and wrote many plays, orchestral suites, incidental film music and film scores. His most famous was Appointment in London (1952), for which he wrote the music and also the squadron song. Wooldridge died in a car accident on 27 October 1958.

88 On 3 April Flying Officer J.H. Brown and Flying Officer Pounder were killed on the raid on the locomotive repair shops at Malines in Belgium, when their Mosquito was hit by coastal flak and finished off three minutes later by two Fw 190s.

89 *Bommen Vielen op Hengelo* by Henk F. Van Baaren, translated in *The Mossie* – MAA, Vol.16, April 1997.

90 They were buried at Maubeuge Centre cemetery on 5 April. On 30 July 1943 Mackenstedt crashlanded his Fw 190A-5 after being hit by return fire from an 8th Air Force B-17, and died of his injuries in hospital. See *The JG26 War Diary,* Vol.2 1943–45 by Donald Caldwell. (Grub Street, 1998)

91 Mosquitoes of 140 Wing, 2nd TAF, flew the eleventh and final RAF raid on Hengelo on 18 March 1944 when they bombed the Hazemeyer works.

92 On 28–29 June 1942 Oberleutnant Reinhold Knacke, Staffelkapitän, 1./NJG1 had been the first Nachtjagd pilot to claim a Mosquito kill, when he shot down DD677 of 23 Squadron at Haps, Southern Holland. Guided by Leutnant Lübke, Jägerleitoffizier of Himmelbett box *Eisbär (Polar Bear)* at Sondel, Northern Holland, Lent power-dived onto a Mosquito west of Stavoren from superior altitude, and at 500kph fired a burst of cannon shells at the Mosquito. NF.II DZ694 of 410 Squadron, flown by Flight Sergeant W.J. Reddie RCAF, and his navigator, Sergeant K. Evans, who were on a Night Fighting Patrol over Holland, were KIA. Lent was noted for experimenting with new methods of attack. He would practice and perfect a diving attack, which would give him sufficient speed to overtake a Mosquito and shoot it down. For being one of the first German pilots to overcome this versatile aircraft he received special praise from Göring. Lent eventually rose to the rank of Oberst with a position of high command in the night fighter arm. He achieved 102 night victories and eight day victories before being killed in a flying accident on 5 October 1944.

93 Shand remained missing while the body of his navigator was washed ashore at Makkum. Linke, with twenty-four night and three day victories, was killed on the night of 13–14 May 1943. After shooting down two Lancasters (W4981 of 83 Squadron and ED589 of 9 Squadron) and Halifax DT732 of 10 Squadron over Friesland, he suffered an engine fire. He baled out near the village of Lemmer in Friesland but he struck the tail unit of his Bf 110 and was killed. Linke's Bordfunker, Oberfeldwebel Walter Czybulka, baled out safely.

94 Flight Lieutenant Harold Sutton DFC and Flying Officer John Morris, and Flying Officer Fred Openshaw and Sergeant Alfred Stonestreet, of 139 Squadron.

95 Unable to find the target by DR, Patterson identified and attacked Weimar railway station from 300ft. Patterson completed two tours of daylight operations on Mosquitoes and he was awarded the DSO early in 1944. Squadron Leader Blessing DSO DFC RAAF was KIA on 7 July 1944 on a PFF marking sortie over Caen.

96 *The Mossie,* Mosquito Aircrew Association, Vol.21, January 1999.

97 Flying Officer F.M. 'Bud' Fisher DFC and his navigator, Flight Sergeant Les Hogan DFM, were prevented from attacking the target by the balloon barrage, and bombed the town from 200ft. (Fisher and Hogan were KIA on the night of 29–30 September 1943 when their Mosquito crashed near West Raynham returning from the raid on Bochum). Flying Officer Don C. Dixon and his navigator, Flying Officer W.A. Christensen, attempted three runs on the target. They were also prevented from bombing by the balloons and intense flak, and so they dropped their bombs on a goods train at Lastrup. Pilot Officer Ronald Massie and Sergeant George Lister, who were last seen as the formation entered cloud prior to reaching the target, crashed near Diepholz and were killed.

98 By March 1945 Roy Ralston was CO of 139 Squadron and still managed to fly on operations. He had been awarded the DSO for 'outstanding leadership and determination' and he was awarded a bar to his DSO after his eighty-third op, promoted to wing commander and given command of 1655 Mosquito Training Unit at Marham. At the end of the war Ralston was listed for a permanent commission but a medical examination revealed that he had tuberculosis and he was invalided out of the RAF in 1946. Wing Commander Ralston DSO★ DFC DFM AFC died on 8 October 1996.

99 Flight Lieutenant William S.D. 'Jock' Sutherland and Flying Officer George Dean, of 139 Squadron in Mosquito DZ605/D, were seen to bomb their target. On their return they flew into high voltage overhead electric cables when attempting to land at RAF Coltishall and they crashed at Wroxham railway station. Both were killed. Flying Officers Alan Rae DFM and Kenneth Bush of 105 Squadron in DZ483/R died when their Mosquito crashed as they tried to land at Marham on one engine.

100 109 Squadron was the premier marking squadron in the RAF, carrying out the most raids and flying the most sorties in 8 Group, which it joined on 1 June 1943.

CHAPTER FOUR – 'MUSICAL MOSQUITOES'

101 In April 1942 109 Squadron was established at Stradishall, Suffolk, to bring *Oboe* into full operational service as a navigation aid for Bomber Command, before moving to Wyton in August where, at the end of the year, it received the first *Oboe*-equipped Mosquito B.IVs. *Oboe* was first used on 20–21 December 1942 when the CO, Squadron Leader H.E. 'Hal' Bufton DFC AFC, and his navigator, Flight Lieutenant E.L. 'Ding' Ifould, and two other crews, bombed a power station at Lutterade in Holland. On 31 December 1942–1 January 1943, on a raid on Düsseldorf, sky-marking using *Oboe* was tried for the first time when two Mosquitoes of 109 Squadron provided the sky-markers for eight Lancasters of the Path Finder Force. 'Sky markers' were parachute flares to mark a spot in the sky if it was cloudy. The PFF markers' job was to 'illuminate' and 'mark' targets with coloured TIs (target indicators) for the Main Force and other 8 Group Mosquitoes. Three types of marking, using names selected by D.C.T. 'Don' Bennett from the hometowns of three of his staff, were later employed. Parramatta in New Zealand gave its name to the blind ground marking technique, which used only H2S in bad visibility or broken cloud. Newhaven was ground marking by visual methods when crews simply aimed at the TIs on the ground, and Wanganui in Australia lent its name to pure 'sky marking'. The TIs themselves were made in various plain colours and used vivid star-bursts of the same or a different colour to prevent the enemy from copying them at their many decoy sites near major cities.

102 Later Group Captain DFC★ AFC AE.

103 Wolstenholme (who became famous after the war as a BBC sports commentator) flew Blenheims on 107 Squadron earlier in the war. On 21 May 1941 he made it back to Massingham with his observer, Sergeant J.C. 'Polly' Wilson RNZAF, dead in his seat after their Blenheim was hit by flak on the operation to Heligoland. Wilson was laid to rest in the lovely country churchyard at Little Massingham, close by the airfield.

104 Later Group Captain Cundall CBE DSO DFC AFC.

105 See *Mosquito at War* by Chaz Bowyer (Ian Allan, 1984), and *Mosquito Thunder* by Stuart R. Scott. (Sutton Publishing, 1999)

106 Pilot Officer R.A. Hosking in a PR Mosquito had photographed a V-1 site at Bois Carré, 10 miles north-east of Abbeville, on 28 October 1942. This was the first V-1 flying bomb launching site in France to be analysed on photographs, and the buildings shown were meant for storage of flying-bomb components. The Vergelrungswaffe I (Revenge Weapon No.1) was a small, pilotless aircraft with a 1,870lb HE warhead that detonated on impact. On 5 December 1943 the bombing of the V-1, or Noball sites, became part of the Operation Crossbow offensive. By 12 June 1944, sixty weapons sites had been identified. Hitler's 'rocker blitz' began on 13 June when ten V-1s, or 'Doodlebugs' as they became known, were launched against London from sites in north-eastern France.

107 Squadron Leader Blessing DSO DFC RAAF was KIA on 7 July 1944 on a PFF marking sortie over Caen.

108 Stead had joined 58 Squadron in July 1941, and he flew six sorties in 1941 as co-pilot to Leonard Cheshire VC before returning to 58 Squadron. He was posted to 196 Squadron, completed his first tour in June and began his second in October 1943. Hauptmann Dietrich Schmidt scored forty night victories in NJG1. He was awarded the Ritterkreuz and survived the war.

109 B-17G 42-97480 and Lieutenant Otto H. Brandau's crew failed to return from a raid on Germany on 13 April 1944. Four crew were KIA and six were taken prisoner.

110 The Mk.IV Mosquito with a 'Cookie' on board was 'just' capable of a take-off on a main runway with favourable wind, and once in the air the aircraft handled sluggishly until 'bomb gone', when the altimeter unwound itself at an alarming rate. At take-off time many a fitter and rigger could be seen sheltering as soon as the aircraft taxied out for take-off. Aircrews learned that the safety height to fly when 4,000lb bombs were exploding was a minimum of 4,000ft.

111 Eaton's immediate award of the DFC for this operation was announced on 17 April 1944. He went on to complete ninety operations by 18 March 1945. On 7–8 March Flight Lieutenant Angus Caesar-Gordon DFM dropped 105 Squadron's first 4,000lb 'Cookie', in the Duisburg area after the primary target at Hamborn could not be identified. (On 11–12 March a 105 Squadron Mosquito, flown by Squadron Leader J.S.W. Bignall and Flying Officer G.F. Caldwell, took off from Graveley in company with two Mosquitoes of 109 Squadron and dropped a 'Cookie' on the Verstahlwerke steel works at Hamborn.) On 10 July 1944 Grenville Eaton and Jack Fox took-off on their first daylight operation when the port engine blew up as they reached the end of the runway, an event that was usually fatal. Eaton somehow flew a circuit and landed safely on one engine but when Fox dropped prematurely through the escape hatch the propeller killed him.

112 Flight Lieutenant Norman Clayes DFC and his observer, Flying Officer Frederick Ernest Deighton, were killed returning from an operation to Châteaudun on 12–13 May 1944, when a Verey pistol was discharged in the Mosquito as they came into land.

CHAPTER FIVE — VALIANTS AND VICTORS

113 The USAAF became the USAF on 18 September 1947.

114 These squadrons were commanded by Colonel Clifford J. Heflin and Colonel Stanley T. Wray, who had commanded the 'Carpetbagger' Group at Harrington in Northamptonshire and the 91st Bomb Group at Bassingbourn, respectively, in the Second World War.

115 On 23 August 1948 the provisional status of the 3rd Air Division was dropped and it was assigned to USAFE. The Division moved from Marham to the former United States Strategic Air Forces in Europe HQ at Bushy Park on 8 September.

116 First to re-equip was 115 Squadron in June 1950, followed in August by 149 Squadron, and 90 Squadron in January 1951. No.149 Squadron remained at Marham until October 1950 and 44 (Rhodesia) Squadron stayed for a short sojourn, 7 February–April 1951. At Marham also, 207 Squadron operated the Washington B.1 from 4 June 1951 and 35 Squadron from 1 September 1951, until both converted to the Canberra B.2 in 1954.

117 *Life On The V-Force*, West Norfolk Aviation Journal, No.1 (October 1993). Alan Gardener joined the RAF in 1952 and trained as a navigator on Dakotas at RCAF Summerside in Canada. After

training he served with 44 Squadron and 76 Squadron on Canberras, then on Valiants with 7 Squadron and in 1968 on PR.9 Canberras at RAF Luqa in Malta. He returned to the UK in 1971 and joined 214 Squadron at Marham on Victor K.1 tankers, transferring five years later to 57 Squadron on Victor K.2 tankers. In 1983 he moved to RAF Honington as Operations Officer and retired from the Service in 1984 as a Flight Lieutenant.

118 Forty-five B.K. Mk.Is equipped for bomber or tanker duties were built and this variant was used by 214 Squadron for flight refuelling trials in 1959.

119 On 3 May 1943 twenty-eight-year-old Squadron Leader Leonard Trent DFC RNZAF, who hailed from Nelson in New Zealand, led eleven Venturas of 487 Squadron in the bombing of the Amsterdam power station. All the attacking aircraft were shot down and Trent survived to be taken prisoner. It was only after repatriation that the full story became known and on 1 March 1946 Trent was awarded the Victoria Cross for his leadership and gallantry. See *The Reich Intruders* by Martin W. Bowman (Pen & Sword, 2005).

120 On 11 October 1956 a Valiant of 49 Squadron carried out the first British operational atomic bomb to be dropped from an aircraft, which was released over Maralinga, Southern Australia. On 15 May 1957 a Valiant of 49 Squadron dropped the first British hydrogen bomb during Operation Grapple in the Pacific.

121 At the International Air Congress in June 1923, Boulton and Paul designer John North suggested refuelling in flight as a means of achieving more efficient commercial aviation. Refuelling experiments were already being made in America and it was urged that similar experiments be carried out in Britain. Following a refuelling demonstration by French aviators in December 1923, the Royal Aircraft Establishment at Farnborough was directed to carry out experiments during February–March 1924 using a pair of Bristol Fighters, between which water was transferred via a 60ft pipeline. The experiment was considered satisfactory and trials were resumed in 1930, during which contact was made between a D.H.9A trailing a 160ft pipeline and the tail of a Vickers Virginia. This method was abandoned in 1932 in favour of a wingtip-to-wingtip method, which was trialled using a length of weighted garden hose! Refuelling methods presented 'considerable problems' with large aircraft, although air refuelling was demonstrated at the 1931 Royal Air Force Display at Hendon with a Virginia tanker and Wapiti receiver. A similar display was given in 1934, and the following year a Wallace and Hart demonstrated the technique.

122 During the following two years, in addition to his National Aviation Day activities, Cobham experimented with refuelling methods, with this long-range flight in view. The RAE was asked to co-operate and, in July 1934, refuelling was demonstrated between the Courier and a Vickers Victoria, fitted up as a tanker. The latter aircraft was then positioned at Aboukir and a 70 Squadron Vickers Valentia, fitted with refuelling equipment, was made available at Hinaidi to refuel the Courier near Shaibah. The need for a satisfactory refuelling method only became urgent in 1935 and the 'towing' method was initially specified, with a strongpoint in the nose gun station of a bomber aircraft for the towing cable, along which the refuelling hose would be passed. In 1936 this was changed to a method whereby two aircraft would fly roughly line abreast, with the refuelling hose being suspended from the openings. In December 1937 the requirement was deleted in favour of additional tankage and more powerful engines.

123 It was still being considered, however, by Transport Command for the supporting freight flights and at the Command's request Cobham's company prepared a report dealing with a refuelled Avro York service between Bengal and Manila, a distance of 2,300 miles. Preparations for the deployment of Tiger Force continued. Units were allocated and advance parties sailed for the Far

East, but before any squadrons could be deployed the dropping of the two atomic bombs on Japan in August 1945 made their task redundant, and the Force was disbanded.

124 In 1948, the USAF decided to adopt air refuelling for Strategic Air Command and British equipment was ordered as an interim measure, pending the development of an improved system. They also asked for a method of refuelling fighters and, during the winter of 1948–49, various schemes were studied, resulting in the development of the 'probe and drogue', first demonstrated in April 1949 and now widely used by the RAF and other air forces. Demonstrations to the Air Staff and Government officials, and the twelve-hour refuelled flight by a Meteor in August, did much to renew official interest in Britain. It was now a practical proposition for jet fighters and had obvious applications, such as long-range deployments, but its use in a combat zone was still considered impractical. Evaluation trials at Horsham St Faith, May–October 1951, with sixteen Meteor F.Mk.8s as receivers and three Lincoln tankers proved satisfactory. Yet Fighter Command was unwilling to adopt the technique if the provision of tankers, which were 'large, expensive and vulnerable', meant a reduction in the number of fighters on economic grounds. It was decided not to adopt the technique 'at least for the present', but future types were to include provision for air refuelling in their design.

125 Evaluation of potential targets during the late 1940s showed that a radius of action of 2,500 nautical miles was desirable for satisfactory coverage, but an aircraft designed to carry a 10,000lb bomb load over this distance would be extremely large and heavy, and present serious runway problems. A radius of 1,500 nautical miles was finally decided upon, and the new jet bombers were designed to meet this requirement. Subsequent range extension might be achieved, it was thought, by overloading and the use of rocket-assisted take-off.

126 Design studies began in 1953, and early in 1954 a Valiant B Mk 2 engaged in formating trials with a Canberra tanker. Trials with a production Valiant B Mk 1 were carried out during 1956, and Valiant-to-Valiant trials began in 1957. By April 1958 the technique had been cleared for service use, and 214 Squadron was nominated as the trials and development unit. During the trials, which ended in May 1960, several long-distance refuelled flights were made and the compatibility was demonstrated with the other V-bombers. 90 Squadron converted to the tanker role in August 1961, but both units retained their bomber commitments until April 1962, when they officially became tanker squadrons. Operational squadrons began converting to the receiver role during 1960. Vulcan receiver training began late in the year in preparation for a non-stop flight to Australia, this being accomplished the following June by a 617 Squadron crew flying a Vulcan B Mk IA. The 9,993-nm distance between RAF Scampton and Sydney was covered in little over twenty hours, the Vulcan being refuelled by Valiant tankers detached to Akrotiri, Karachi, and Tengah. This, and other long-distance flights by Vulcan squadrons, demonstrated the global mobility and extended range now possible. Victor squadrons began conversion during 1962. Fighter Command introduced the air-refuelling technique in June 1960 when 23 and 64 Squadrons, equipped with the Javelin FAW Mk 9, began receiver training.

127 Flight Lieutenant W.A. Gallienne was buried at Marham village cemetery. The rest of his crew were Flying Officer R.S. Morton (aged twenty-six); Flight Lieutenant K.J. Peacock (thirty-one) and Squadron Leader M.T. Doyle (thirty-nine). The Canberra crew were Flight Lieutenant J. Flabber (twenty-five); Flying Officer S. Cowie (twenty-four) and Flying Officer J.H. Woolnough (twenty-four). See *The Night A Miracle Saved Holt* by Antony King-Deacon, *EDP Magazine*, August 1998.

128 All three of the V-bomber designs – Valiant, Vulcan and Victor – had provision for Martin Baker ejection seats for the two pilots only. The three crew in the back sat facing the rear.

129 It was not until 1978 that it was announced that a number of VC 10s were to be brought back into RAF service for conversion to tanker aircraft to supplement the Victor K.2 force.

130 617 Squadron were the second Tornado unit to form, the first being 9 Squadron at RAF Honington on 1 June 1982.

131 The Vulcan B.2 (MMR)s of 27 Squadron that had specialised in the maritime radar reconnaissance (MRR) role had been disbanded on 31 March 1982 and the Nimrod force had taken over MMR duties, but only the Victors had the refuelled range to operate as far south as the Falklands. (In 1983 27 Squadron reformed as a Tornado GR.1 operator at Marham). Squadron Leader John Elliott and his crew in XL192 flew the first operational Victor sortie during Operation Corporate on 20 April. The primary purpose of the MMR (and two similar MMR sorties flown by Victors on 22–23 and 24–25 April) was to provide data on surface shipping and ice conditions etc to HMS *Antrim*, the ship leading the small naval Task Group responsible for recapturing South Georgia (Operation Paraquat). Having reached its target area Elliott descended from its transit height to around 18,000ft and for ninety minutes Beedie and Cowling carried out a radar sweep of 150,000sq. miles of ocean. Nothing untoward was found and the information was made available to Antrim. The 7,000-mile sortie took fourteen hours forty-five minutes. South Georgia was recaptured on 26 April. On 29 April Vulcan B.2s XM598 and XM607 were tanked from Waddington to Ascension. The Victors air-refuelled the Vulcans twice en route and the tankers required numerous fuel transfer themselves to complete the nine-hour flight.

132 BLACK BUCK I.

133 Russell, who had just turned fifty, was an experienced Victor AAR instructor at Marham.

134 The last refuelling bracket took place 3,000 miles south of Ascension, and Tuxford had to transfer more fuel than planned, which left XL189 with insufficient fuel to return to Wideawake. The need for radio silence meant that the Victor could not call Ascension and arrange for another tanker to meet him on the return. Tuxford and his crew could only pray that another tanker from Widewake would intercept them before they ran out of fuel and had to ditch in the freezing South Atlantic, where death would be almost instantaneous. BLACK BUCK I was the first time that a Vulcan had dropped bombs in anger in its twenty-five-year history.

135 Bob Tuxford was awarded the Air Force Cross for his part in the mission and his crew – Squadron Leader Ernie Wallis MBE, Flight Lieutenant Mick Beer, Flight Lieutenant John Keable and Flight Lieutenant Glyn Rees – each received the Queen's Commendation for Valuable Service in the Air. Bob Tuxford joined the ETPS in 1983 and left the RAF in 1987 to fly for Monarch Airlines.

136 One of the results of the Falklands experience saw six Vulcan K.Mk.2 tankers quickly organised to meet the urgent need for extra tanker capacity, and they continued in the tanker role until 1984. Victor deployment support to the South Atlantic continued until Mount Pleasant Airport opened in May 1985 and Wing Commander Martin Todd, OC 55 Squadron, flew the last Victor out of Ascension and back to Marham on 10 June. 101 Squadron, with its five VC 10 K.2 and four VC 10 K.3s, became operational in 1984 and added a significant improvement in AAR capability. The requirement for a strategic tanker to meet commitment of the kind demonstrated in the South Atlantic led to an order for six TriStar tankers with an additional three authorised for conversion in 1986.

137 In November the squadron lost a second Tornado when the crew ejected safely from ZA603 during a training sortie in Germany. On 8 November 1984 Tornado ZA604 of 27 Squadron was involved in a collision with a USAFE A-10A close support aircraft. Flight Lieutenant Edward Smith and Squadron Leader Gareth Williams ejected without injury. The A-10A was landed safely.

138 The RAF first entered giant voice in 1951, but in thirty years recorded success only in 1974 when one Vulcan crew won the Mathis Trophy and another won a navigation trophy.

139 The Curtis E. LeMay Trophy, awarded to the crew with the highest number of points scored in high and low-level bombing and time control, was won when two 617 Squadron crews gained first (Squadron Leader Peter Dunlop and Flight Lieutenant Dick Middleton) and second places (Flight Lieutenant Steve Legg and Squadron Leader Vic Bussereau). The John C. Meyer Trophy, awarded for 'the best low-level damage expectancy', was won by Squadron Leader Dunlop and Flight Lieutenant Middleton with 90.4 per cent, beating an F-111F of the 48th Tactical Fighter Wing by almost four percentage points. Another Tornado was placed third. In the Mathis Trophy, awarded to the team with the highest points for both high and low-level bombing, Tornado crews were placed second and sixth. In thirty timed-bomb releases 617 Squadron achieved an average timing error of less than one second. In bombing accuracy during the high-speed, low-level attacks of both phases, the average mean point of impact was less than 20 yards from the target. During the high-level bombing of Phase 2 the average mean point of impact was 21 yards from the target. See *Tornado* by Francis K. Mason (PSL, 1986).

140 In the Meyer Trophy the winning 'team' comprised Squadron Leaders Mal Prissick and Terry Cook, and Squadron Leaders Dan Walmsley and Jack Stone, gaining a damage expectancy of 94.97 per cent. Squadron Leader Barry Holding and Flight Lieutenant John Plumb, and Flight Lieutenants Beveridge and Bentham, came second. Tornadoes took first and second places in the Curtis E. LeMay Trophy, the aircraft being flown by Flight Lieutenant Dave Beveridge and Flight Lieutenant Benny Bentham (with 2,619 points, or 98.8 per cent) and Squadron Leaders Prissick and Cook (2,607 points, or 98.3 per cent) respectively. The trophy for the Best Tornado Crew was awarded to Walmsley and Stone. Right up to the closing stages 27 Squadron was heading for a clean sweep and it only needed a moderate score by one aircraft for the Tornadoes to take the first two places in the Mathis Trophy. Unfortunately over the last target an aircraft had one of its practice bombs 'hang up' and, accordingly with the rules of the competition, its crew was awarded the score of the lowest-placed aircraft, dropping 27 Squadron to second place in the contest. See *Tornado* by Francis K. Mason (PSL, 1986).

141 Flight Lieutenants Dave Beveridge and Benny Bentham with 2,619 points (98.8 per cent) and Squadron Leaders Mal Prissick and Terry Cook with 2,607 points (98.3 per cent).

CHAPTER SIX — 'TANKER TRASH' AND THE TORNADOES

142 Each JP233 contained thirty SG3657 concrete-cratering bomblets and 215 HB876 area-denial mines, which were timed to explode during the following twelve hours to pose a serious and long-lasting threat to vehicles and personnel engaged in repair activities. This system delivered both types of submuntion simultaneously from jettisonable, captive dispensers.

143 'On 19 January an additional Victor was sent to supplement the other six. Up to a maximum of 14 sorties were flown over the Persian Gulf in support of attack missions and air defence patrols and together with 138 olive trails and numerous other patrols, 299 sorties were flown over the 42 day war, an average of 33 missions per crew. The Victor detachment achieved every objective and did not fall down on any operational sortie. It was tight at times and the need for flexibility, excellent engineering support and good airmanship saved the day and produced a 100% success rate.'

144 On 18 October Squadron Leaders Ivor Walker and Bobby Anderson of 16 Squadron ejected from Tornado GR.I ZA466/FH following a take-off collision at Tabuk, with an incorrectly-raised

arrestor barrier at the approach end of the runway. On 13 November, while piloting Jaguar GR.1A XX754, Flight Lieutenant Keith Collister of 54 Squadron was killed on a low-level training flight over Qatar. On 13 January 1991 Flight Lieutenants Kieran Duffy and Norman Dent of 14 Squadron were killed when Tornado ZD718/BH crashed during a low-level training sortie.

145 Wing Commander Jerry Witts of 31 Squadron would also lead four Tornadoes from Dhahran to the same target.

146 Flight Lieutenant Rupert Clark (aged thirty-one) and Flight Lieutenant Stephen Hicks (twenty-six) of XV Squadron were flying ZD717 on 14 February when they were the last aircraft in an 8-Tornad/4-Buccaneer package in an LGB attack on Al Taqaddum air base. General radio chat drowned out warnings and they were hit by two SA-2 SAMs. Clark survived and was taken prisoner but Hicks was killed.

147 One of ZD791's AIM-9L Sidewinders was hit by flak, exploded and 'took out' the engine, forcing Flight Lieutenants John Peters (twenty-six) and Adrian 'John' Nichol (twenty-seven) of XV Squadron to eject. They were captured by the Iraqis and endured a brutal imprisonment before their release on 4 March 1991.

148 Author's interview with Wing Commander John Broadbent/Presentation to the RUSI on 23 October 1991 by Wing Commander Broadbent, Royal Air Force Staff College, Bracknell. ©RUSI Journal August 1992. John Broadbent was awarded the DSO.

149 The bodies of Wing Commander Elsdon and Flight Lieutenant Collier arrived in the UK on 19 March 1991.

150 In an interview with Mark Nicholls of the EDP, January 2001.

151 Mohammed Mubarak was shot down on 17 January when eleven out of the twelve A4KU Skyhawks despatched from Dhahran dropped their bombs on Saudi territory. Major Jeff Scott Tice and Captain Harry M. 'Mike' Roberts of the 401st TFW (Tactical Fighter Wing) were flying F-16A/Cs on a combat strike from Doha AB on 19–20 January, when they were shot down over Baghdad when SAMs detonated close to their aircraft. Both Roberts and Tice parachuted to safety but became POWs. Another F-16 went down on 21 January when a MK-84 bomb detonated before release. US Navy helicopters rescued the pilot at sea. All eight USAF pilots and three USN pilots became POWs in the Gulf War.

152 Dave Waddington and Claire Holderness were married in the chapel at RAF Cranwell on 17 August 1991. Promoted to Wing Commander, Dave Waddington assumed command of IX (B) Squadron in June 2006.

153 On 20 January Squadron Leader Peter Battson and Wing Commander Mike Heath of 20 Squadron experienced a control malfunction aboard Tornado ZD893 just after take-off from Tabuk. They flew around for one hour twenty minutes burning off fuel, jettisoned eight 1,000lb bombs and made two landing attempts before they ejected. They were airlifted home on 24 January. On 22 January Squadron Leaders Gary Lennox (thirty-four) and Kevin Weeks (thirty-seven) of 16 Squadron were killed when their Tornado (ZA467) was shot down during the attack on Ar Rutbah radar station. On 23 January Pilot Officer Simon Burgess, at twnty-three the youngest pilot in the conflict, and Squadron Leader Bob Ankerson (forty) of 17 Squadron, ejected after the explosion of one of their bombs on release detonated the others aboard Tornado ZA403/CO. Both men were taken prisoner, although their families were unaware of this until they were released on 5 March. These losses, plus Peters and Nichol's loss on 17 January, Elsdon and Collier's on 18 January and Clark and Hicks' loss flying ZD717 on 14 February took overall RAF Tornado combat losses in the Gulf War to six. ZD843 made an emergency landing at Dhahran on 24 January with severe damage caused by a SAM explosion.

154 Some 218 Buccaneer-Tornado missions were flown and twenty-four bridges and fifteen airfields were attacked, during which 169 LGBs were dropped (forty-eight by Buccaneers).

155 Between 10–27 February, seventy-two successful TIALD sorties were flown and twenty-three were aborted.

156 On 10 February Flight Lieutenants Gareth Walker and Adrian Frost, plus the four bombing aircraft, accompanied Wing Commander Iveson and Flight Lieutenant Chris Purkiss in ZD848.

157 In the months leading up to the second Gulf War, which began on 20 March 2003, Coalition aircraft patrolling Iraqi 'no-fly' zones bombed eighty air defence sites. Over the first three weeks of the war USAF crews flew nearly 40 per cent of the combat sorties and delivered of the munitions tonnage. The rest was divided between the USN, USMC, RAF and RAAF. In all, 15,000 precision-guided munitions were dropped and 750 cruise missiles were launched. In Operation Iraqi Freedom, 68 per cent of the 29,199 munitions used were either laser-guided or satellite-guided. By 25 March the Coalition could claim 'total dominance of the air.' In all nearly 2,000 US and allied warplanes flew 41,404 sorties over Iraq (of which the US Air Force flew 24,196) in the campaign to oust Saddam Hussein. An American Patriot missile shot down a Marham-based Tornado GR.4, flown by Flight Lieutenant Kevin Main and Flight Lieutenant Dave Williams, as it returned from a bombing mission over south-west Baghdad on 22 March. Both crew were killed. On 9 April Baghdad fell and on 16 April 2003 US Central Command (CENTCOM) officials declared the end of major combat action in Iraq).

158 The GR.4 is an up-rated GR.I/IA with new cockpit displays, full compatibility with the TIALD pod for autonomous Precision Guided Munitions (PGM) delivery, integration of NVGs with an upgraded FLIR (Forward Looking Infra-Red) and an enhanced self-defence suite.

159 On 10 November 1943 138 Airfield HQ formed at Lasham, as part of No.2 Group within 2 Tactical Air Force. The wing finally comprised 613 Squadron, 305 (Polish) Squadron and 107 Squadron, which were equipped with Mosquito VI fighter-bombers. The Wing's operations became legendary with precision attacks on Gestapo headquarters at The Hague, the German barracks at Arnhem during Operation Market Garden in Holland, and many other pinpoint targets until VE Day in May 1945. See *The Men Who Flew The Mosquito* by Martin W. Bowman. (PSL, 1995; Pen & Sword Aviation 2003, 2006); Between 1954 and 1956 twelve wings were deployed in the 2TAF area, controlling a total of thirty-five squadrons as at 1 January 1956. 551 Wing at Gütersloh disbanded on 1 November 1956. Between September 1957 and September 1958 six wings were disbanded (121 Wing at Gütersloh, 123 at Wunstorf, 124 at Oldenburg, 125 at Althorn 139 at Celle and 148 at Wahn). After September 1958 the strength of 2TAF (renamed RAF Germany (Second Tactical Air Force) with effect from 1 January 1959) stood at six wings, controlling eighteen combat squadrons. The last RAF wings in Germany (34 at Laarbruch, 121 at Gütersloh, 122 at Jever, 135 at Brüggen, 137 at Wildenrath and 138 at Geilenkirchen) were all disbanded on 1 January 1960.

BIBLIOGRAPHY AND FURTHER READING

Boiten, Theo and Bowman, Martin W., *Battles with the Nachtjagd: The Night Air War Over Europe 1939–1945*. (Schiffer Publishing, 2006)

Boiten, Theo, *Nachtjagd: The Night Fighter versus Bomber War over the Third Reich 1939–45*. (Crowood Press, 1997)

Bowman, Martin W., *RAF At War*. (PSL, 1997)

—, *De Havilland Mosquito*. (Crowood Aviation Series 1997, 2005)

—, *Mosquito Bomber/Fighter-Bomber Units 1942–45*. (Osprey Combat Aircraft 4, 1997)

—, *English Electric Lightning*. (Crowood Aviation Series 1997, 2005)

—, *Wellington: The Geodetic Giant*. (Airlife 1989, 1998)

—, *RAF Bomber Stories*. (PSL, 1998)

—, *The Men Who Flew The Mosquito*. (PSL 1995, Pen & Sword Aviation 2003, 2006)

—, *Sentimental Journey*. (Erskine Press, 2005)

—, *Stratofortress: The Story of the B-52*. (Pen & Sword Aviation, 2005)

Bowyer, Chaz, Mosquito At War. (Ian Allan, 1984)

Bowyer, Michael J.F., *2 Group RAF: A Complete History 1936–1945*. (Faber & Faber, 1974)

—, *Action Stations* 1: East Anglia. (PSL, 1990)

—, *Action Stations Revisited: No.1* Eastern England. (Crecy, 2000)

Broadbent, Group Captain John DSO, Presentation to the RUSI on 23 October 1991, RAF Staff College, Bracknell. (August 1992)

Chorley, W.R., *Royal Air Force Bomber Command Losses of the Second World War, Vols. 1–6*. (Midland Counties Publications, 1994–98)

Delve, Ken, *RAF Marham: The Operational History of Britain's Front-Line Base from 1916 to the Present Day*. (PSL, 1995)

Eastern Daily Press

Fairhead, Huby and Tuffen, Roy, *Airfields & Airstrips of Norfolk & Suffolk*. (Norfolk & Suffolk Aviation Museum)

Freeman, Roger A., *Bases of Bomber Command Then and Now*. (After the Battle, 2001)

Jones, Barry, *V-Bombers: Valiant, Vulcan and Victor*. (Crowood Aviation Series, 2000)

McKee, Alexander, *The Mosquito Log*. (Souvenir Press, 1988)

Mason, Francis K., *Tornado*. (PSL, 1986)

Middlebrook, Martin and Everitt, Chris, *The Bomber Command War Diaries: An Operational Reference Book 1939–1945*. (Midland Publishing, 1996)

Morse, Stan, *Gulf Air War Debrief*. (Aerospace Publishing, 1991)

The Mossie. Various volumes. (Mosquito Aircrew Association)

Narborough Airfields Research Group, The Great Government Aerodrome, *RFC Narborough: The Story of a First World War Airfield*. (NARG, 2000)

Noble, Bernard, *Noble Endeavours*. (Privately Published)

Scott, Stuart R., *Mosquito Thunder*. (Sutton, 1999)

Sharp, C. Martin and Bowyer, Michael J. F., *Mosquito*. (Faber & Faber, 1967)

West Norfolk Aviation Journal. No.2 (summer 1994)

—, No.1 (October 1993)

White, Rowland, *Vulcan 607: The Epic Story of the Most Remarkable British Air Attack since WWII*. (Corgi, 2006)

Wooldridge, John de L., DFC★ DFM, *Low Attack: The Story of Two Mosquito Squadrons 1940–43*. (Sampson Low, Marston & Co Ltd 1943)

INDEX

If you are interested in purchasing other books published by The History Press, or in case you have difficulty finding any History Press books in your local bookshop, you can also place orders directly through our website

www.thehistorypress.co.uk